W9-BOM-891

Giancarlo Masini

# MARCONI

*Foreword by Frank D. Stella*

*Preface by Emilio Segré*

Marsilio Publishers
*New York*

Copyright © 1976
by Giancarlo Masini

Translation copyright © 1995
by Giancarlo Masini

Of this edition copyright © 1995
Marsilio Publishers
853 Broadway
New York, NY 10003

ISBN 1-56886-057-9

Distributed by
Consortium Book Sales & Distribution
1045 Westgate Drive
Saint Paul, MN 55114-1065

The publication of this book was made possible in part by a generous
contribution from the National Italian American Foundation (NIAF)

*All rights reserved*
PRINTED IN THE UNITED STATES

# CONTENTS

Guglielmo Marconi was a multi-faceted genius: inventor, man of technology, man of science, he was not constrained by the limited knowledge of his time. He successfully carried out the first wireless telegraph transmission in the summer of 1895 when he was just twenty-one years old. He developed the means of transmitting and receiving radio signals at increasing distances, bridging the Atlantic Ocean and, eventually, the entire world. With this feat, he initiated the "modern world of telecommunications".

Marconi had an exceptional entrepreneurial mind as well. He understood that radio- and telecommunications could not be developed without the support of a commercially productive and technologically up-to-date industry. The first wireless telegraph company was founded by Marconi in London, followed by many others in the most important countries in the world. RCA (Radio Corporation of America) was the first of Marconi's companies in the New World.

The combination of scientific genius, technological accomplishment, and entrepreneurial ability were the key factors in Marconi's success and in the rapid development of radio (and later, television and radar) technology. Marconi gave humanity the means to communicate at any distance in real time, a fundamental contribution to

Western civilization, considering the impact telecommunications have on the cultural, social, economic, and political activities of the entire world.

Marconi's work has been one of the few, throughout all history, to deeply affect the habits and actions of the entire mankind. His contribution to human progress has been compared to the invention of printing. We can easily recognize the many elements of modern technology that directly stem from his achievements: satellite telephone and video communications, television, telefax, weather report images of the earth from space, radio beacons to guide airplanes, and other contemporary marvels such as the microwave ovens found in most kitchens. We would have none of these without this great Italian genius.

In the preface to this book, Nobel Laureates Emilio Segré praises its scientific and historical significance. Itt would be difficult, he writes, to find a better account of Marconi's complex personality and immense work, than the one given to us by Giancarlo Masini. Awarded the "Campione d'Italia" Prize for nonfiction in 1976, Masini's book does indeed provide an unparalleled portray, factually accurate and entertainingly written, of the eventful life and accomplishments of the "father of the radio."

Masini, a physical chemist and historian of science, is one of the best known European science journalists. In 1961 he was the initiator of the Science section in the Italian daily *Corriere della Sera*.

For this biography he worked for eight years documenting Marconi's activities in Italy, the United Kingdom, Canada, and the United States. He enriched his research through interviews with those who could give direct reminiscences about the life and work of the inventor: Marconi's oldest daughter, Degna Marconi Paresce; his first wife, Beatrice O'Brien; his second wife, Cristina Bezzi-Scali; and some of his assistants, including engineer L. Gallarati. Because of its scope and exhaustive research, Masini's work has been hailed as the definitive biography of Marconi.

In commemoration of the Centennial of Marconi's wireless telegraph invention, I am proud that the National Italian American Foundation has played a part in bringing his story to the American people.

Frank D. Stella, Chairman
NIAF, Washington, D.C.
September 1995

# PREFACE

Modern technology has evolved from an initial period plagued by business and practical engineering problems, through a second era in which the inventors prevailed, to the present era of scientific programmed research. The nature of these first two periods is best exemplified by the work of individuals such as James Watt and Thomas A. Edison, respectively. It would be difficult to affiliate the present era with a single individual because the protagonists are teams of people working in institutions or laboratories. Working at the end of the second era, Guglielmo Marconi's inventions can be attributed to his individual work. Not only an inventor but also a great entrepreneur, he was motivated by a combination of technological curiosity and business interest. Today, technology operates in a way that makes the appearance of a new Marconi unlikely. The technologists on the San Francisco Peninsula or on Route 128 in Massachusetts are scientifically much more sophisticated than Marconi, but it is unlikely that they would accept a challenge such as his on an individual basis.

Marconi made a first class scientific discovery: the ionosphere. This discovery did not derive from any specific insight but from his utterly pragmatic attitude. His only aim was to transmit signals as far as possible.

The consequences of Marconi's inventions are far-reaching; it is not an exaggeration to say that they have deeply affected modern civilization. For this, Marconi's name is known to everybody as the symbol for telecommunications in all its forms. But what kind of man was he?

Marconi's life is extremely interesting, especially the early years. At times, it reads like fiction. Dr. Masini has been very successful in telling Marconi's story, demonstrating solid documentation of facts that must have required considerable research. Because of the strong feelings aroused by Marconi and the empty rhetoric with which he has been sometimes celebrated, especially in Italy, Masini's sympathetic and level-headed approach is especially commendable. It allows one to gain serious insight into Marconi's unusual family background, early development and complex personality.

I thoroughly enjoyed the book, although it left me curious about Marconi's way of working. Dr. Masini, who had the same interest, tells me that Marconi's original notebooks, if they ever existed, have unfortunately disappeared. Thus the primary source for this important period in the inventor's life is missing. Furthermore, Marconi was interested in Patent Applications, not scientific papers, and for this reason he was rather secretive about his procedures, a habit that has presented additional difficulties for anyone trying to reconstruct his way of methodology.

With the coming of the First World War, both Marconi's role in telecommunications and his lifestyle changed significantly. While we know it changed, we can only speculate why. Masini chose to give only the facts and not to guess at the reasons. Could it be that the refined scientific technology, which entered the field with the vacuum tube, was beyond Marconi's methods? Masini has chosen, in my opinion properly, to let the reader guess for himself. At times, Marconi's life creates the impression that we are reading the biographies of two different people: an extraordinary technologist and businessman, and a passionate lady's man. But these two sides coexisted, with one occasionally overwhelming the other.

From well-known scientists and lawyers who had extensive contacts with Marconi, I had received contrasting impressions of the man. When I was a young assistant professor, I saw and heard Marconi give an official speech to a physics conference. Soon after, to my astonishment and completely by accident, I overheard a loud conversation at a railway station between the inventor and an intimate friend of his on most personal subjects. The coherent picture of the man presented in Masini's book has allowed me to put these various facts of Marconi's character in perspective.

The reader could hardly find a better introduction to Marconi's interesting personality and to the permanent value of his work than Masini's wonderful biography.

Emilio Segré
Nobel Prize for Physics


Berkeley, California 1984

# MARCONI

## A True Love Story

One morning late in the summer of 1895, three young men from the countryside near Bologna were participants in a remarkable discovery—the invention of the wireless telegraph. The leading actor in this momentous drama was twenty-year-old Guglielmo Marconi, a precocious farm boy with a passion for electronics. The supporting roles were played by Marconi's able assistants: his older brother, Alfonso, and a young tenant farmer named Mignani. Eventually, the three youths' discovery lead to some of humanity's most spectacular achievements—the invention of radio and television, radiation for heating and medical therapies, satellite communications, and even the means of intercepting radio waves from distant stars and galaxies—but on this particular morning, there were few signs of what was to come.

At the time, the only evidence that something unusual was taking place was the single report of a rifle, fired into the sky from the edge of a vineyard in a valley to the southwest of Bologna, along a tributary of the river Po. It is here that the last foothills of the Apennines of Tuscany and Emilia empty into a series of hilly fields, dotted with trees and old farm buildings. To the local farmers, already immersed in their day's labor, the shot that rang across these hillsides and fields was an unwelcome annoyance, since rifle fire usually announced the presence of unauthorized hunters among their fields. The shot was not fired on their behalf, however, but was intended only for the ears of young Guglielmo, who now waited anxiously in the attic of his parents' home almost a mile away. For the young inventor, the shot—a prearranged signal to announce that his latest experiment had been successfully completed—was a glorious inerruption of the morning stillness.

Guglielmo had labored for months in virtual secrecy, shut up day and night in an improvised laboratory in the family home, preparing for that morning's experiment. With the exception of Alfonso, no one in the family knew of his intentions. The young man had become increasingly fascinated with electromagnetic waves and the untapped possibilities for transmitting and receiving them. Scientists such as Heinrich Hertz and Augusto Righi had inspired the young inventor with their important theories and experiments, but these distinguished researchers had done very little to further the practical applications of their discoveries. Guglielmo believed that their inventions could be used to transmit messages across great distances—without the use of wire. During the past few months, this idea had become the single passion of his life.

Nobody will ever know—Marconi avoided the subject of failures throughout his life—how many modest successes and crushing disappointments were necessary before he achieved his goal.

Marconi's first wireless transmission covered the distance of his attic laboratory. This was nothing new. By the time of Marconi's experiments, scientists in a number of places were regularly conducting short-range wireless transmissions over similar distances. What was impressive about Guglielmo's early research, however, was the fact that he successfully completed his modest experiments without the sophisticated instruments used at the university research centers where such tests were routinely conducted. What puzzled the young inventor was that it had apparently never occured to any of these distinguished scientists to put their discoveries to practical use. Although the young inventor realized he would never, on his own, be able to keep pace with the progess of university laboratory research, he knew that his quest for practical applications for his invention gave him an edge over his more-sophisticated competitors—an advantage he was determined to keep.

## The Little Hammer Moves

Marconi's childhood home, the Villa Griffone, was the headquarters for his earliest experiments. Still standing, the villa is a solid country house with few architectural pretensions. Built in 1600 by the Griffone family, it is an unadorned structure with plastered walls, revealing both the practical spirit and extreme frugality of the wealthy landowners of the day. The building's original owners were clearly not ones to waste money on decoration; every cornice and doorway of the structure was designed strictly for its functional value, and nothing more. Though it is perched on a hillside, with a dominating view of the Reno Valley below, the entire building has only a single balcony.

The villa is composed of two upper stories, with three rows of square windows arranged at regular intervals, and a ground floor pierced on two sides by the heavy doors of coachhouses, cellars and other storage areas. The main body of the house is topped by a long triangular-shaped attic, which was probably once used for storing cereals. This was the site of Marconi's original laboratory.

In front of the Villa Griffone, another hill, the Celestini, rises abruptly to the southwest. A large cross still stands on the hill's summit, a sight that was clearly visible from the Marconi house and perfectly in line with one of the windows of the young inventor's laboratory. Guglielmo chose the top of the hill as the site for his receiving apparatus. The transmitter was installed in the attic, with the wires and plates of the antenna sticking out of the window.

On the fateful morning in 1895, after so many experiments within the walls of the Villa Griffone, Guglielmo transmitted his message from his attic laboratory to the spot where his two accomplices were waiting. The message was a simple one—the three dots designating the letter S in Morse code—but it traveled almost a kilometer across the fields in front of his home. In comparison with the few meters inside the laboratory, this was a huge step forward. But, as the young man knew, his achievement did not represent any real advance in the transmission of messages. A ray of light reflected from a mirror, the flashing of a lamp, even, in some conditions, the human voice—all these could exceed such a distance.

Guglielmo had entrusted the young tenant farmer Mignani with the responsibility of monitoring the transmission with the inventor's homemade receiving apparatus. Mignani's assignment was to wait on the Celestini hillside, at a farmhouse near a spot called the Pines, almost a mile from the Marconi villa. Then, at the precise moment when the key of the simple receiver began to vibrate, Alfonso, who had accompanied Mignani to the farmhouse, was to take up his rifle and fire the prearranged shot into the air. Give the signal, Guglielmo had instructed, "when you see the little hammer move three times." In past experiments, Mignani had been instructed to wave a handkerchief to signal a completed transmission. This time, however, the distance was too great for the inventor to see any form of visible communication.

As soon as the shot rang out, Guglielmo realized that he had demonstrated that electric waves could be transmitted at a considerable distance, provided that the power of the transmitter was suitably increased. But this was only the first step in a long, demanding journey. If the signals were incapable of overcoming obstacles—a hill, for example—then the wireless telegraph would only remain a dream. What enormous power, he wondered, would be able to penetrate a mountain range? And even if such power could be supplied, how could electromagnetic waves, traveling in a straight line, overcome the problem of the earth's curvature? These were problems that the young inventor realized he would be forced to solve if his dream of wireless telegraphy was ever to become a reality. But for this day, at least, Guglielmo Marconi had plenty of reason to celebrate.

This is Marconi's account of the episode, and it has been faithfully handed down by all of the inventor's biographers, including his closest and most enthusiastic collaborator, the Marchese Luigi Solari. In order to be faithful to the facts, however, another, slightly different account deserves to be heard. Many years later, Antonio Marchi, one of the many tenant farmers who worked the Marconi family's fields, reported a conflicting account of the events leading to Marconi's momentous discovery. Marchi died in 1948 at the age of 105. Throughout his life, the old farmer maintained that Marconi's receiver was not, in fact, on the hilltop with Mignani and Alfonso when Marconi transmitted his first long-distance message, but safely encased in a wooden box in the tenant's modest home about a mile from the Villa Griffone. Marconi had entrusted the box containing his equipment to Marchi's care, along with strict orders that everything he heard should be reported in detail. According to Marchi, the young man would first transmit his impulses from his laboratory at the Villa Griffone and then run to the Pines to learn of the success—or failure—of his attempt from Marchi's own lips.

Marconi's own version of the episode is supported by the inventor's careful records that he kept of all his experiments. Though he was a decent and basically honest man, Marchi may have rearranged the facts in order to share the glory of his famous neighbor. Yet, his story is also quite plausible. Throughout his life, Marconi conducted his experiments in the utmost secrecy, a fact that casts some suspicion on his reported decision to use rifle fire as a signal. Also supporting Marchi's story is the inventor's lifelong practice of protecting his equipment in wooden or metal boxes, a habit the old farmer could not have known about—unless his young neighbor had somehow included him in his experiment. We shall probably never know which of these stories is true.

## Hill Farmers

According to the parish registers of Capugnano, Marconi's paternal ancestors were members of the country gentry. Though they were not extremely wealthy, the family owned a huge stretch of land running from Capugnano to Porretta, and they commanded enough power and respect to develop a rather arrogant confidence in themselves. Like their other landed neighbors, the family members were privileged and well-to-do in relation to the population at large, and determined to hold onto their money and property. Their ideas and opinions were rooted firmly in their own narrow culture. They loved hard work and a good table, and their life together was governed by rigid family traditions. They looked suspiciously at new ideas and were dedicated, more than anything else, to increasing the value of their inheritance—or at least keeping it intact. They organized every aspect of the work of their servants and the sharecroppers, and they enjoyed giving orders. Yet, they deserve credit for transforming a stony soil into fertile fields and prosperous farms, producing rich harvests of barley, maize, corn and wine. Interspersed with the cultivated lands were chestnut groves, a source of fuel, stakes for building and carpentry, and abundant supplies of dried food.

It was the custom, at that time, that the sons of landowners—if they wished to and had the intellectual capacity—continued their schooling beyond the elementary stage, usually in a church-supported institution. Many young people were also encouraged to pursue an ecclesiastical career, not only out of piety, but also for practical reasons. In the first place, almost all educational institutions were run by the church. Moreover, at a time when most parish churches were involved with the ownership of farms or other small holdings, having a son in the priesthood satisfied a common need among the area's landowners to connect spiritual comfort and material well-being.

Domenico Marconi, Guglielmo's grandfather, was not one to act differently from his fellow landowners. In keeping with the practice of the day, he sent two of his sons, Arcangelo and Giuseppe, to the seminary to study for the priesthood. (Another son, Gianbattista, would forego the seminary and later become a lawyer in Bologna.) Arcangelo, the younger of the two, would complete his training and enter the priesthood, only to be murdered a few years later by a thief he caught robbing the presbytery. Unlike his younger brother, Giuseppe did not feel drawn to the ministry. Before completing his education and preparing for religious orders, he left the seminary and returned to the family farm. But after having seen and learned so much, Giuseppe soon grew impatient with the rural, uncultured atmosphere of Capugnano and Porretta. He devoted himself entirely to the management of the family properties, and a few years later moved to Bologna. There he soon met and married Giulia de Renoli, the daughter of a rich banker, who died only nine months later while giving birth to her only child, a son named Luigi.

Now a widower with a small child on his hands, Giuseppe decided to bring his father Domenico, who was now old and living alone, down to the city from his mountain home. Giuseppe somehow persuaded the older man to sell the property at Porretta and move to a house in Bologna. Collecting only his most prized possessions, Domenico completed the move with three cartloads and a gig. But after spending a lifetime in the peaceful countryside of the Apennines, the old man found city life was just too much for him, and the two men compromised by moving to a small place at Pontecchio, seventeen kilometers from Bologna. For Giuseppe, this was certainly not the city life for which he longed, but it was still a vast improvement over the harsh isolation that awaited him in Poretta.

Giuseppe took charge of running the new property, while old Domenico made quite a success of raising silkworms. Financially, everything went well. Giuseppe Marconi had remained on good terms with the de Renoli bankers; he visited their home on occasion, and they in turn came to stay with him at the Villa Griffone. It was through these in-laws that Giuseppe met the woman who was to become his second wife and the mother of Guglielmo.

## An Irish Girl

During this same period, Andrew Jameson was living with his wife and four daughters in Ireland, at Daphne Castle in County Wexford. Jameson was also a wealthy man, the founder and proprietor of a flourishing whisky distillery. His elder brothers also dealt in the traditional liquor of their country, setting up a business in Dublin.

The Jameson home was a fine old mansion, complete with a moat and parkland enough to express the owners' social position as worthy members of the Irish gentry, who took pride in the country's traditions.

Annie, the youngest of the daughters, had a marvelous voice and a real passion for singing. From adolescence, she was permitted to take lessons and to develop her musical gifts, but when she was invited to perform in London, at Covent Garden, the Jameson family drew the line. Jameson would never allow his youngest daughter to pursue a career on the stage. To console Annie for the loss of Covent Garden, her parents decided to let her travel and study in Italy, where the family had business connections with the de Renoli bankers.

Disappointed by the loss of a career in the theater but eager to visit "the land of sun and song," Annie arrived in Bologna as guest of the de Renolis, where she soon met Giuseppe Marconi. A widower with a young child, Giuseppe was nonetheless still in his prime. He was handsome and charming with a temperament and expressiveness not easily found in the British Isles.

The two quickly fell in love, although Giuseppe was a full seventeen years her senior. Annie recognized from the beginning that marriage to Giuseppe would be even more difficult to achieve than her dream of singing at Convent Garden, but it may have been precisely this realization that led to her unshakable determination to marry the Italian—whatever the cost. Half Scot and half Irish, the Jamesons were much more conservative and set in their ways than the country landowners of the Italian provinces. She was well aware that her father and mother, her sisters, and all her relations would deny their consent. Not only was Giuseppe Marconi a widower, much older than she was, and the father of a child—he was also an Italian. Even if he had been a king, he was still, in her father's eyes, an incomprehensible foreigner—someone to be treated politely, even to accommodate as a guest, but certainly not to be thought of as a member of the family.

Even though she was fully aware of this, Annie still acted the part of the dutiful daughter. She returned home to Wexford to ask for her family's blessing. The response was just as she had foreseen—an adamant refusal. Annie was forced to submit to her family's wishes.

There were to be no trips abroad to console her this time; instead she was encouraged to plunge into the society of the county, with its dances, parties and introductions to the most eligible young men. Annie showed no outward sign of disappointment; she remained serene and obedient, leading Andrew Jameson and the family to believe that the foreign widower left behind in Italy would be easily forgotten. The truth proved to be quite different.

Foreseeing opposition to their hopes, Annie and Giuseppe had agreed to write to each other in secret, intending to wait until she came of age before fulfilling their plans to marry. When the day finally came, Giuseppe left Bologna and crossed the Alps to France, while Annie sailed for the continent. The couple met and embraced at Boulogne, where they were married on the same day.

The honeymoon returned them to the city where they had first seen each other and where they were to make their home. Giuseppe had furnished the Villa Griffone as his summer home but had also taken a house in the center of Bologna, in via delle Asse (today's via Quattro Novembre) for the winters. It was to the house in Bologna that the bridegroom led his beautiful Annie. She was small and graceful, barely five feet tall, with blue eyes, rosy cheeks and chestnut blond hair.

It would be a mistake to portray Marconi's mother as a poetic soul who was out of touch with the practical side of life—far from it.

Annie Jameson Marconi had unusually acute common sense, uniting the pragmatism typical of the British Isles with an intuition for the most appropriate course of action in any situation. All this was held together by an extraordinary tenacity already evident in the way she had overcome her family's prohibition to marry the man she wanted.

These qualities enabled her to understand, earlier than anyone else in the family, the importance of the work of her prodigious son— and to lead him, almost by the hand, down the first difficult steps on the road to worldwide success.

Annie quickly settled down in Bologna, feeling little nostalgia for her home in Ireland. The old buildings of Bologna, the porticos and cathedral of San Petronio, the monuments of the city in Emilia, were not a bad exchange for the old mansion back in County Wexford. The house in Via delle Asse was also a fine building for its day, with large windows at the front, high decorated ceilings and extensive gardens in the rear. And in late spring, there was also the Villa Griffone, surrounded by green fields, vineyards and chestnut groves, with the scent of hay, and the song of crickets, cicadas, and chaffinches.

## One Saturday Morning

In 1866, just a year after their romantic elopement to Bologna, the love of Giuseppe Marconi and Annie Jameson bore its first fruit, a fine baby, christened Alfonso. The boy was born at the Villa Griffone, where Annie had decided to spend the final months of her pregnancy.

Almost nine years would pass before the birth of the couple's second child, on 25 April 1874. According to the parish records, the birth took place on a Saturday morning, at a quarter past nine.

Spring that year was unusually cold in the hills at Pontecchio and
the birth took place in the house in Bologna. There had also been
difficulties in the pregnancy, and Giuseppe felt it best to keep his
wife in the city, where medical assistance was more quickly and easily
available. Even with theis precaution, Annie almost died giving birth.
Everything turned out well in the end, and when the mother and
baby were both safe, the midwife ran to give Giuseppe the news that
he had another son. According to one of the family anecdotes, an
old servant, seeing Guglielmo for the first time in his mother's arms,
exclaimed "What big ears he has!" To which Annie replied, "All the
better to hear the still small voices of the air."

Marconi's earliest years were spent in perfect tranquillity, even if
the head of the house had developed over the years something very
close to miserliness. A closer look at this aspect of Guglielmo
Marconi's father's character, might be useful in gaining insight into
the great inventor's personality and behavior, as well as understanding how the wireless telegraph came into being in the midst of all
kinds of difficulties.

Giuseppe Marconi was certainly no spendthrift. He could not
possibly have been—either as a hill farmer in the atmosphere in
which he lived, or in the spirit of the times themselves. His lands,
farmed on a share-cropping system, gave a reasonable livelihood,
provided they were carefully managed. This explains his shrewdness
in choosing his crops and varying them from year to year as he read
the markets and harvests. It also accounts for his severe supervision
of the tenants, whom he considered to be little better than thieves,
ready to steal what was rightfully his the moment his back was
turned. On the other hand, the sharecroppers had always considered
the owners as exploiting the toil of others.

Annie Marconi must have put a considerable strain on her husband's income, if one considers her numerous holidays and visits to
the thermal baths, along with her journeys from Bologna to

Florence, Leghorn, and England. Annie visited her family on a number of occasions. Sensible Irish people, the Jamesons refused to turn the elopement at Boulogne as a tragey. They quickly resumed relations with their daughter, and it is not unlikely that at least part of Annie's dowry found its way into her hands. At any rate, Annie remained on intimate terms with each of her three sisters.

## A Crowded Life

As the years went by, especially after the birth of Guglielmo, old Marconi seldom moved far from his fields and the Villa Griffone. Annie and the two boys, however, never spent an entire year at Pontecchio. After the birth of her second child, Guglielmo's mother, who had always been delicate, felt the cold and damp which characterized the Bologna countryside for most of the winter months. The house at the Villa Griffone—in spite of its numerous fireplaces— had no adequate form of heating. At the beginning of October, when the fog and heavy rain started, Annie, along with Alfonso and Guglielmo, would pack up and move to a more gentle climate. Usually the chosen retreat was Leghorn, not only because it was warmer and had the benefit of the sea air, but because Elizabeth Prescott had virtually settled there with her four girls; in fact there was quite an English colony in the town.

The two Marconi boys and their four little cousins became inseparable playmates. Annie and her sons went to England on two occasions during this period, staying first in Bedford (only fifty miles from London) and then at Rugby. But like other British expatriates, Annie was happiest when she could spend a few months in Florence, where the English had always been more numerous and more cultured than at Leghorn. Here the Jameson-Marconi and the Jameson-Prescott sisters met many old and dear friends of the family.

Florence also held another attraction. From there it was easy to get to Prescott, the place where Giuseppe had been born. Annie and her boys made the journey not out of family duty but for more practical reasons. The famous thermal baths at Poretta were already in existence and were highly regarded for their capacity to rejuvenate the skin—something to which Annie attached particular importance. Giuseppe Marconi accompanied his family to Poretta, happy to revisit his native haunts and to chat with former friends.

When good weather arrived, the whole family returned to the Villa Griffone, and for long periods the five ladies of the Prescott family came there too. These trips are further evidence that Giuseppe was never the scrooge-like figure that many believe him to have been, though it is equally clear that Guglielmo's father was a stern parent who required respect and obedience.

Organized by Annie with her husband's unenthusiastic consent, the annual migrations prevented the two boys from attending school regularly. Guglielmo went to elementary school at Casalecchio sul Reno, but he received most of his early education at home. A schoolmaster from Pontecchio, Germano Bollini, was engaged to teach the Marconi boys Italian, and they learned English from their mother. Each day the exiled Irish woman would call her sons to her room and give them their lessons. She eventually added religious instruction to their study of English, in the hope that they would be brought up in the Anglican faith.

Surprisingly, Giuseppe did not object to his wife's wishes. Since leaving the ecclesiastical college where he had studied for the priesthood, the elder Marconi had been relatively indifferent to questions of religion.

## Language and Religion

Annie devised an extremely effective method of bringing together study of religion and of the mother tongue. Each evening after dinner, she would read the boys two chapters of the King James Bible. When their knowledge of the language was good enough, she had them read aloud while she corrected any mistakes in pronunciation or intonation. During their stays at Leghorn or Florence, Annie and her sons attended the services of the Waldesian church, the closest in her opinion to the Anglican style of worship.

The boys received a full-time education: English and religion from their mother, Italian from Germano Bollini, and the other subjects from the school in Casalecchio. For diversion and to relieve a mind already bubbling over with ideas, Guglielmo frequently used his father's library. Though Giuseppe's collection hardly boasted anything special, there was still plenty to feed a young boy's imagination and awaken an appetite for knowledge. Two books, in particular, caused Guglielmo to develop a new passion: a life of Benjamin Franklin and a reprint of Faraday's Lectures to the Royal Institution on Electricity. The boy was particularly fascinated by the scientific adventures of the great American statesman and inventor. The kites that Franklin launched to demonstrate the electrical nature of lightning appealed to Guglielmo's imagination and roused in him a desire to investigate the American inventor's questions for himself.

Guglielmo's passion for reading and experimenting outside the classroom contributed to a lack of progress in the classroom. The future inventor was twelve years old before he succeeded in getting his elementary diploma. In that year, 1866, he was able to enter a secondary school, the "Cavallero" Technical Institute, situated in via delle Terme in Florence.

Annie Marconi scarcely concealed her preference for Guglielmo—perhaps because he was her youngest, or because she had almost died giving birth to him, or because she detected more of herself in the boy than in her other children. Certainly, her predilection for him increased during the many lessons in English and religion. Through that close contact—as teacher to pupil as well as mother to son—she discovered his extraordinary intellectual resources and his determination to work out solutions to all kinds of problems for himself.

Giuseppe Marconi, in contrast, never managed to understand the strange nature of his youngest son. As a provincial landowner, Giuseppe could only envision one kind of family behavior: it was the children's duty to learn the ways of their elders. To Giuseppe, the first signs of Guglielmo's passion for electrical phenomena and his subsequent experiments could only have appeared to be useless, even dangerous childish games—and expensive to boot.

From childhood, Guglielmo had been fascinated by all kinds of mechanical and electrical devices. Whether it was a turnspit or a sewing machine, he seemed to understand at once how each instrument worked. He would take them apart and put them together again, often making similar or better devices himself.

The traditions of the Marconi family include the story of a trick played by Guglielmo on one of his four Prescott cousins. A sewing machine had been bought for Daisy, his favorite, and Guglielmo dismantled it and turned it into a turnspit. But when he saw the dismay that his cleverness had caused his little cousin, he immediately began to reassemble the machine. Though it is impossible to determine if the episode actually took place, it is certainly what one would expect from the young Marconi

2

# THE MOTHER'S INTUITION

## A Difficult Student

As a student at the "Cavallero" Institute in Florence, Marconi had no more success making friends with his schoolmates and teachers than at the Primary school in Pontecchio. He also remained distanced from the private tutor who taught him Italian at his father's house. Years later, the "old boys" of the Cavallero Institute still remembered Marconi, but none of them could recall a single incident involving his friendship with another student.

Florentine teenagers—even those belonging to the upper classes at the "Cavallero" Institute—have always been the same. Tricks, teasing and practical jokes enjoy great popularity, directed especially against teachers and those schoolmates who are soft-tempered, easily embarrassed, or simply different from their classmates. The young Michelangelo, when he was still an apprentice painter, had his nose broken by a young man of his age during a fight. Michelangelo reportedly started the conflict by sneering scornfully at the other man's painting style.

Guglielmo was frequenly teased and mistreated by the other children—perhaps because of his formal dress and serious disposition; or perhaps for the extravagant style of his mother's dresses. More than anything else, he was an easy target for his fellow students because of his problems with pronunciation. Every time the lean, well-groomed youth answered a question, read a piece of prose or recited a short poem by heart, he would emit a succession of phonetic oddities. Florence is, after all, the cradle of the Italian language, and misuse of the language is a serious offense, one not easily forgiven by the other students. Guglielmo must have suffered horribly because of his unusual intonation, which betrayed traces of Irish, English and the vernacular speech of Bologna. "Your Italian is appealing," a teacher once told him: "Let us hear the poem you were asked to learn by heart; speak loudly so that everyone can hear you." Marconi could not complete a single line before his recitation was drowned out by the laughter of his classmates, followed by jokes and teasing that often continued for days. These experiences increased his natural shyness and contributed to the solitary, quietly reflective attitude that would continue throughout his life.

Marconi's first daughter, Degna, would later write that Guglielmo started his lifelong friendship with Luigi Solari during his year at the secondary school in Florence, where the latter was also enrolled; this does not seem very likely, if one considers what happened years later. Solari's solemn account of Marconi's life and work—the first book ever written about the inventor—has set the standard for all following biographers. Each page of Solari's work makes a strong case for his intimate friendship with the inventor and his important contributions to Marconi's ideas and experiments. About their shared experience in Florence, Solari was able to write only a single sentence, essentially denying the existence of even a casual early acquaintance. "When in Florence," recalled Solari, "by a strange coincidence, we attended the same school, the 'Cavallero' Institute of via delle Terme, but we knew each only by sight because I was in the next form higher and therefore did not allow him to fraternize with me." It would be several more years before the two men would meet again.

Guglielmo's failure to fit in with boys of his age group in Florence helped to mold his individualistic personality and reserved nature. Although shy and withdrawn, he was already sharply aware of his intelligence and confident that he would achieve something truly extraordinary in his life. Years later he would write of this crucial period in his life:

> The memory of my childhood which has most vividly remained impressed in my mind is the care with which I would try to hide from everybody—in order not to be teased—my irresistible feeling that one day I would be able to do something new and great. More than hopeful, I was certain of this—since I was eight or ten years old, which gave me solace when I was occasionally rebuked by my teachers when I had not diligently prepared the lessons which did not interest me at all. They will realize one day—I used to say to myself—that I am not as dumb as they think."

## Life in Livorno

Mercifully, the school year in Florence finally came to an end, and the following summer Giuseppe Marconi—perhaps wishing to satisfy his wife or maybe because the traveling from Pontecchio to Florence was simply too expensive—decided to move the family to Leghorn. An elegant house was rented in viale Regina Margherita and Guglielmo was enrolled at the Istituto Nazionale in Via Cairoli, a private technical school where the genial young man could devote himself to his favorite subjects—the scientific disciplines. But his study habits continued to be irregular, even in the more favorable climate, and he never received a diploma.

Guglielmo's failure to finish school prevented him from being accepted by the Italian Navy Academy of Leghorn. The young inventor wished to join the navy because of both his love for the sea and the fact that his two best friends, Filippo and Giulio Camperio, had already been admitted. Filippo would remain one of Guglielmo's closest friends throughout the inventor's lifetime, and though Giulio would die in his youth, Marconi would later honor the youngest Camperio boy's memory by naming his only son after him.

At school in Leghorn, Marconi was most fascinated by the lessons of his physics tutor, Professor Giotto Bizzarrini, whom he would later remember with great enthusiasm. When school was out, Guglielmo would use what he had learned in Bizzarrini's class to improve his homemade electrical equipment.

Annie Marconi Jameson, who had never forgotten her early passion for singing and music, gave her children a refined musical education by sending them to private music classes. Once again, Giuseppe Marconi honored her wishes without a blink, both happy and proud to please the woman who had given up her own artistic vocation to become his wife.

Marconi's school education was varied and irregular, not only because, as one of his biographers would later write, the precocious youth had little tolerance for the "traditional and pedantic curriculum suitable for mediocre students," but also for two more essential reasons. First, wealthy people in Italy at that time did not have to send their children to state schools; there were a number of fine private institutions as well as the option of studying at home, for which it was easy to find willing teachers who needed the opportunity to increase their modest salaries.

The second reason is to be found in his mother's typically British attitude. Annie Jameson was unimpressed with the Italian educational system and the then-fashionable idea that, in order to be received in a better class of society and make one's way in life—one had no choice but to learn Latin.

In line with her "nonconformist" approach to education, Annie Jameson was also exceptionally lenient with her son, compared with other parents in the region, allowing him to forego those classes he either did not enjoy or in which he was less than brilliant. Convinced that physics and electrology enraptured Guglielmo's mind more than anything else, she arranged for additional private classes in those subjects. She even sought out the best electrophysics instructor in Livorno, Vincenzo Rosa of the Liceo Niccolini, and invited him to her home to tutor her son. Throughout his life, Marconi would recall, "the clear and practical method with which Professor Rosa initiated me to the study of electrophysics."

## A Blind Telegraphist

Since he first read about the scientific adventures of Faraday and Franklin, Marconi's deep interest in electrical phenomena and instruments had been kindling inside him. Vincenzo Rosa's teaching quickly turned the curiosity of a child into the passion of a man. What had been game now became an experimental discipline, despite the limits imposed by rudimentary equipment and the lack of solid theoretical preparation or a well-equipped university laboratory in which to work.

During the time he lived in Leghorn, Marconi met an old, retired telegraph operator named Nello Marchetti near the harbor where he often fished and went sailing. Marchetti, who was almost completely blind, grew fond of the precocious lad. Guglielmo returned the old man's affection, and often spent time with him, asking for explanations about his experiments as they chatted about electrical phenomena. Marchetti owned a small telegraph with which he trained Marconi in Morse code.

During the time the Marconis lived in the house in Viale Regina Margherita, Guglielmo devised an odd gadget made with an arrow-shaped piece of zinc. When placed on the roof, it picked up atmospheric electricity during a storm. When connected to an appropriate circuit, the instrument produced discharges which rang a bell. There was nothing extraordinary in this, but to his family and friends the mechanism must have seemed like magic. Outside of Professor Rosa's classes, Marconi eagerly absorbed any books and reviews which dealt with electricity. It was during this period that he began to take a particular interest in everything that was written about electric waves.

To understand what was known in the field at the time, it is necessary to step back as far as 1815, when a young French engineer, Jean-Augustine Fresnel, carried out the now classic experiments on light diffraction phenomena. Fresnel proved that the diffraction of light rays was due to interference in the atmosphere. His findings would prove to be a fundamental contribution to the so-called "wave theory," by means of which the classic optics phenomena were eventually explained. According to the theory, light rays were likened to the waves that can be observed in a pond into which a pebble has been thrown, or the vibrations of guitar strings that have been plucked by a player's fingers. In these cases, the waves are obvious and visible. But what of the invisible waves in light rays? What was their nature? What originated them, and how?

An explanation to these questions was finally provided in 1864 by the Scottish physicist J. Clerk Maxwell, with his theory of electro-magnetic waves. Before Maxwell, the frequent and well-known experiments of Michael Faraday had already demonstrated the close relationship between magnetism and electricity. Exploring the intimate links between variations of electrical and magnetic quantities, Maxwell proved in theory that the radiation of light rays was a result of electromagnetic wave radiation.

The Scottish scientist's work has played a crucial role in the development of modern physics. His theory demonstrated that light waves are conducted by an electromagnetic field, a fine, impalpable substance which permeates every inch of the universe.

Before Maxwell, no one had been able to "see" the waves, just as scientists had continually failed to prove the existence of ether. Physicists were finally forced to acknowledge that the latter substance did not actually exist but had simply been conceived to account for certain otherwise-unexplainable phenomena. Many people were similarly suspicious about the existence of electro-magnetic waves.

The task of experimentally demonstrating the existence and the propagation of electromagnetic waves was undertaken by the brilliant German scholar Heinrich Rudolph Hertz. In his experiments, Hertz used the well-known induction coil, invented by Heinrich Daniel Ruhmkorff. The instrument consisted of a core bundle of soft iron wires; over this was wound a primary coil of thick wire and then a secondary coil of up to 50,000 turns of fine wire. Currents generated by a battery passed through the primary circuit, which included a make-and-break system. The operation of the make-and-break system caused the primary current to rise and fall, generating another current in the secondary coil. This process could then be accelerated to produce a difference of more than 10,000 volts at the output terminals of the secondary coil. Today, the most common example of an induction coil is the ignition coil in a car, which raises the low voltage of the battery to the high voltage necessary to produce sparks in the engine.


## Hertz's Work

Electric transmission without the use of wire had already been observed in the eighteenth century. In 1750, the well-known "abbot electrician," Jean Antoine de Nollet, succeeded in sending an electric discharge, without conducting wires, from one bank to the other of the Seine. The "electric flow" had obviously passed through the water.

In 1791, the Italian zoologist Luigi Galvani, noticed, while conducting tests on frogs, that the muscles of the hind legs of one dissected creature moved with quick jerks when he activated a particularly powerful electrostatic machine. The machine had been placed at a great distance from the small wooden board on which the two legs were placed. This was the earliest recorded example of the transmission of waves through the air.

In 1838, Carl Steinheil discovered that the electric current passing through a conductor generated an electric flow in another conductor. Four years later, the electric telegraphic code inventor, Samuel Morse, succeeded in broadcasting telegraphic signals through a wire which had accidentally broken. In 1881, many years closer to Marconi's experiments, Alexander Graham Bell, one of the fathers of telephony, managed to send a message by telephone from one ship to another at a distance of one and a half kilometers. Not until Hertz's work on electromagnetic waves, however, did the phenomenon acquire the value and the dignity of an authentic scientific theory, verifiable by methodical experimentation.

When Hertz began his research, he did not simply carry on "experiments at random." The German scientist was absolutely convinced of the validity of the Maxwellian theory. In his laboratory at the University of Bonn, he had set for himself the goal of finding the most convincing evidence of what Maxwell had described. Hertz's experiments were successful, thanks to the Ruhmkorff coil and the spark gap, an apparatus formed by a pair of brass rods mounted on ebonite pillars. The rods end in a pair of adjustable brass spheres which face each other, thus forming the spark gaps. When the distance is correct in relation to the electric tension, sparks occur between the gaps.

Connecting a spark gap to a powerful Ruhmkorff coil and making use of the high tension discharges obtained in this way, Hertz was able to generate electromagnetic waves of varying lengths, depending on the dimensions of the machine. He called his new instrument an "oscillator", a device capable of producing the oscillating motions of electromagnetic waves.

## The Electric Resonator

The first of Hertz's receivers was a simple copper wire bent to form a loop whose extremes ended with two tiny spheres almost touching the detecting instrument. Minute sparks were produced between these two spheres.

Carrying on with his experiments, Hertz greatly improved his detectors and oscillators by using half-cylindrical reflectors; in their flare he placed small discharging spheres. Hertz used his new invention to produce and measure electromagnetic waves up to eighty centimeters long.

Hertz's discoveries aroused a great deal of interest among the world's scientific elite. His test were immediately reproduced in several universities and his instruments were improved to make them more powerful. New ones were devised and the electromagnetic waves which were obtained were more accurately studied and measured.

In Italy, at the University of Bologna, the prominent physicist Augusto Righi was making a name for himself with the invention of powerful and precise oscillators and detectors. One of these oscillators (the "three-spark" oscillator) was made of two brass spheres suspended in a glass container full of paraffin oil; the device increased electric resistance and therefore generated more energy. The two spheres were at a distance of two millimeters from each other and were connected with two conductors which were also spherical and which could be electrically charged with sparks obtained from a spark gap linked to a Ruhmkorff spark coil. Professor Righi used his machine to demonstrate that electromagnetic waves and light waves behaved in similar ways but had different lengths

Also in Italy, Temistocle Calzecchi-Onesti, an unknown physics researcher whose work has only recently been reappraised, invented a machine which turned out to be of fundamental importance in the first steps of wireless telegraphy. Calzecchi-Onesti's device consisted of a small glass tube containing metal filings, in contact with two electrodes. When a spark was produced in the proximity of this instrument, the metal filings acquired a special characteristic and yielded to the contact between the two electrodes. If they were inserted in a circuit with an electric bell, the flow of electromagnetic waves was signalled by the sounding of a bell.

The Italian researcher's instrument was the first coherer. It remained unknown to the rest of the world for a number of years—

perhaps because of the excessive modesty of the inventor—though he published the results of his research in 1884 in the "Nuovo Cimento." The same instrument was invented independently in 1890 in France by Professor Eduard Branly, who called it the *radio-conducteur*. Sir Oliver Lodge, who improved the instrument considerably, was the first to use it to demonstrate electromagnetic waves. This is why Calzecchi-Onesti's invention has always been known by its English name—except during the Fascist regime when all English names were banned and it was referred to as the "coesore".

The coherer was based on a previous discovery by David H. Hughes, the inventor of the printing telegraph. Hughes discovered that a tube of silver and zinc filings, loosely packed, was sensitive to an electric spark from the discharge of a Leyden Jar. The spark caused the metallic filings, which normally offered a very high-resistance electrical path, to coalesce, or cohere. This reduced their electrical resistance to a low state and allowed current from the battery to flow through them.

The device was improved by Professor Lodge, with the inclusion of a timed mechanism that gave the tube a regular light tap, restoring the coherer to its original high-resistance state. In 1893, Lodge detected electromagnetic waves as far as forty meters from the transmitter, using the coherer in a circuit with a battery and a galvanometer.

As we have seen, the principle on which wireless telegraphy is based was already known, but none of Marconi's predecessors foresaw the possibilities inherent in it. Hertz was a pure scientist, whose single aim was to demonstrate the validity of Maxwell's theory; he had not interest in the practical applications of his discoveries. The same can be said for the equally non-pragmatic Augusto Righi. Following Hertz's research, he reached the previously described conclusion that Hertzian waves and light waves were identical, but he never ventured beyond the frontiers of pure research, acknowledging the possibility of radiotelegraphy only after Marconi had already realized it.

Only the English physicist Sir William Crookes, the discoverer of cathode rays, foresaw in 1892 the possibility for telegraphy with Hertzian waves, but he did not apply his intuition in a practical way. Oliver Lodge had been the first to try to transmit signals through space, making use of the induction effects between wide-range circuits installed on two nearby islands. But his experiments demonstrated only one fact—transmission by induction could not be used to overcome great distances.

This was the situation inherited by the young Marconi at the time he began his experiments.

# THE LIGHTNING MACHINE

## The Meeting with Augusto Righi

In the summer of 1894, Marconi's mother decided to take a holiday in the Alps near Biella. She packed her bags, and with her husband's consent, went off to Oropa with her sons. The little town attracted her because of its splendid mountain walks, its invigorating air and bright sun, and, most of all, its healing natural waters. After sampling the Spa at Porretta, Annie was anxious to try the waters at Oropa.

It was here, in the relaxed atmosphere of this resort, that the young Marconi first developed the idea of wireless telegraphy. The initial inspiration came from a newspaper review commemorating Hertz for his work. (The German scientist had prematurely died at the beginning of the year.) It has been suggested that Marconi read the newspaper by accident. It is more likely, however, that before leaving home for the holiday, the young man packed into his suitcase all the books and publications which most interested him, including the article.

During the leisure hours at Oropa, the young Marconi read and re-read the piece on Hertz's work until he knew it by heart. It was probably during one of his lengthy walks that the idea of using electromagnetic waves to transmit intelligible messages over long distances first flashed through his mind.

The future inventor of radio was endowed with a sharp pragmatic sense. It was this, much more than any attraction for scientific speculations, which encouraged him to study electronic phemonena. But there were other reasons too which aroused his enthusiasm and determination.

It was the last decade of the nineteenth century, and the industrial revolution which had started more than a hundred years earlier was in full swing. Imperial powers, such as Great Britain and France, had increased trade and military operations to every part of the world—creating a pressing need for effective and dependable long-range communication. Both the telegraph and telephone had already been invented, yet intercommunication by means of wires, although extremely useful, still presented tremendous difficulties.

For centuries, people had been searching for the fastest and most efficient way to send messages, an endeavor that had produced signal lamps, heliographs, and various types of signalling systems. But none of the means devised had provided a fundamental solution to the problem.

Marconi was not deterred by the fact that, though he had succeeded in transmitting his waves over a distance of forty meters, Hertz had failed to realize the practical applications of his achievement; nor was he depressed that a leading light in physics such as Augusto Righi, along with his most distinguished colleagues in the field, had declared that it was impossible to communicate words at a distance by means of Hertzian waves. Considering the scientific knowledge available at the time, Righi and the other scientists were perfectly correct, at least in theory. But the more theoretical obstacles Marconi encountered, the more he felt driven to challenge them experimentally, following his own intuition and depending on the technical ability of his own hands.

Marconi's acquaintance with Professor Righi had not been a coincidence. The physicist, who worked and lived in Bologna, took his holidays at a country house in Sabbiuno, not far from the Villa Griffone. Guglielmo's father held a position of some importance in Bolognese society and therefore had access to homes which were not open to other people, while Annie found it easy to befriend Professor Righi and maintain useful contact with the scientist.

## Scientists and Inventors

Guglielmo was unable to attend either the Navy Academy of Livorno or the University of Bologna because of his lack of a secondary school diploma. Thanks to the relations between his family and Professor Righi, however, he was granted permission to enter the library of the Physics Institute at the University and access to the scientist's laboratory, as well as the additional honor of private meetings with the distinguished professor.

There is no written record of what the young Marconi and Augusto Righi said to each other the first time they met; but it is likely that Marconi approached Righi with some anxiety, but also with a strong desire to learn as much as he could from the gifted scientist. Righi, for his part, was probably surprised by the young man's impressive knowledge and by the sharpness of his observations. With an indisguisable appreciation for the young man's intellectual gifts, Righi granted Guglielmo permission to use his laboratory for some of his experiments—experiments which Guglielmo would then try again at home.

The two men never became close friends. Many years after that first meeting, when Guglielmo's fame had already crossed the ocean, it would have probably been tempting for the physicist from Bologna University to support the claims of those who wrote that he had been Marconi's scientific mentor.

On the contrary, Righi was always careful to distinguish the role and work of scientists devoted exclusively to research and exploration, the category to which he belonged, from the activity of those who would utilize the discoveries they made and invent systems for their practical application. Marconi was proud of belonging to the latter group.

On this subject, Professor Righi was to write on 12 March 1930:

Therefore might I be allowed to point out once more that as a general rule the work of those who, devoting themselves to science, have provided the opportunity for and even encouraged such applications. In particular, nobody I imagine would dare to claim that without knowing my experiments on electric waves, Marconi would have been able to conceive his brilliant invention.

Righi went on, admitting with surprising humility,

I also understand that recently I have repeatedly been honored as Marconi's master. I should be very happy to deserve such a title, but it would be necessary to give the word a wide meaning to apply it to someone who had only a few conversations with the young inventor, mostly about projects which were not those which have deservedly made him famous, and someone, moreover, who at the utmost, happened to be in a position to provide him with explanations, clarification and advice on those projects".

On another occasion, Righi vigorously defended Marconi's preeminence in the field of wireless telegraphy, only to add the following observation:

> As far as I am concerned the question of priority is of entirely secondary importance, compared with the ability he has shown in incessantly improving the necessary equipment and in launching his invention towards practical objectives. In a word, Marconi's value lies more than in the imaginative development of his lucky find, but in what he did to derive a practical result from it."

## The Real Master

Marconi never recognized Augusto Righi as his teacher. That honor was reserved for Vincenzo Rosa of Leghorn, a modest secondary school teacher whose ideas first captured the young inventor's imagination. Speaking at the Royal Academy of Sciences in Stockholm, on 11 December 1909, Marconi recalled his early education:

> In outlining briefly the history of my contribution to the realization of radiotelegraphy, I must say that I never followed regular courses in physics and electronics, though I have felt the most vivid interest in these subjects since I was a boy. I did, however, follow a course of lessons in physics held by the late Professor Rosa of Livorno, and I certainly kept myself diligently informed of all the publications of the time related to scientific topics, including the work of Hertz, Branly and Righi. In Italy, in my home near Bologna, back in 1895, I started tests and experiments to establish whether it was possible to transmit telegraphic signals and concentional signals at a distance by means of the Hertzian waves, without the help of wires. After

some preliminary experiments with Hertzian waves I rapidly became convinced that if it were possible to transmit and receive these waves or similar ones, reliably and at considerable distances, a new communication system would be possible, with excellent advantages in comparison with signal lamps or other optical methods whose practical use is so much dependant on favorable weather conditions.

In my first tests I used a common Hertz oscillator and, as a detector, Branly's coherer; but soon I realized that Branly's coherer was not sufficiently stable and reliable for practical use. Some improvements were made using reflectors both for the receivers and the transmitters. As transmitter I then adopted Righi's oscillator.

At the end of the summer of 1894, when the holidays at Oropa were over, Marconi's family gathered again at Pontecchio at the Villa Griffone. Guglielmo immediately applied himself to the idea which now haunted him. He consulted regularly with Professor Righi; he applied himself intensely to anything that could give him a better understanding of the methods of generating and receiving Hertzian waves. Many years later he would write:

By the time I was twenty, I was fairly well acquainted with the published results of the work of the most distinguished scientists who had occupied themselves with the subject of electric waves; men such as Hertz, Branly, Lodge, Righi and many others. With regards to Professor Righi, much criticism was levelled at me in the early days because in my first experiments, I used a form of oscillator which had been devised by him and which itself was a modification of Hertz's oscillator. By availing myself of previous knowledge and working out theories already formulated, I did nothing but follow in the footsteps of Howe, Watt, Edison, Stephenson and many other illustrious inventors. I doubt very much whether there has ever been a case of a useful invention for which all the theory, all the practical applications and all the apparatus were the work of a man.

The university laboratory was simply not sufficient for Marconi's experiments. It was absolutely necessary for him to work with his own hands, without supervision and therefore without the risk of someone stealing his ideas.

For these reasons, Marconi sought his parents' permission to use the attic at the Villa Griffone as his laboratory. This odd request discouraged the elder Marconi even more about his son. Apart from the money involved, he was worried about Guglielmo's continuing failure to pursue a professional career. In Giuseppe Marconi's way of thinking, setting up a laboratory, even a rudimentary one, for the young man's "electrical games" was a complete waste of time.

In spite of his misgivings, the elder Marconi gave in to his wife's insistent requests, even agreeing to provide money for the purchase of the additional instruments and materials that Guglielmo needed for his work.

## A Detecting Bell

Desperate to realize his ideas—and terrified that someone might get there before him—Marconi locked himself up at the top of the house and started to work day and night. He was totally indifferent to sleep and hunger, and to his father's complaints about his absence from the family gatherings at meal times. He completely forgot the peaceful country walks, as well as his devotion to fishing. He left his workshop only when he needed a piece of equipment or information from the university library.

The young man spent his time in this way throughout the autumn of 1894. The family had planned to move back to Bologna at the beginning of winter, but Guglielmo informed his mother that it would be absolutely impossible for him to interrupt his work until the following spring. Annie did not need to be told twice. She happily sacrificed the conveniences of her home to support her son's work, using the opportunity to save money as a means of receiving her husband's consent.

Deeply convinced that Hertzian waves could transmit signals at a distance, the young inventor's first concern was to produce these elusive emissions for himself and to observe their effects in practice. His first task, therefore, was to repeat some of the experiments that Hertz and Righi had previously conducted.

Among his innovations since the time he had worked in the laboratory of Professor Rosa in Leghorn was the lightning-revealing machine. This basically consisted of an electrical circuit which included a battery, an electric bell and a tube of iron-filings, devised by Calzecchi-Onesti and Branly, that was used as a switch. In normal conditions, the metal dust would not conduct the current and the bell remained silent. When a storm erupted in the vicinity, however, and lightning began to flash, the iron filings were subjected to "cohesion." The electric current from the battery passed through and the bell began to ring. Marconi's house must have echoed to these trills a thousand times. But if the acoustic signals seemed to Annie to be further proof of her son's technical ability, they aroused little enthusiasm in Giuseppe. For the older Marconi, a bell was always and only a bell. The system was not even useful for warning the farm-hands that a storm was approaching, since thunderbolts announced their arrival.

Guglielmo was making progress, however. This simple and rudimentary piece of equipment helped him to make his invention more sensitive. The electric waves caused by the lightning discharges were far more powerful than the Hertzian waves which a Ruhmkorff spark-coil—no matter how large it was constructed—could produce.

For Marconi, the fact that the waves produced by lightning set off the alarm demonstrated beyond doubt that the waves could cover kilometers. "While admiring the country around Biella," he would later write, "I was convinced that man could find new energies, new resources, new means of communication in space. The free roads of space as avenues for the transmission of human thought have exercised a spell over me ever since. In them there are inexhaustible sources of inspiration for new works for the benefit of mankind."

Between the idea of wireless telegraphy and the actual realization of working machines, a host of difficulties and obstacles needed to be overcome. Guglielmo knew that he could not duplicate nature's powerful "radiators," and he could not count on the electric power of lightning to conduct his experiments.

At best, he had been able to put together some modest oscillators—first of the Hertz type, then in the style of Righi. He now faced a threefold problem that was difficult to solve from a technical point of view. First he had to increase the power of the oscillators, since they were to be used as transmitters. Once he had succeeded at this, he then had to invent devices which would augment the capacity without scattering its power. Finally, he had to substantially increase the sensitivity of the detectors.

## Working Method

Although Marconi worked on these problems incessantly, he did not reach the results for which he was hoping until the first months of

1895. In fact, his first attempts were total failures. Other young, less-dedicated young inventors might have abandoned the task, particularly since his conversations with Professor Righi were far from encouraging. But in those difficult months when everything seemed to conspire against him—from his father's lack of sympathy to the frequent failure of his experiments to the disappointing talks at the University—Marconi revealed the other formidable aspect of his personality: a stout determination. In the years to come, this would prove to be one of the essential and decisive factors in his final success.

Once Marconi conceived of the possibility for a system to transmit intelligible signals over a distance, nothing could quench the fire of his astonishing creative enthusiasm—neither his numerous experimental failures nor his ongoing lack of theoretical support. On the contrary, each new problem seemed to increase both his stubborn commitment and his remarkable inventiveness.

Silent and pensive by nature, Marconi retreated even more into his shell during those months at the end of 1894 and the beginning of 1895, opening his heart only to his mother. There is no written evidence of his state of mind during this period; but a number of events demonstrate how he must have been feeling. Professor Righi later recollected that Marconi limited himself to hearing only "a few pieces of advice" and to explanations of events and experiments which, to the professor, had nothing to do with radiotelegraphy.

Here we have a picture of the young Marconi's method of working. Carefully concealing his secret ambition, he asked Professor Righi for only the scientific and technical information necessary to clarify the behavior of a phenomenon—avoiding so far as he could any mention of his real intentions. Even as a young man, Marconi could easily anticipate the negative opinion which would have been expressed if his goals had been made public; and he also realized that the less he said, the less he risked being overtaken by somebody else.

Marconi was forced at the time to rely on a very rudimentary workshop in the attic at the Villa Griffone: a few tools lying on the table which had once been used by his grandfather to breed silkworms; makeshift instruments that the older man had either made with his own hands or bought second-hand or broken and then repaired. In sharp contrast with this, the laboratory of the University of Bologna had many sophisticated instruments with which men such as Righi himself and his assistants could have easily shot ahead of him—if they had only understood the importance of his experiments. The young inventor was certainly conscious of this and behaved accordingly.

After he had repeated Hertz's experiments—adopting as wave detector the two small terminal spheres of a copper conductor shaped in a ring—his next concern was the coherer. Marconi's first important change to the coherer would prove to be one of the fundamental reasons for his success. By this time, the inventor must have constructed dozens of little tubes filled with metal filings; on a purely empirical level, he had found that, of all metal dusts (copper, tin, lead, silver, nickel), the best yield was regularly offered by a mixture containing ninety-five percent nickel and five percent silver; the small grains of the metal dust also had to be extremely fine and as similar to one another as possible. After a whole series of experiments, he felt confident that the best results could be obtained with a mixture of nickel and silver filings placed between two plugs also made of silver. Eventually, he would produce a vacuum in that same little tube, bringing the sensitivity of the coherer to a level that is still unsurpassed.

In his first real breakthrough, Marconi finally managed to generate a ring from the bell of a detector circuit, placed at the end of his laboratory on the side opposite the transmitter. He had finally reproduced the effect of lightning discharges, using the small sparks of a Hertzian oscillator. The ringing of that tiny bell would prove to be the signal of his success.

## The Aerial and the Earth Plate

It was late at night. At the Villa Griffone everyone else was asleep, but the young man could not resist waking his mother to break the news. He then repeated the experiment just for her.

"Reproduced with rather rudimentary means," Marconi was later to write, "an oscillator similar to that used by Righi; I likewise reproduced a resonator using as a detector a glass tube with pulverized metal. By means of curved zinc sheets, I made two reflectors which I placed one opposite the other, at the maximum height allowed by the laboratory; at the center of the far room I placed the electric wave detector, and I linked it to a battery."

In the meantime, he had already moved into a room next to his original workshop in order to increase the distance of the transmission. When he switched off the circuit-breaker between the Ruhmkorff spark coil and the two little spheres of the spark-gap placed in the center of the semicylindric zinc reflector, the detector started to work. To measure the energy that the instrument could receive, Marconi would insert a voltmeter into the circuit of the metal dust tube, either in series with the electric bell or as a substitute for it.

Along with its many advantages, the coherer had one limiting and frustrating drawback. Every time the device received a signal, it had to be gently struck before it could receive further signals. Marconi soon corrected the situation by putting an electromagnet at the beginning of the circuit. The electromagnet set in motion a small hammer which tapped against a tube of filings every time a train of waves reached the detector and the coherer dust made contact with the instrument. In this way, the coherer was able to detect the arrival of Hertzian waves and to receive subsequent waves. This was the first device equipped to transmit and receive radioelectric impulses quickly and reliably.

As soon as he was able to test the new device and register its perfect performance, Marconi received the first confirmation that radiotelegraphy was effectively possible. To his delight, he could now progress to the next step in his experiments.

"The extremely weak current which I could generate with the material I had available," said the inventor, "was not sufficient to make a Morse apparatus work. I at once thought of reinforcing it by means of a relay, which I later did. For the moment I thought it was necessary above all to study the behavior of the electric waves at a greater distance, in the open air, outside the limited space of my laboratory. I had complete faith in that possibility. I went to talk to Professor Righi about it; he expressed serious doubts as the practicality of my project. And he was actually right, without the earth terminal".

Meanwhile, things were changing at the Villa Griffone. In the last months of 1894, Guglielmo was hard at work, shut away in his attic-workshop. As the young inventor labored in seclusion, tormented by his father's lack of understanding and the failure of his first experiments, the four daughters of his aunt, Mrs. Prescott, arrived in Pontecchio. Annie Marconi happily welcomed her sister's arrival, since the girls—particularly Daisy, Guglielmo's favorite cousin—who would bring, if nothing else, an amosphere of carefree cheerfulness to the large, isolated house.

Guglielmo had no intention of allowing the boisterous young girls into his laboratory, and, to prevent misunderstandings, he began locking himself inside. He instructed his mother that he did not want to be disturbed, even for his meals. She often left his favorite dishes outside the laboratory door, but began to worry because he appeared to be losing weight (as one can clearly see in pictures of the period).

After the experiments had finally started to yield results and the hope of success grew stronger, Guglielmo, in a rare display of good humor, actually allowed Daisy to visit his secret retreat. To the young girl's eyes, the modest workshop must have appeared more fabulous than a wizard's cell, particularly after one experiment that her cousin showed her.

Daisy was so impressed and spell-bound that she could not stop talking about it with her sisters, her aunt and even her uncle Giuseppe—as far as she was actually allowed to talk with the head of the Marconi household..

Daisy's enthusiasm, along with Annie Marconi's unceasing diplomacy, as well as reports by Vornelli, the carpenter, and the laborer Mignani (the two men sometimes did a few things for the inventor and were bound to have seen something), gradually convinced the incredulous Giuseppe that the young man was really working on something serious.


## Five Hundred Lira

After this, even Guglielmo's older brother, Alfonso, entered the inventor's world and started to help him when needed, and an atmosphere of excitement and expectation came to pervade the Villa Griffone. Guglielmo badly needed money to buy materials and instruments, and one day, probably on his mother's advice, he suddenly decided to talk openly with his father about his work and his needs. He told the older man of the successes he had already obtained and announced others to come.

The shrewd farmer was not easily persuaded, however. He had already seen one experiment, involving the bell and the little hammer applied to the coherer of the detecting machine, but he asked for a more convincing demonstration. He insisted that the detector's vibrations could have simply been a coincidence, and he asked his son to transmit the Morse signal of the letter "S," with its well-known and unmistakable three dots. This would involve the transmission of three rapid electromagnetic vibrations at very short regular intervals. Guglielmo, who had substituted a telegraph tapper for the primitive switch in the transmission circuit, immediately agreed to his father's proposal.

The demonstration was a complete success. From that moment on, the three dots of the letter "S" became the testing signal for all of Marconi's conquests in radiotelegraphy.

It seemed that Giuseppe's disbelief had finally been overcome. But when Marconi asked his father for money, Giuseppe demanded that his son first explain to him, in comprehensible terms, the principles of his invention and the grounds on which he based his hopes for future successes.

Giuseppe's argument was flawless. After all, if Guglielmo's invention was really open to future industrial application, he would later need a lot of money and would have to ask financial help from bank managers, businessmen and politicians. Such men, he insisted, would certainly not be inclined to invest funds on the inventor's word alone. Guglielmo then told his father the whole story of his research; he talked of his past successes and described what he would do in the immediate future. Giuseppe did not betray any enthusiasm at his son's "report." He understood that the young man was really on to something, but he also warned his son that wireless telegraphy would have no future if he did not succeed in transmitting and receiving signals at a great distance.

"Keep me informed of your progress, then we shall see," he counseled. Guglielmo was disappointed and confused by his father's response. Without money, how could he carry on and enlarge his experiments? Perhaps Guglielmo looked his father straight in the eye, convincing the older man of his seriousness. Or perhaps Giuseppe sensed his son's panic and desperation. Whatever it was that provoked him, Giuseppe suddenly searched through his pockets and put into his son's hand five hundred lira—even more than Guglielmo had requested, and more than enough to continue his experiments.

Within the family, Guglielmo had won a victory that he had probably been dreaming of for years. From that moment, his father not only stopped grumbling and saying "rubbish" each time he referred to his son's equipment; he also became both an admirer of and a wise adviser to his son's experiments.

Encouraged by the confidence placed in him after his initial success, Marconi redoubled his efforts and, in a relatively short time, he essentially completed his first real radiotelegraph transmitter with the introduction of an aerial and an earth plate.

In previous experiments with Hertz and Righi apparatuses, Marconi had used various kinds of reflecting metal plates to transmit and receive waves, but he soon understood the limitations of such instruments. Probably thinking back to his earlier experiments with "zinc arrows" in Leghorn, he now replaced the two outside balls of Righi's oscillator with two metal sheets. He then linked one to the earth while he lifted the other up in the air. The three spark Righi oscillator was, as had been demonstrated, more powerful than the original Hertzian instruments and permitted more intense and easily manageable wave train emissions. By substituting the balls with the earth plate and serial, Marconi widened the range of the oscillator emissions to an extent which was unthinkable at the time, even for someone like Righi. With the introduction of the earth-aerial system, Marconi was basically capable of generating and radiating waves which were much longer than any that had ever before been studied.

## From a Petrol Tank

In a letter to Luigi Solari, Marconi reported that, in order to achieve "waves longer than any which had been used at that time" (waves thirty to forty meters long), he had removed the earth and the aerial sheets from an old petrol tank. He continued:

> I then discovered the way to transmit waves at distances of hundreds of metres. By chance I set one of the iron sheets at a considerable distance from the ground and the other on the earth. Thanks to this position, the signals became so strong that I could extend the transmission range to a kilometre. I saw then for the first time a great new way opened to me. Not yet a triumph. Triumph was still very remote, but I understood at that moment that I was on the right road. My invention was born. Immediately afterwards I had the idea of replacing the sheet suspended in the air with copper wires. I kept the wires separated from each other by means of wooden sticks. A piece of copper buried in the earth was substituted for the plate on the ground. Once more the result was impressive. The earth-aerial system had been invented.

In the letter, Marconi claims that his recent achievement, the antenna-terra, was primarily a product of chance. It is hard to accept this statement. As at least one writer has pointed out, Marconi's attempt to credit the antenna-terra to "chance" is like the buyer of an entire lot of lottery tickets saying that the winning tickets were due to fate. Marconi had, in fact, conducted numerous experiments on the antenna-terra system. Moreover, this kind of apparatus had already been set up some years before by Calzecchi-Onesti, the inventor of the coherer—even if the earlier invention was somewhat different in structure and purpose.

Guglielmo certainly knew this, and it clearly gave a particular pattern and direction to his tests. He would later describe the events leading up to his discovery in the following way:

> When in 1895 I was making a series of experiments in Italy, I used an oscillator with one pole on the ground and the other linked to an insulated capacity, while the receiver was also placed on the ground and connected to a similar aerial. Aerials were formed by tin-plated iron cubes thirty centimeters wide (each side) and I realized that when they were placed on the top of a pole two metres high, it was possible for me to transmit the signals at a distance of thirty metres. With the aerial placed at the top of poles four metres high I was able to receive signals at a distance of one hundred metres from the transmitter, and with the same cubes placed eight metres above the ground, though keeping the rest unchanged, I could easily reach distances of about four hundred metres. Using larger cubes, one hundred centimeters wide, fixed at a height of eight metres, clear signals could be received within a radius of two thousand four hundred metres, which approximately corresponded to a mile and a half. These results seem to indicate that transmitting and receiving devices set up according to the plan in figure n. I [the reference is to an original sketch Marconi included with the text of a lecture he read on 2 March 1899 at a gathering of the Institution of Electric Engineers in London], that is to say, a radiator of the Hertzian type with a pole on the ground and the other linked to a vertical, or almost vertical, conductor, or to an aerial

placed at a certain height, and a resonator formed by the required receiver, also with the terminals connected one to the earth and the other to an insulated vertical conductor, form a transmission and reception system which could work at distances above those reached when using the normal Hertzian radiators and resonators".

"The results just quoted also indicate that the distance at which the signals could be received varies approximately with the square of the distance of the capacity (of the antenna) from the earth or perhaps with square root of the length of the vertical conductor."

By this time, Guglielmo had achieved results and acquired experimental data unimagined based on earlier research. On a theoretical level, he had arrived at notions ignored by everyone else at the time. In contrast with the scientific opinion of the time, which claimed that Hertzian waves could not radiate sufficiently in space for practical purposes, he was not deterred by the fact that "Hertzian waves seemed to vanish within a few metre range."

According to Maxwell's and Hertz's theories, sound waves obey laws that are analogous to those governing light waves. Marconi wondered why then was it not possible to extend their range simply by increasing the power of the apparatus radiating them and the sensitivity of the receiver? "If we had attributed to the power of light only the possibilities offered by a candle," Marconi wrote at the time, "we would never have built lighthouses and reflectors."

These are the simple considerations from which Marconi's idea had originated, and as Orin E. Dunlap has observed, this is why wireless telegraphy, by the time the earth-aerial device was used, was already more than an accidental episode. For Marconi; it was a typically premeditated discovery.

In test after test, Guglielmo increased the range of his transmitters and the sensitivity of the receiving instruments. The broadcasting station was a fixed apparatus on the top floor of the Villa Griffone. A wire ran out of the house wall and joined the transmitters to a copper plate buried in the earth; another wire ran to the antenna, which had a variety of shapes. They were either isolated plates hanging on a piece of wood, or a series of wires stretched between two poles. The receiving apparatus, which repeated the fundamental aerial-earth system, was portable.

After additional experiments that ranged as far as the edges of the field around the house, the signals sent by Marconi widened remarkably: first one hundred, then two hundred, four hundred, and finally six hundred meters. On the transmission tapper, he would strike the three dots of the letter "S"; his brother Alfonso, his eye fixed on the coherer of the detecting instrument, checked the reception of the signals and waved a handkerchief so that the inventor could see it from the laboratory window. A vertical wave meant "received"; a horizontal one meant the opposite. Soon the morning of the famous gunshot would arrive.

4

GREAT BRITAIN UNDERSTANDS

## Disappointment from Rome

Now that he had demonstrated the possibility of broadcasting
signals over physical obstacles—even those formed by hills—
Guglielmo no longer had any doubt that he had invented something
exceptional. But how could he get his new telecommunication system accepted and applied in a way that would earn him the credit he
deserved? More specifically, how could he now protect the propri-
etorship of his method of wireless telegraphy?

The Marconi family discussed these problems at length among
themselves and also sought advice outside the family. There were
two people in Pontecchio whose opinion Giuseppe held in great
esteem. One was the family physician, Doctor Gardini, and the other
the parish priest. The two men were invited to the Villa Griffone
and informed of the experiments and of the results achieved by
Guglielmo. Consultations lasted several hours; at the end everyone
agreed that a proper letter should be written to the Ministry of
Posts and Telegraphs. The resulting missive was a masterpiece: on

the one hand, it placed great stress on the importance and future possibilities of Marconi's invention; on the other, it revealed nothing about the design or functioning of the apparatus that would allow for the possibility of plagiarism. The letter asked the Italian state to cooperate so that Guglielmo's work could continue "in the interests of the nation."

The letter was sent by registered mail to the Minister of Posts and Telegraphs. Waiting for an answer from Rome was an exhausting business for the entire family. Giuseppe was the most anxious, but Guglielmo continued stoically with his experiments, seemingly undisturbed by the delay.

At last the postman from Pontecchio brought the long-awaited reply. The reply was written by a Ministry civil servant. According to a deeply rooted tradition of Italian bureaucracy, he issued neither a denial nor an approval of the request. It was simply: the sort of expedient which allowed the bureaucrat to put the document on file and his "conscience" at rest. Observing that wireless telegraphy might be useful for sea communications, the letter's author did encourage the inventor to continue with his experiments. About possible help and direct interest from the Italian state, however, there was not a word.

Everyone was, of course, disconcerted and embittered by both the delay in response and the inconclusive answer, especially Dr. Gardini. Although he was also disappointed by the news, Guglielmo did not lose heart, nor did he doubt for a moment the importance and practical possibilities of wireless telegraphy.

"First of all I offered wireless telegraphy to Italy," Guglielmo Marconi would later write, "but it was intimated to me that perhaps, in view of the close connection between wireless telegraphy and the sea, it would be better to go to England, where the maritime activities are more highly developed, and, after all, it was logically the best country for my first attempts at overseas signalling. My mother's English relatives also gave me some help. But do keep this in mind, Italy never said that the invention was useless, only that wireless telegraphy in those days seemed to be promising for sea activities, and this was how I came to London".

Marconi's explanation came at a time when he had already made the overseas transmission tests and was enjoying a wave of success, with strong support from the Italian Government. The events which carried him to England were much more complicated. But Marconi had his own reasons for describing the events in this way. In addition to his lifelong patriotism, he had also become a captain of industry—though he also remained an experimental scientist. He therefore had the discretion not to offend the Italian authorities, a courtesy that they would later reciprocate with honors and financial assistance.

In 1895, at the Villa Griffone, Marconi's family had quickly passed from enthusiasm over Guglielmo's amazing invention to bitterness at the Ministry's denial of aid to uncertainty about the next step to take. Radiotelegraphy could become a working reality only if it received recognition and acknowledgement from authorities in the government and in the scientific world. Marconi might have talked to some eminent scientists—inviting Righi, for example, to watch some of his experiments—but his well-founded fear of being upstaged prevented even this option.

Marconi knew that, if his work and equipment were leaked before the invention was protected with a patent, there was always the risk that someone might steal his thunder. Once again, it was Annie who came up with the solution.

After all, she consoled her son, the Italian Ministry of Posts and Telegraphs had already hinted at the endless possibilities for radiotelegraphy at sea. And England, she reminded him, was then the most important maritime nation. These considerations, plus the fact that Mrs. Marconi had a vast and influential number of relatives in the British Isles, prompted her to write to England. Among her relatives, Annie had a nephew, Henry Jameson Davis, who, after earning a degree in engineering, had served in Queen Victoria's army as a colonel and had a number of friends and useful acquaintances in scientific and technical circles in London. It is impossible to know how many letters Annie sent to England or the tone of the replies; the result, however, was that, at the end of this intense correspondence, Guglielmo Marconi's future was arranged. He would go to Britain together with his mother. There he would present his equipment and experiments to that country's authorities.

## The First Patent

On 2 February 1896, Annie Jameson and her son boarded the train at Bologna station that would take them to London via Paris-Calais. Giuseppe and the rest of the family saw them off. The two passengers had packed more than their share of luggage, including a black metal box which had been carefully built under Guglielmo's special supervision. The box contained the inventor's most valuable radiotelegraphy instruments.

Before Guglielmo and his mother's departure, Dr. Gardini had written a letter to his friend, General Ferrero, the Italian Ambassador in London, providing the young man with a formal introduction:

"Guglielmo Marconi," explained Gardini to the ambassador, "has succeeded in sending signals by means of the wireless telegraph a distance of one thousand five hundred metres with a machine he has invented. He has been invited to London, but before leaving Italy he would like to offer his invention to the Italian Government. He would welcome Your Excellency's friendly and invaluable advice."

General Ferrero replied:

I advise young Marconi to protect his invention with regularly authorized patents all over the world, to maintain liberty of action for future dealings with the Italian Government in any commercial agreement for the transfer of his patents, and to feel free to go wherever he can most easily find the large funds he requires to launch such a new and important invention which will not be a secret for long.

This was obviously the best reply that the ambassador could give under the circumstances. On the one hand, he had no choice but to allow Marconi to go to England, where he could find both more generous assistance and understanding; on the other hand, Ferrero was careful to safeguard the future interests of the Government he represented.

When they reached London, Annie and Guglielmo found the young man's cousin, Henry Jameson Davis, waiting to meet them at Victoria Station. Davis remembered his aunt very well, but he could not possibly have recognized Guglielmo, whom he had last seen on a visit to the Villa Griffone when the inventor was barely three years old. The meeting was a friendly one, and as they had agreed in the letters they had previously exchanged, Henry took mother and son to another relative's house, since there was no room in his own.

Guglielmo related his experiments in detail to his engineer cousin; he told him of the results and also showed him the equipment he had with him in the black metal box. Unfortunately, a disastrous accident had occured during the journey from Bologna to London. At English Customs, one of Her Majesty's zealous officers opened the black container, saw its strange contents and refused to let them through without making sure that the odd instruments were not intended for some assassination attempt. He insisted on unscrewing clamps, unplugging wires, and otherwise meddling with the coherer to "investigate" the Ruhnkorff spark-coils. Before he had finished his investigation, the officer had tampered with the various instruments so much that they could no longer be used. His suspicions, of course, were probably exasperated by the inventor's mumbling in response to many of his questions. Guglielmo was not about to reveal his secrets to anyone—not even a custom's officer.

Once in England, Guglielmo's first concern was to repair the instruments. Henry was eager to help. Aan engineer himself, he immediately understood the importance of his cousin's work. He took upon himself the task of finding the necessary materials. After the instruments had been adequately repaired, there was still the problem of protecting the invention of radiotelegraphy with an English patent. Henry took his cousin to one of the best lawyers in London, a specialist in patents, in order to identify the best course to adopt. Meanwhile, Henry and the other relatives, with the agreement of Marconi and his mother, plotted the best way to identify and approach an English authority suitably qualified in the field of communications.

They soon agreed on a definite course of action. First, the inventor would buy the patent. After that would follow the launching phase and the commercial development of the invention. But things did not go exactly as planned.

The formulation of the patent request was extremely laborious. Marconi wrote it, corrected it, and rewrote it several times before he was satisfied with the results. Finally, on 2 June 1896, the application, along with the necessary documentation and the expedients suggested by the lawyer, was filed at the London Patent Office.

In the document, Guglielmo reserved the right to include a further note with more detailed explanations. This extra document was filed almost a year later, on 2 March 1897, under the title, "Improvements in Transmitting Electrical Impulses and Signals and in Apparatus therefore." The patent was officially recognized on the 2nd of July of the same year with the number 12039.

"I, Guglielmo Marconi, of 71, Herefore Road, Bayswater, in the County of Middlesex," began Marconi's patent statement, "do hereby declare the nature of this invention to be as follows: according to this invention, electrical actions or manifestations are transmitted through the air, earth or water by means of electric oscillations of high frequency."

The document also describes the legal patent claims against possible plagiarism including modifications of some parts of the circuit or the equipment.

## The Engineer-in-Chief of the British Post Office

Even before the application for a patent, several important events had taken place in the Marconi-Jameson household. Mrs. Jameson, after staying for some time with her relatives, realized that Guglielmo's activities required both time and tranquillity, and decided that it would be best for the two to rent a house of their own. They chose one at 71 Hereford Road, in Kensington, with Giuseppe once again covering the expenses. This allowed the inventor more time and space to carry on his work, continue his studies and increase his contacts with English society.

Nor did Marconi neglect his contact with the Italian ambassador, General Ferrero. In the following months, he took full, advantage of the previous introduction by Dr. Gardini. As Guglielmo would later write, "Almost immediately on my arrival in London, I called on General Ferrero, the Italian ambassador, and subsequently had numerous meetings and interviews with him."

Marconi's family connections, along with the value of his ideas and experiments, put him right at the center of London high society. Among Guglielmo's many admirers was Campbell Swinton, a distinguished and much admired scholar who was introduced to the inventor by the latter's cousin Henry. The English scientist immediately understood the value of Marconi's work and the vast possibilities it offered. On 30 March 1896, he wrote a letter of introduction for Guglielmo to the chief engineer of the English Post and Telegraph Services, Sir William Preece.

Even as it marked the effective arrival of wireless telegraphy to England, the letter was extremely laconic, in keeping with the traditional English style. Nevertheless, it included all the elements necessary to raise Preece's curiosity. Not only did Swinton know his own authority in the scientific field, he was also fully aware of Preece's own attempts at wireless telegraphy based on induction—attempts which, up to that time, had proven unsuccessful.

Swinton's letter began:

Dear Mr. Preece,

I'm taking the liberty of sending to you with this note a young Italian of the name of Marconi who has come over to this country with the idea of getting taken up a new system of telegraphy without wires, at which he has been working. It appears to be based upon the use of Hertzian waves, and Oliver Lodge's coherer, but from what he tells me, he appears to have gone considerably beyond what I believe other people have done in this line.

It has occurred to me that you might possibly be kind enough to see him and hear what he has to say, and I also think that what he has done will very likely be of interest to you.

Hoping that I am not troubling you too much.

Believe me

Yours very truly,

A.A.C. Swinton

## From the Office to the Laboratory

The first encounter between Marconi and Preece was witnessed by an assistant to the head of postal services, a young man who went by the name of Mullis. This is how he described that historical meeting which took place at the Head Office of the British Postal Service in St. Martin's-Le-Grand:

Mr. Probert [the electric-light superintendent] brought into Mr. Preece's room a young foreigner who was introduced as Signor Guglielmo Marconi. He had with him two large bags. After mutual hand shaking and while the Chief cleaned his gold-rimmed spectacles, the contents of these bags were placed on the table and seemed to consist of a number of brass knobs fitted to rods, a large spark coil and some odd terminals, but most fascinating of all a large-sized tubular bottle from which extended two rods. So far as could be seen, these terminated inside the bottle on two discs, very close together. Between them could be seen some bright filings or metal particles.

This immediately took the Chief's eye and was obviously, by the careful way it was handled, something of great importance and certainly of particular interest to Mr. Preece.

Mullis does not add anything else to his account. He reveals neither the content nor the tone of the conversation between the Italian inventor and the technologist who took an immediate liking to the "naive and open" young man (Preece's own words). The pieces of equipment that Marconi eventually displayed, along with their relative diagrams, excited considerable admiration. Perhaps Mullis had had to leave the room while the equipment was being displayed—a suggestion later offered by Marconi's daughter Degna. Whatever the explanation for the lapse in observation, Mullis continued his description at midday, when Preece called him and said: "It has gone on twelve. Now take this young man over to the refreshment bar and see that he gets a good dinner to my account, and come back here by two o'clock."

At two o'clock sharp (we can be sure of this because Marconi was punctuality itself; he fiercely hated habitual late-comers and on this particular afternoon had excellent reasons to be on time), the two men were back at Preece's office. Mullis continued:

> The Chief came along, and as we entered the room, I noticed that everything was just as left, with the exception of a piece of paper which had been placed under the contact of the telegraph key. This was removed and after one or two preliminary adjustments to the connections and brass balls by Mr. Marconi, the key was depressed and immediately the bell on the adjacent tube commenced and continued to ring. Mr. Marconi then went over to the glass tube, gave this a few sharp taps and the bell ceased ringing.
>
> I knew by the Chief's quiet manner and smile that something unusual had been effected. The following day and the rest of the week experiments were run off.

If Mullis's report gives a faithful picture of what took place at Preece's office, it seems that Marconi brought Sir William only a few of his instruments, intending to bring out the others for the next experiments.

In fact, Marconi had already invented the automatic "decoherer" by the time he met Preece. This instrument could not possibly have been the "large bottle" described by the English Post Office clerk, nor would Marconi have needed to move in order to reactivate the coherer after the first discharge had been registered—if he had brought all his paraphernalia with him.

All this seems perfectly logical, since Marconi's initial introduction to Preece took place in an office, while the subsequent experiments described by Mullis were conducted in the well-equipped laboratory of the British Telegraphic Services, where Sir William was the director.

## A Genuine Friendship

During the weeks following his introduction to Preece, Marconi's experiments were frequent and, for the most part, fully justified his hopes.

A warm friendship quickly developed between Sir William and the young Marconi, despite the differences in age and position. As the tests continued and Marconi's invention proved capable of more and more fruitful applications, the chief engineer of the English Post Office no longer restricted participation in the experiments to his most direct collaborators and assistant; instead he started to invite technical experts from the General Post Office. Preece also allowed one of his most skilled technicians, a former naval officer named George Stevens Kemp, to become the inventor's first assistant. Kemp would eventually become one of Marconi's most faithful and trusted disciples, remaining with the inventor until the end of his life.

One of Marconi's first open-air demonstrations, carried out with Preece's assistance, consisted of transmitting signals from the roof of the Post Office to the roof of another building in Queen Victoria Street. The two places were approximately one mile apart, but several tall buildings obstructed communications.

In spite of the threat of interference, the test was a complete success, and Preece suggested Guglielmo should move on to long range experiments in the open countryside.

This is how Degna Marconi later described her father's successful initial introduction to Kemp, during his experiments over the roofs of London:

> When he looked over the ornate stone balustrade, he saw a red-headed fellow watching him curiously. The man on the pavement caught my father's eye and shouted up, 'What are you doing there?' Marconi called back, 'Come on up and I'll show you.'
>
> "The onlooker arrived on the roof with such remarkable promptness that my father believed he had scrambled up the drain. (I sincerely hope not for the Post Office is a towering building eight stories high.) The second that George Kemp reached the rooftop, he went to work for Marconi, and continued to work for him forever after. In 1896 he was an ex-petty officer of the Navy,
>
> employed at the Post Office as one of Preece's helpers. Marconi's staff was beginning to form."

Though first-hand, the account tells only part of the story. If it was true that Kemp was working at the British Post Office as Preece's assistant, then the red-haired fellow was certainly not a new face to Marconi; on the contrary, Guglielmo probably already knew of Kemp's skill and had him in mind as a possible collaborator. It is also likely that Preece appointed Kemp, at least in part, to keep an eye on Marconi and report what he was doing. Whatever the reason for or the circumstances of his initial meeting with Kemp,, Marconi was capable of arousing immediate enthusiasm in the people who came into contact with him, and the inventor's future assistant was clearly not an exception.

The London experiment took place on 27 July 1896, in the presence of scholars and other eminent figures officially invited by Preece. By that time, Marconi had already improved his invention to a point where he could connect a Morse recorder to the receiving circuit—an achievement which aroused the admiration and wonder of the entire British scientific community.

A Morse receiver consists of a stylus attached to a lever operated by an electromagnet. A clockwork motor moves a slip of paper under the stylus, on which it leaves ink marks—dots and dashes of the Morse alphabet—whenever the electrical circuit is completed or broken. Guglielmo had already tried an apparatus that included this type of receiver while he was in Pontecchio. In a lecture he gave on 3 March 1905 at the Royal Institution in front of the Duke of Northumberland, Marconi reported:

> The author, between 1895 and 1896, carried out his first tests with an apparatus based on principles which have allowed the success of radiotelegraphy over long distances. This initial apparatus is represented by Figures 1, 2, and 3. Figures 1 and 2 illustrate the receiving and transmitting apparatus; in Figure 3 are shown the circuits of the receiver

Here, the inventor is referring to diagrams that he himself had drawn. The last of these showed the electric circuit of the apparatus, in which he had included a Morse receiver.

## An Italian Without a Monkey

According to one of the many anecdotes surrounding Marconi's life, the first five hundred lira that he received from his father was spent on an old Morse receiver from a junk shop in Bologna.

The Morse receiver originally used by Marconi was fed by an independent battery and plugged into the circuit of the receiving apparatus by means of a relay (involving an electromagnet). The device was activated when the coherer—picking up the Hertzian waves—released the current to the electromagnet. Also connected to the electromagnet was the little hammer, which would "decohere" the tube of metal filings and govern the motion of the stylus.

Marconi's breakthrough had startling repercussions. When the test was about to start, Preece informed Marconi publicly: "Young man, you have done something really exceptional; accept my deepest congratulations."

Apart from the Post Office officials, Marconi's work also began to attract the attention of the technicians of the Army and Navy; the story was soon taken up by the newspapers. With the press coverage, of course, came many malicious comments. One newspaper, obviously recalling experiences with earlier immigrants from Southern Italy, had this to say:

> It may be another Italian with his barrel-organ, but without the monkey, and the organ doesn't play, though it seems to be making plenty of noise all the same.

In spite of the incredulity and opposition from the press, however, Marconi was proving triumphant among the leading authorities in the field. In successive tests in the countryside near Salisbury Plain, Guglielmo managed to transmit signals over a distance of fourteen kilometers. The transmitter was housed in a shed and the receiver on a small cart, so that it could be moved. This was in accordance with Marconi's requirements, to enable him to study, in more detail than had been possible in Pontecchio, the wave propagation with copper parabolic reflectors concentrating the radiated energy in a particular direction. With the completion of the first large-scale campaign, the newspaper were finally convinced of the significance of Marconi's experiments, and the news even spread to Italy.

Marconi's first interview with the Italian press was published in *La Tribuna* on 23 December 1897, and signed by Olindo Malagodi. A few days earlier, William Preece had given a much-discussed lecture in London. Malagodi's account, published under the title, "Wireless telegraphy; Important invention by an Italian - Interview with the inventor," follows, including a brief preface by the interviewer.

London, December 23rd—(O.M.)

Last week Mr. Preece, leading English expert on telegraphy, delivered a lecture at Toynbee Hall on the unusual subject of the possibilities of wireless telegraphy. After recalling that as long ago as 1838 the German scientist Steinhiel had announced this possibility, he listed some of the events which have taken place in his own department, leading the English government to allocate a sum of twenty-five thousand francs for experiments. The money was spent, but without serious results.

"But I have a great surprise in store for you. A short time ago a young Italian electrician came to see me, with a new system, which we immediately tested on Salisbury Plain with excellent results, over a distance of a mile and three quarters. This young man is Signor Guglielmo Marconi, who is present here today and who will be able to repeat some of these experiments for you in miniature.

According to Preece's later recollections, the experiments were a complete success and the young man was warmly applauded. Preece then announced that the English Government had ordered further experiments with the new invention, with no expenses spared.

Preece continued before the delighted audience:

For further information about the nature and the uses of the new invention, I asked Signor Marconi for an interview which he kindly gave. Marconi is a young man: he was born in Bologna in 1874 of an Italian father and a British mother. He has not studied regularly at the university, but is self-taught according to a characteristic Italian tradition. Only lately has he studied some problems in physics with Professor Righi of Bologna University. He came to London about ten months ago, on private business and it was only a series of casual circumstances that led him to inform the British Government of his invention.

"What is the nature and the aim of your discovery and how did it come about?" asked Malagodi, in the interview with the inventor that followed the transcript of Preece's lecture.

"My discovery," the young electrician answered, "does not contain any new principle, but the applications and extension of principles already known. It took shape in my mind little by little. I never thought of exploiting it immediately, and I did not expect to see it welcomed so suddenly and with such great interest by the British Press. Mr. Preece's lecture has now involved me in a massive correspondence ."

"Could you explain to me, as simply as possible, your invention and the scientific principles on which it is based?" Malagodi inquired further. Marconi responded:

Very well. Some time ago Hertz discovered electric rays or vibrations which radiated in a straight line exactly as light rays do and which had similar properties of refraction and so on. He also succeeded in registering the effects of these rays on machines which are now known as Hertz resonators. But the effects received by Hertz did not go beyond a distance of fifty metres. Moreover, though they could overcome many obstacles, they were intercepted by a metal plate or by a land mass. Therefore, thinking at first only of this problem, I tried to obtain a more sensitive receiver and, so to speak, to reinforce the power of these rays. And in fact I have succeeded in getting these electrical vibrations to act at a distance of three thousand and five hundred metres, seventy times more than Hertz's distance. In the second place I have succeeded in making the vibrations travel through metal plates and through a mountain as they do through the air. This fact is important because over a distance of a few kilometers when there is no obstacle, other means of communication can be used and mine would be redundant. The idea of telegraph communication by these means and without metal wires came to me later in the summer of 1895 while I was at the Bagni di Adorno."

Noticeable here, once again, is Marconi's postponement of the date of his discovery in order to avoid discussing his disappointments and failures in 1894. The interview, therefore, deals only with the principle which led him to include the independent circuit of the Morse machine with a simple relay, fed by the circuit of the radio receiver, with the antenna, the coherer and the earth plate as its basic elements. Marconi told the interviewer:

The obstacle I then had to face, was that the action of these vibrations was too weak and could not start the telegraph machine.

But I succeeded in overcoming this difficulty too. I thought, that if these vibrations were not powerful enough to act directly themselves, they would still be powerful enough to operate another electric force. To explain this idea, I shall use a simple simile. Isn't it true that the driver of a railway engine doesn't have enough strength to turn the wheels? And yet with an action requiring a limited strength, he opens a tap and releases the steam power which sets them in motion. I thought of getting these electric vibrations to play the part of the engine driver by linking them on a battery connected with the telegraph machine, so obtaining the emission of the force necessary to do the job."

"Would you like to say something about the consequences and practical applications of your discovery?" asked Malagodi. Marconi continued.:

It is hard to foresee them all. To start with, I shall mention those which the English Government is now trying. It is thought that my invention is applicable above all in wartime, during military operations and in the Navy. During a war, this wireless telegraphy will make quick and easy communications possible between those divisions which would otherwise find themselves cut off, as at the Battle of Adua. However, even more important will be its applications at sea. When one of these devices is fitted in a lighthouse and ships have their receivers, as soon as they come within three or four thousand metres, an alarm bell will ring. This is important in rain and fog, when the lighthouses are not visible. In this way, we shall have an electrically controlled lighthouse, which will always operate, unlike the one depending on light, which is so uncertain. In the same way we shall be able to avoid collisions between ships, and so on.

"And is this system going to be used for everyday telegraph communications at long distances?" asked Malagodi in closing.

"In theory there are no obstacles," replied the inventor, "but it will certainly be first necessary to overcome many practical difficulties. Meanwhile we shall consider the applications which are already possible; and at the beginning of the new year we shall start experiments ordered by the English Government at Penzance."

Malagodi concluded the interview and the article by summarizing the following disclaimer from Marconi:

> With this I ended the interview. I should report that Signor Marconi then added that the explanations just given are expressed in popular language, his aim being to give a simple idea of what the invention involved, and that his words cannot therefore be taken as a basis for scientific analysis; this will be possible when the overall theory of the invention and details of the experiments are published.

## Unusual Maturity

Even in the form of short-hand notes taken by the journalist Malagodi, these statements reveal once again Marconi's remarkable skill and caution in disclosing details concerning his inventions. As always, he discussed his work only so far as it suited him, offering not one word more than was strictly necessary to achieve his ends.

He makes it clear that wireless telegraphy is not based on new principles, but that it uses information which has been available to physicists for some time. He does not advance any of the arguments underlying the details, and in order to protect himself from criticism from the academic community (he may be thinking of people such as Righi), he warns that the example he has given of the engine dri-ver is strictly for the layman; he rightly underlines (and asks the journalist to report) that his declarations cannot be used as material for scientific discussion. Scholarly objections will, of course, have to wait for the right time and place when the theory of his telegraph system and his results will be explained in full, he says.

Reading this first interview, one can see the outlines of the figure who will dominate the following chapters: a far-sighted captain of industry and a broad-minded business man who knows exactly how to single out the area in which his "products" can be introduced with high profits and great success for himself—military communi-cations. Marconi's reference to the then-recent battle of Adua is not at all accidental, nor are his comments on sea communications. And like a consummate marketing expert who does not want to alarm his competitors, he wisely cautions that, though there are no theoretical obstacles to the eventual use of his invention for long-distance tele-graph communications, considerable difficulties will first have to be overcome before his invention can possibly challenge the dominance of the telegraph in long-distance communications.

Other inventors, riding high on the winds of success, might have been carried away by enthusiasm and held nothing back from the interviewer. Amazingingly for one so young and inexperienced in such matters, Guglielmo, at the age of 22, had already acquired the sagacity and self-control of an old hand.

The reference to the Army and Navy, in an interview with the largest Italian newspaper of the time, must certainly have been directed at the authorities of his own country, who were growing increasingly curious about his invention, as Marconi had learned from his conversations with General Ferrero.

The article was written after the British and European press had given wide coverage to the Italian inventor's successes, following both

Preece's and Guglielmo's lectures and the public demonstrations at the Royal Institution on 11 December 1896.

During the first experiments on Salisbury Plain, which started on 2 September 1896, Marconi's apparatus had succeeded in transmitting signals at a distance of almost two miles. During those tests, apart from the distance problem, Marconi was mainly concerned with the mechanisms regulating the action and the radiation of waves. In March 1897, when further research was conducted in the same area, transmissions reached still longer distances (from four to fifteen kilometers) and were also used to make a whole series of tests on the different modes of behavior of Hertzian "rays". At the time, Marconi was operating with waves whose length ranged from seventy to three hundred meters and with short waves of about sixty centimeters, gathered and reflected by means of a copper parabolic mirror one meter in diameter. This enabled him to demonstrate on a large scale what he had first realized in Pontecchio as a boy—that short waves could be directed "in a beam" to specific areas, and that longer waves could overcome obstacles such as hills and mountains.

To explain this phenomenon, the inventor frequently used the following analogy: "Short waves behave like short quick ripples which hit a rock and come back; while longer waves go beyond the rock by going round it."

It would later be discovered, of course, that the propagation of electric signals from one end of the globe to the other takes place for completely different reasons—the zone around the earth which reflects electromagnetic waves like a mirror. At the turn of the century, however, geophysics was still far from these future acquisitions. Aware of the theoretical limitations of his discovery, the young Marconi was proceeding cautiously—exactly as the scientific method from Galileo onwards had taught—basing each step strictly on experimental results and leaving all theoretical interpretations to others.

He was interested in developing a system which could transmit human words at a great distance, overcoming all obstacles of time and space. He wanted the facts to speak for themselves, proving that his idea was not a dream and that the instruments he had invented, when improved or at least modified for his own purposes, were perfectly adequate to transmit and receive telegraph messages without the aid of wires.

## Giuseppe's Almanacs

After the first experiments over the roofs of London and on Salisbury Plain, Marconi was overwhelmed with letters from all over Europe. The correspondence increased even more after the historic lecture by Preece at the Royal Institution and the related experiments by Marconi—all diligently reported by Olindo Malagodi in *La Tribuna*.

The letters included many incredible offers and requests. One writer offered himself as wireless telegraphy agent for a country or region. Others offered money and admiration. Others, of course, were skeptical and sarcastic. There were even bizarre protests; one lady strongly objected because "the waves sent by Marconi in the ether" had caused an annoying form of pins and needles in her feet. There was also mail from Italy. Degna Marconi later recalled that a Milan bank offered the incredible sum of 300,000 Lira for the rights to Marconi's invention.

The latter offer had, of course, interested Guglielmo's father, who was still running a very large farm at the Villa Griffone. From time to time, Giuseppe sent his wife and son the money necessary to remain in London in suitable style. He also corresponded regularly with both his wife and son, and was very proud of the ongoing triumph of the boy whose extraordinary talents he had been slow to recognize.

In this instance, the elder Marconi urged his son to accept the bank's offer. Faced with his own financial pressures, he could not help but consider the immediate possibility of investing in an attractive piece of property bordering his own, the Villa Banzi at Pontecchio. He sent his son full details, including the number of cattle and the condition of the various agricultural products.

Giuseppe's advice to sell to the first bidder may also have been prompted, at least in part, by fatherly affection and a desire to have his son back home. For years he had neglected his, and he now longed to make up for the past with his son settled comfortably, and prosperously, beside him. The older man must certainly have felt lonely ever since Guglielmo and Annie first departed for England.

During the period from the inventor's departure for the British Isles, on 2 February 1896, through his return to Italy in the summer of 1897, Giuseppe sent many moving letters to his son, even if written in the undemonstrative style of a country gentleman. There is also a series of notes in Giuseppe's "almanacs," which include brief descriptions of the sale of agricultural products, purchases of shoes and bills paid to the blacksmiths—along with accounts of the most important events of his life, including remarks on letters received from his wife and his son; the answers he sent; his money orders mailed to England; and details of his journey to Great Britain after Guglielmo's triumph. Thirty-two of Giuseppe's "diary-calendars" are now contained in the library of Bologna University, carefully documenting the lives of Giuseppe and his son from 1857 to 1901.

## General Ferrero

While in London, Guglielmo had tried to keep on good terms with the authorities in his own country, in spite of the initial disappointment from Rome, through his contact with the Italian ambassador in London, General Ferrero. Marconi made no secret of his strong patriotic sentiments and his desire to place the invention of wireless telegraphy at the disposal of the Italian Government.

One does not need to be a cynic to suggest that the inventor behaved in this way for reasons that were not entirely patriotic; certainly Marconi's passion for his native Italy was sincere, but he also needed to allow himself room to maneuvre in case things did not work out in England. It is worth citing an official communication on this matter from the Italian Embassy in London, preserved in a note by Marconi:

> Royal Italian Embassy in London—20, Grosvenor Square, London, W1—4th January, 1896.
> Dear Sir,
> I am delighted to be able to offer you my congratulations on the successes that, according to what you say, your experiments in wireless telegraphy transmission have achieved. I should be happy to come and see your equipment. Have the kindness to accept my invitation for lunch at the Embassy next Thursday, at one o'clock. Afterwards, we shall be able to see your instruments or arrange a suitable day for an appointment. Accept, dear Sir, the expressions of my high esteem. The royal ambassador, A. Ferrero.

The memo's date is obviously a typist's mistake; in fact, Marconi had left Pontecchio for the British Isles on 2 January 1896, and could not possibly have been in the British capital on the fourth. Since it was only the fourth day of the year, the typist must have inadvertently written 1896, instead of 1897.

Of interest, the letter bears the following address: "Signor G. Marconi - 67, Talbot Road, Westbourne Park, W." Guglielmo's mother, after a brief stay at Hereford Road had decided with her son's consent to rent a house more suited to the inventor's new position. For this reason, the two had moved to the house at Talbot Road, which was to be Guglielmo's residence for many years.

In a recent study published in the *Giornale della Società Fisica Italiana* (July-September 1973) in the Archives of the Italian Embassy in London, Professor M. Gervasi presents an original letter in Marconi's own hand-writing, dated 20 December 1896. It was in answer to this letter that General Ferrero wrote the previously quoted invitation.

Guglielmo's letter follows in its entirety:

67, Talbot Road,
Westbourne Park,
London, W.
20 December, 1896.

Excellency. As your Excellency will remember I had the pleasure approximately ten months ago to inform you that I had discovered a system of telegraphing between two places without the need for conducting wires.

I now believe it is my duty to inform Your Excellency that, as I have been introduced by some of my mother's relatives to Mr. W.H. Preece F.R.S. Chief Engineer of the British Telegraphs, he has kindly offered me the assistance of the Post Office in carrying out some experiments with my system.

These experiments have taken place in London and near Salisbury.

Before describing the results obtained, I will say a few words about the system adopted.

As a transmitter I use an instrument reproducing electrical radiations (oscillations which are similar to those discovered by Hertz). These radiations are projected by a parabolical reflector and falling on the receiving instrument through a device (which I think I have invented) activate an ordinary telegraph such as a Morse key.

If the radiations sent by the transmitter are sent forth and interrupted according to the signals of Morse code, the receiver acts in such a way as to reproduce the signals.

This system's advantage over the heliograph or optical telegraph is that its signals are unaffected by darkness or fog, and even obstacles such as trees or houses do not prevent the transmission of signals.

Moreover with another system of mine, which has also been tried out at Salisbury, we have discovered something which is of considerable scientific interest, that a hill more than one kilometre wide between the transmitter and the receiver would not obstruct the transmission in the least.

In the tests at Salisbury we have used small and primitive pieces of equipment which I have built myself. With these we have obtained good signals at 2800 meters from the transmitter; at 3200 metres, we have also obtained signals, but rather uncertain.

The transmitter was operated by a small battery providing 8 volts and 3 amperes.

The British Government has shown a great interest in these tests, and I have been notified that it intends to spend whatever is necessary to test and develop my invention, and it has already decided to spend Lira 200 in tests which will take place near Cardiff immediately after the beginning of the New Year.

As there no longer seems [to be] any doubt about the possibility of obtaining wireless signals at a distance of 20 or 30 kilometers by means of more powerful and highly developed apparatuses, I believe the system will be of great use to the Italian Army.

I have applied for the patents for this system of mine in the most important countries of the world.

I will be very pleased and honored if Your Excellency would like to see the instruments I have made. I have the honor to declare myself the most obedient servant of Your Excellency, Guglielmo Marconi.

The first thing once notices about this piece, written by the twenty-two year old Marconi, is the inventor's limited familiarity with the Italian language. (There are even some spelling mistakes in the original document.) Upon closer examination, however, the letter reveals two other interesting details. The first is Marconi's ongoing desire to attract the interest of the Italian Government in the practical application of his invention. Secondly, the letter clearly shows that, at least at that time, General Ferrero was not the great friend of the family that Marconi later claimed. Marconi would write in a separate note, later published in England: "I applied for a patent, a letter was written to General Ferrero, a particular friend of my family, who was at that time the Italian ambassador in London". It is difficult to believe in such a friendship, however, when Marconi writes a letter like the one quoted above in which he identifies himself as "Your Excellency's obedient servant." Though Marconi's extreme formality and respect for authority may account for at least part of the letter's reverent tone, it is more likely that Guglielmo may have told an innocent exaggeration about his friendship with the Italian ambassador to raise his standing at a time when ambassadors were important and influential personages.

## A Sailor in London

Nevertheless, Marconi did write at the time that he had discussed with General Ferrero the "question whether or not the Italian Government wished to buy the exclusive rights to my invention."

"General Ferrero told me," Marconi continued, "he had had some difficulty in obtaining a direct opinion from the Italian Government and therefore he advised me, as friend of my family, to wait some time before making any decision about the rights to the invention."

Marconi had other reasons (apart from the invention's use by the Italian Government) to keep in touch with General Ferrero during this period. The time had finally come for Guglielmo to return to Italy to do his military service. This was a responsibility that he would otherwise have welcomed, but he realized that the army would have put a stop to his research in England at the very moment when the most promising results were in view. As the son of Annie Jameson, he certainly had a valid excuse for avoiding military service in Italy, provided that he was willing to accept British citizenship. But, despite his mother's strong influence and the fact that the best prospects for his work beckoned in the British Isles, Guglielmo felt strong ties to Italy and fully intended to remain Italian—an affection for his homeland that he maintained for the rest of his life.

According to Luigi Solari, General Ferrero referred the problem of Guglielmo's military service to the the Minister of the Italian Navy, Benedetto Brin, in a confidential letter. "I am sure that Brin will arrange for you to do your military service," Ferrero reassured Marconi, "without asking you to interrupt your important work."

Brin's response to Ferrero's request delighted the young inventor. "Contrive to show me that Marconi has participated in some activities at sea," Brin wrote, "and I shall know what to do."

"Very well excellency!" Marconi rejoiced when Ferrero gave him the news. "In Leghorn I had a fishing boat; I often went out fishing. Some of my friends, such as, for instance, Arturo Ciano, who now is at the Naval Academy, could testify to it."

A few days later, Marconi was attached to the navy and posted to the embassy in London as an ordinary seaman. Each month thereafter he received a modest salary as a sailor, which he never collected. By the end of his national service, his salary amounted to a considerable sum, which he donated to the Italian Hospital in London.

As it turned out, Minister Brin's decision was a propitious one, both for the young inventor and the rest of the world. Between February 1896 and the summer of the following year, Guglielmo Marconi was at the center of a series of events which marked both the public success of wireless telegraphy and the beginning of the inventor's fame.

## Slaby's Acknowledgement

Marconi's experiments were not received with enthusiasm by everyone. On the contrary, there were many denigrators and sceptics, as well as those who claimed to have anticipated Marconi's work. It was these latter, ill-founded claims that particularly angered and embittered the young inventor. Much of the opposition and disbelief came from Marconi's fellow scientists. According to one account, one of the fathers of modern thermodynamics, Lord Kelvin (who would later become an enthusiastic supporter of Marconi), scoffed condescendingly when first told of the results of Marconi's experiments: "Wireless is all very well, but I would rather send a message by a boy on a pony."

Based, as they were, on irrefutable evidence, Marconi's demonstrations attracted the attention and support of the people who really counted—including the technologists of the telegraph services and the experts among the general Staff of the Army and the Navy. The latter group was particularly impressed by the experiments which Marconi conducted in March 1897, with the assistance of the faithful Kemp, at the lighthouse across the Bristol Channel near Cardiff between the islands of Steep Holm and Flat Holm. These tests gave Marconi the opportunity to demonstrate, even more clearly than before, the importance of the size, shape and height of the antennae. When Guglielmo needed to raise the antennae higher than a pole planted in the ground would permit, he decided to use kites—an idea that may well have originated with the inventor's childhood memories of Franklin's experiments with lightning.

The tests at Flat Holm, where the transmitting station had been installed, attracted the attention and presence of onlookers and specialists, including many important figures in the worldwide scientific community.

Among others, William Preece had invited Professor Adolph Slaby of Charlottenburg, a German scientist who had been studying wireless telegraphy for many years. Slaby had succeeded in transmitting signals over a distance of one hundred meters, but had not been able to extend it.

Slaby later recalled:

It was an unforgettable occasion. Five of us stood around the apparatus in a wooden shed as a shelter from the gale, with eyes and ears directed towards the instruments with an attention which was almost painful. The hoisting of the flag was the signal that all was ready. Instantaneously we heard the first tic-tac, tic-tac and saw the Morse instruments print the signals which came to us silently and invisibly from the island rock [Flat Holm], whose contour was scarcely visible to the naked eye—came to us dancing on that unknown and mysterious agent, the ether."

The German scientist would later cause Marconi a great deal of trouble; but for now, Slaby was full of enthusiasm and praise. "I saw there something quite new. Marconi had made a discovery," he continued. "He was working with means the entire meaning of which no one before him had recognized."

At the time, the specialist from Charlottenburg had access to many of Marconi's secret instruments. After his return to Germany, he was able to repeat some of the experiments for himself, and for many years people in Germany talked of the Slaby radiotelegraph system. The Kaiser's Government, wanting to claim a great part of the merit of the invention of the wireless telegraph for Germany and to make the country independent of foreign systems of communications, later formed the Telefunken Society. The firm, which took its name from the word the German word funk (or "spark," since the transmission of Hertzian waves was obtained through sparks), would become the greatest rival of Marconi's Radiotelegraph Company.

## Return to Italy

The reports of so many leading authorities who had been present at the experiments in the Bristol Channel helped to publicize Marconi's invention even further. The Italian Government sent an attentive observer, a captain in the naval engineers, named Vittorio Malfatti, who was on permanent assignment in London, where he was attached to the superintendent of naval supplies. Malfatti's task was to observe Marconi's work as closely as possible and report back to Rome "without making himself conspicuous."

Malfatti's report was fully ratified by ambassador Ferrero, through the naval attache, Captain Bianco. He told the Italian authorities exactly what they wanted to hear. The experiments at Flat Holm and the other small islands in the area had shown that wireless telegraphy could work even in bad weather. Slaby's reference to the storm is further evidence of this. There was clearly much in Marconi's work to interest the technicians and the communications experts in the Italian Navy.

Thanks to Malfatti's report, Marconi was officially invited by the Italian Government to return to Italy to display his work. The tests across the Bristol straits had continued until the end of May 1897, while additional experiments, independent of Marconi, had been organized at Dover by the English Government. According to documents collected by Jacot and Collier in "Marconi: Master of Space," the latter experiments were conducted under the direction of William Preece.

The results of these latter attempts were significantly inferior to those achieved by Marconi. In the early days of June 1897, the inventor and his mother began their return trip to Italy. Annie stopped at the Villa Griffone, while Guglielmo continued to Rome.

Marconi had been happy to accept the Italian invitation for a number of reasons, including, but not limited to, his passionate love for Italy and his understandable desire to be repaid for the indifference which had greeted his initial experiments. But the days of indifference had finally ended for Marconi. Many influential people in London had already taken a great interest in his work and were putting forward proposals for the industrial use of his invention. Preece had become increasingly active (and very successful) in his efforts to obtain substantial financial backing for the inventor's experiments, and the idea of a Marconi Company seemed more and more like a possibility.

Since the patent rights for his invention were safe, a short time away from England could only have a positive effect on Marconi. He must certainly have realized that his departure would highlight the importance of his presence, especially on the heels of the poor results of the experiments at Dover, in which he was not personally involved. Following his success in England, Marconi had good reason to believe that he could convince the Italian Government of the usefulness of the radiotelegraph.

A deep scientific and technical interest also lay behind Marconi's decision to return home. Minister Brin informed him of the decision to place at the inventor's disposal everything necessary to test his instruments at sea. In the past, Guglielmo had made his tests only from fixed stations, even if some of them had been separated by water.

Marconi's first demonstration for the Italian Navy Ministry came within a hair's breadth of failure. He intended to transmit a message from one floor of one building to the next, but after preparing the equipment, he suddenly realized that he did not have a pole to support the aerial. After a brief moment of panic, the inventor noticed a broom, hooked it to a wire, and asked one of the people in the room to hold it in the air. A similar solution was found at the receiving end. Once the equipment had been suitably arranged, Marconi sat down at the telegraph key and speedily tapped out a message, causing enthusiasm and surprise among everyone in attendance. On the narrow ribbon of paper connected to the Morse receiver, the words, "Viva l'Italia" were spelled out in dots and dashes.

The news caused a sensation throughout Italy. Marconi soon gave a similar demonstration at the Quirinale, the Royal residence, in the presence of King Umberto I and the Queen. Invitations to the demonstration were sent to ministers, senators, members of Parliament, admirals and also to some scientists. It was a moment of triumph for Marconi. Nevertheless, the doubts, the reservations and the uncertainties still persisted in some scientific circles. After all, some claimed, to transmit and receive signals from one floor to the next was really nothing extraordinary. There was still plenty of room for doubts until longer range transmissions were achieved.

But Guglielmo was now ready to proceed his with his experiments—and to respond to those who continued to doubtthe validity of his work.

5

# A Captain Of Industry

## Experiments at La Spezia

After his triumph in Rome, Marconi was instructed to start immediately with his experiments at La Spezia with the Italian Navy. Admiral Ernest Simion, who was present at the experiments, later described them in the lengthy passage that follows:

> The instruments provided by Marconi for the tests were identical with those he had used in the experiments in the Bristol Channel in May 1897. Throughout the course of the experiments, the transmitter was set up in the electronic laboratory at San Bartolomeo: the aerial was twenty-five metres high. On July 10th, 11th, 12th and 13th, tests were carried out on land; I remember one organized for teaching purposes for the department's officers, in which the receiver was placed in the square at the entrance to the arsenal on the side of the Headquarters building. The tests were illustrated by Cavaliere Pasqualini and by Marconi himself.

During those days we had clear communications between San Bartolomeo and the receiving station at the headquarters over a distance of 3000 metres.

On July 14th, sea tests were started; the receiver was installed in the tug-boat N.8 on which the aerial could be lifted 16 metres high; the aerial was formed by an insulated piece of wire covered with a terminal plate. The transmitting station of San Bartolomeo, ten minutes after the departure of the tug-boat from the quay, was to signal the dots and dashes for fourteen minutes, at intervals of ten seconds; it was then to stop the transmission for five minutes and restart with an interval of five seconds instead of ten between one signal and the next. These conditions for transmission, except for slight variations, were followed in all the subsequent tests.

After the masts of the tug-boat disappeared from view, reception was still clear up to 400 metres, then it became impossible to read it, and at a distance of 12,700 metres, we received only a few letters.

On the 15th, the experiment was repeated and the aerial of the tug-boat was raised to 30 metres. At the beginning, the presence of storm clouds caused a lot of interference, making it impossible to decipher the signals. Once the clouds had disappeared, the reception became clear up to a distance of 5,500 metres. These tests were also meant to see what effect the land masses between the stations had on communications and therefore, once reception had been ensured, the tug-boat was so directed that the point of Castagna covered San Bartolomeo. The reception stopped and it started again when the tug-boat stood out to sea so that the land no longer intervened.

On July 16th, the test was repeated in much better weather conditions; the reception was good up to 7,400 metres, became occasional up to 9,000 and incomprehensible up to 10,500; some signals were still received at 12,500 metres.

On July 17th, the receiver was installed on the San Martino. the reception remained excellent, both when the receiver was on the main deck, on the gun deck and even when inside the central lounge behind the 4 inches iron plates of the ship's side. Less good was the transmission with the receiver installed below the water line in the bow hold.

On July 18th, the tests started again and the San Martino went outside the breakwater.

Reception which was clear up to a distance of 12,500 metres, became irregular and ended by stopping at 13,500 metres. The ship turned then its bows in the direction of the gulf of La Spezia and, after having set the receiver in a better position and slightly improved the insulation of the aerial, contact with San Bartolomeo started again at a distance of 6,000 metres.

The San Martino headed out to the open sea once more and reception was perfect up to a distance of 16,300 metres. Then there were interruptions: a few rare signals, hardly intelligible, reached us even from as far as 18,000 metres.

After the ship reversed course to move towards the land contact was resumed at a distance of 12,000 metres from San Bartolomeo.

San Martino then steered west of Tino in order to find out if this island and that of Palmaria, when screening San Bartolomeo would prevent reception. At 1,000 metres from Palmaria reception was good but then all signals stopped when the ship was at about 7,000 or 8,000 metres from San Bartolomeo.

They then wanted to see at what distance communication could be reestablished with the ship steering away from the land but still keeping San Bartolomeo screened. The result was negative up to a distance of 9,000 metres. Then reception became clear again, when there was no more screening, at a distance of 6,600 metres.

These experiments, which were made at La Spezia and which were the first with the receiver on board ship, showed beyond dispute the value that the system could have for the Navy.

As Simion's testimony clearly shows, the experiments arranged at La Spezia were another huge success for Marconi. They demonstrated; among other things, the great possibilities for radiotelegraphy at sea, in addition to providing the inventor with a rich supply of experimental data which he immediately put to use.

The Navy had given Marconi the lion's share of the credit and all the resources he needed to continue his experiments, including a substantial daily allowance for the entire period he was to spend away from London. The following letter was written to Guglielmo by his father on 7 July 1897, during the period while the inventor was staying in Rome:

Dearest Guglielmo:

Yesterday evening I received your letter telling of the welcome shown you by ministers and officials, and that today you were going to show the King and Queen your experiments. A lot of newspapers have reported it and our Carlino has a good article from its Rome correspondent. As you can get this paper there, I have not forwarded it to you, for who knows if you would have time to read it.

As you have heard, the Italian government would like your discovery [to be] developed under your name. It seems that, on the contrary, the English company  plans not to use it. As I have written you, the new company should bear your name.

I beg you to write immediately to the lawyer you have charged to negotiate the formation of this company, telling him to suspend further action until your arrival. Then we shall have time to talk together and agree what is best to be done.

Do not pay attention when people try to hurry you, saying that supporters and investors will get tired of waiting; these are only artifices to make you accept what is in their interest, rather than yours.

I hear with pleasure that the Government is paying you 60 lire a day during your absence from England, beside your journey and food expenses—and for your assistant, too.

It is a small compensation for the gift you have made of your patent to the Italian Government, an action that does you much honor, as it shows how disinterested you are in benefits for yourself when it comes to serving your country.

While you are at Spezia, write us a line giving news of yourself and indicate if possible how long you will be there so that we may know when and how long you will be able to stop at Griffone, to be with us and the rest.

In the meantime, accept my most cordial 'saluti'.

I leave a little space for your Mama.

I am yours affectionately,

G. Marconi

Annie Marconi, who was staying at the Villa Griffone at the time, added her own regards at the conclusion of the letter, echoing her husband's concerns regarding the formation of the company.

"My dearest Guglielmo:

We were delighted to get your dear letter yesterday and to hear that your experiments are getting on so well, and that the King and the Queen wish to see them and like you very much too, for everyone seems to like you. I hope you will keep well, dear, and that at Spezia your experiments at sea will be equally successful.

Your Papa is anxious about the Company and hopes no bad terms for you will be made. I trust that if Mr. Owen arranges anything with the Company, he will do it in a way to protect and guard you against them. Your Papa and everyone say that the Company should be called after your name, "Marconi's Telegraphy Without Wires," that if it is not it takes the honor from you and might be called after some other person's name to make money. I hope you keep the money safely, and have not lost the Post Office order.

I trust you have got yourself some cool clothes.

Fondest love in which Alfonso joins.

Praying the Lord to bless you

your very loving
Mama

This letter gives us an insight into a series of interesting facts, situations, and states of mind either forgotten or unknown until now. Realizing that his son's invention had whetted the appetite of governments, armies, and businessmen, Giuseppe was obviously no longer thinking about buying a landed property for his son, no matter how convenient and close to home. He had finally realized that wireless telegraphy would become efficient and profitable when supported by industry and commerce; he also realized, however, the challenges and potential pitfalls of the business world. Drawing on his experience as a highly efficient country administrator, he felt that it was his duty to warn his son not to trust lawyers; he even advised him to suspend all negotiations for setting up his company. Giuseppe also reminded his son of a suggestion he had made earlier, that both the discovery and the company should bear his own name. Fearing that Guglielmo's success in Rome might have gone to the young man's head, the older Marconi asked him not to make any hasty decision until the two had the opportunity to speak together in person.

Even this, however, was not enough to assure Giuseppe. Fearing that Guglielmo might feel in some way obliged by the generous allowance of sixty lira a day, he reminded his son that it was only "small compensation" for the extraordinarily generous gift he had made of his patent to the Italian Government.

Giuseppe Marconi was correct. In London, wireless telegraphy was reaching an exciting stage. After the experiments on the Salisbury Plain and in the Bristol Channel, both government and business had become even more interested. Finally, the decision was made by Marconi and his supporters to set up a company. Guglielmo was gratified by the decision; he knew that, without the serious financial support that only a corporation could provide, he would never have the financial capital he needed to extend his research and gain commercially from what he had achieved. He did not wish, however, simply to be taken over in the manner of many other successful inventors, such as Pacinotti and Meucci. Initiated by Preece, the negotiations had been left in the hands of Colonel Henry Jameson Davis. Realizing that the inventor's absence from London could be dangerous at the present juncture; Davis decided to suspend the deal until Marconi was back in England.

### The First Company Is Founded

After the experiments in La Spezia, Marconi went back to Bologna and stayed for a short while at the Griffone. There, he spoke directly with his father, promising to follow the older man's advice.

In London, even before Guglielmo's departure for his experiments in Italy, William Preece had given two important lectures at the Royal Institution and to the Royal Society, the world's leading scientific foundation since Newton's day. The second of the two lectures ended by praising Marconi for creating a new telegraph system that could reach places previously inaccessible. Both lectures were widely reported, encouraging the supporters of the Company to proceed with their plans. Finally, on 20 July of that same year, the company was officially launched as the Wireless Telegraph and Signal Co. Ltd., with an initial capital of one thousand pounds.

Marconi returned to London in time to finalize the negotiations. As a partial reimbursement for his worldwide patent rights (Italy was, of course, excluded), he was given a controlling majority of the shares. As compensation for his patent rights, he received a cash payment of fifteen thousand pounds.

Guglielmo did not ignore his father's advice. The young inventor possessed a strong business flair of his own, however, and when compelled to choose between the desire to see his name in the official title of the radiotelegraphy company and a few thousand pounds more in his pocket, he opted for the latter. In any event, he would soon have his own way about the company's name, since the majority of the shares were in his control. This would enable the inventor and his supporters to determine Company policy within the limits imposed by the financiers.

No other inventor, before or after Marconi, has proven so skilled in practical matters, including business, industrial management and public relations. It is difficult to imagine a Newton or an Einstein giving answers like Guglielmo's to hypothetical offers from a group of financiers interested in launching their discoveries? Marconi was only twenty-three at the time his company was formed, yet he was able to persuade a prestigious and sophisticated group of London businessmen to accept the following agreement: "You put up the money, which represents only a part of the payment for the use of my patents; then you award me an absolute majority of the shares, plus 15,000 pounds. But that's not all. I reserve for myself the administration of the patent rights for Italy."

Some detractors of Marconi's work have seen this episode as further evidence that the inventor of the radio was a ruthless businessman, but that was hardly the case. Marconi rightly felt that he deserved a suitable financial reward for his invention and all the successive improvements to it. He also refused to allow a group of outsiders to reap huge profits from his endeavors, leaving him with only the crumbs. Marconi was fully aware of the value of his work.

But money was never Marconi's primary concern. In his mind, it was an inadequate reward for what he offered. Not only had he fully taken his father's financial advice, he also wanted to safeguard his future research and to ensure that he would be able to finance the necessary initiatives to propagate the use of radiotelegraphy. Without substantial financial backing and the support of a well-equipped industrial organization, radiotelegraphy might never have developed. It would certainly have developed apart from (perhaps even in competition with) the contributions of the inventor himself.

Guglielmo was determined to see his invention develop and his company prosper, and he kept his father, who had remained at the Villa Griffone with the other son Alfonso, constantly informed.

Degna Marconi later reported the following information about the early days of the Wireless Telegraph and Signal Co. Ltd.:

> The first money invested in the company came chiefly from the family, the Davis and Jameson branches and their friends the Saunders and Ballentynes. Outside money came later. To forward his experiments it was essential [for Marconi] that the company make money. The name that so concerned Giuseppe was at first 'Wireless Telegraph and Signal Company,' soon changed to 'Marconi Wireless and Signal Company,' and offices were established at 28, Mark Lane, in the City alongside Tower Hill.

The first part of this might indeed be true. If the funds of the company had really been provided primarily by Marconi's family and relatives, however, it is difficult to understand the reasons for the worries Giuseppe frequently expressed at the time. In the letter quoted above, for instance, he speaks of people "who will get tired of waiting." Even the fierce struggle over the name of the Company would be hard to understand if Marconi's relatives constituted the core of the initial group of financiers. Certainly the Jameson and Davis families would have had few objections to using the name of a relation, to whom—as we have seen—they had always given their warmest support.

A far more likely explanation is that Marconi's relatives and closest friends provided the encouragement for the first large group of financiers. Evidence of this is given in a letter that Marconi sent his father from London on 14 August 1897:

67 Talbot Road
Westbourne Park
London W. 2

August 24, 1897

Dearest Papa,
I received your letter of the 12th yesterday with the enclosed article from the Resto del Carlino.

The article of the Corriere della Sera is not accurate, like so many others, as I have never been to Berlin.

However my contract with the Company is public, as it is compulsory here in forming a new company to disclose the contracts which the company has stipulated.

There is a mistake in the paper when they say that I received £10.000 in cash; I received £15.000.

Yesterday I saw Mr. Preece, who was extremely kind to me, as always. He says that the fact of my having made a contract with the Company concerns myself only, and that if the Company continues to be friendly he will do all he can, as in the past, to make known and to forward my discovery. He has also promised to help the Company in the experiments to be made with my system by loaning the help of military civil engineers. He says he thinks the discovery will be taken up very soon by the British Government who will come to an agreement with the Company as to the compensations to be paid.

The boxes with the apparatus have already arrived in a passable state; the cost was £ 2 15s. od.

I have not yet received news from the ministry, pertaining to those French gentlemen who would like to use my discovery in Africa.

Someone here is preparing an article on my work which will be published next week.

As soon as I have it, I will translate it and will have it published in the Italian newspapers, as I am acquainted with all the correspondents.

My best love to you and Alfonso, from Mother also

Your affectionate son,

G. Marconi

The letter's last three lines give further proof of Marconi's ability as an effective publicist for his company and himself. He understood perfectly that good relations with newspaper men were essential. Public opinion depended both on what the journalists wrote and the decisions of politicians.

This is what the Marconi Company's official history, *Wireless at Sea: The First Fifteen Years*, has to say about the original company:

For the commercial exploitation of his already patented system of "telegraphy without wires" Guglielmo Marconi received the advice and assistance of his cousin, Col. HENRY JAMESON DAVIS of Enniscorthy, Northern Ireland. The latter was the son of Mr. A. Grubb Davis, who married Marconi's maternal aunt, a Miss Jameson.

Col. Davis was a flour milling engineer whose London Office was at 12 Mark Lane. It was from among some of the principal Irish millers with whom his business was mainly conducted that he sought financial backing for the purpose of launching the new enterprise. Hence the predominance of Corn Factors or Merchants among the nine original subscribers at the foundation of the Company.

These subscribers were:

James Fitzgerald Bannatyne of Limerick, Gentlemen.
H. Jameson Davis of Mark Lane, E.C., Milling Engineer.
Thomas Wiles, 2 Catharine Court, E.C.
Henry Obre, 6 Crosby Square, E.C.
M.T. Goodbody            "            "
C.F. Bennet,              "            "
S.W. Ellerby, Southsea House, Threadneedle St., E.C.
R.A. Patterson,          "              "            "
Frank Wilson,            "              "            "

The seven last named above were all Corn Factors or Merchants.

The terms on which agreement was reached for the purchase of all Marconi's patent rights by the Company on its formation were as follows:

Marconi was to receive an immediate cash payment of £15,000, from which was deducted the legal and other expenses of forming the Company. In addition, Marconi was to receive, as fully paid shares, 60,000 of the 100.000 Shares of Lira, each of which comprised the authorized capital. The balance of 40,000 shares was to be put on the market for public subscription, the proceeds of which were to be used to compensate Marconi with Lira 15,000 for his patents and to provide Lira 25,000 as working capital.

On these terms the new company was incorporated on 20 July 1897 as "The Wireless Telegraph Signal Co. Ltd.," with registered Office at 28 Mark Lane, E.C.

The Board of Directors had to comprise not less than three or more than ten persons, qualifications for a Director being the holding in his own right of not less than 100 shares in the Company.

There were five "First Directors":

Edgar Appleby
William Smith
James Fitzgerald Bannatyne
Henry Jameson Davis (First Managing Director)
Guglielmo Marconi

The last named held the right himself to appoint one additional Director before 1 February 1898 and this right was exercised in the appointment of Mr. William Woodcock Goodbody.

The name of the Company was changed to "Marconi's Wireless Telegraph Co. Ltd." by a resolution passed at the Annual General Meeting of Shareholders on 23 February 1900, the new name being registered on 14 March.

Marconi asked Preece to join, but the chief-engineer of the English Post Office refused, because, being a State official, he could not be connected with a private firm.

## On the Sea Cliffs

The relations between Marconi and his protector always remained very friendly, even when Guglielmo, on hearing of the experiments carried out at Dover in his absence, had written to him:

> If, as I fear, the department does not intend continuing in the friendly bona fide relations as you and I believed it would, I shall be obliged, immediately after settling experimentally certain little theoretical points at Salisbury, to proceed to Russia, Austria and other countries which are very anxious to have extensive experiments carried out at there [sic] expense."

Preece succeeded in soothing Marconi's resentment, and his task was probably made easier by the fact that, without the inventor's help, the English technicians had failed to get the expected results. At the time, wireless telegraphy clearly meant Marconi. Moreover, Preece not only allowed Kemp to keep on working for Marconi, but also made other technicians and engineers of the telegraph department and the Army available, when the service was required.

From his experiments in La Spezia, Guglielmo had gained valuable data for other sea tests. Once back in England and after settling all the problems concerning the foundation of the Company, Marconi began an even more intense schedule of work than the previous one. He took advantage of the time he was compelled to spend in London to make a fuller study of radio electronics and the theory underlying it—using the libraries of both the Royal Institution and the Royal Society.

There were a number of meetings at which Marconi met on equal terms with leading figures in the various fields of physics. Guglielmo

read the theories of his peers and compared them with the huge bulk
of experimental data he had collected; he then discussed them with
scientists and prepared new and more advanced experiments. Begun
in the summer of 1897, all this work was carried on for many years.
In short, the young man—full of enthusiasm but lacking any real
underpinning of scholarship—had finally become a personality to
be reckoned with. Though not primarily concerned with disputing
current theories or proposing new ones, he was always ready to
answer his interlocutors with the extraordinary results of his experiments.

For both Marconi and Preece, the most promising future for
radiotelegraphy had seemed to lie in the field of naval activities.
Communication between one point and another on the ground were
already adequately served by wire telegraph, but this kind of telegraphy would never be able to handle contacts between one ship and
another. For this reason, Marconi began to direct all his efforts to
extending and improving the quality of his sea tests.

In order to conduct his experiments in peace, Marconi needed a
place which was not too distant from London but was still sufficiently
uninhabited. After carefully studying the map and visiting a variety of
sites on the coast of Great Britain, he decided to move his equipment
to the Isle of Wight, on the rocky cliffs of the Needles, near Poole.
The name itself describes the shape of the island's sharp rocks, which
rise out of the sea against the sky. Along with his valued collaborators
Kemp and Paget, Marconi set up his quarters at Alum Bay at the
Needles Hotel, a residence for wealthy people in search of solitude
and open spaces. The Wireless Signal Co. had hired a tug-boat and
fitted it with a receiving station with an antenna eighteen metres high.
On land the transmitter serials were entrusted to small aerostatic
balloons or simple kites, but the changeable weather conditions made
similar devices extremely unpredictable.

The attempt to establish regular and effective communications was continually frustrated by winds and storms, which were never to be taken lightly in that part of the world. In November 1897, Marconi built a thirty-six-meter fixed antenna. He then embarked on the boat and began to travel to and from Bournemouth, Poole, and Swanage, regardless of the sea conditions. He wanted to demonstrate that bad weather did not prevent transmissions, a crucial finding necessary to support his campaign to install wireless telegraphy on ships. Ships generally find themselves in need of a good communication whenever the weather is very bad. Apart from this, Guglielmo acquired another very important piece of experimental information. Maintaining perfect contact with land up to a distance of more than 30 kilometers, he proved that his waves could radiate and be received in spite of the feared obstacles of the earth's curvature, at least for short distances.

## A Contract with Lloyds

After the experiments at the Needles, Marconi decided to build another station on land near the town of Bouremouth, at Madeira House, an isolated hotel opposite the Isle of Wight. Tests followed tests, and the results were very encouraging. After the first working sessions at Madeira House, however, Marconi removed his staff of assistants and technicians, his laboratory and his transmitters to the village of Poole because the owner of the Madeira House would no longer tolerate the aerials in the hotel park. This same stretch of English coast would remain the inventor's operative center for the next twenty-eight years.

Back in London in April 1898, Marconi conducted a much-publicized experiment connecting Saint Thomas's Hospital with the House of Commons. Other tests followed, between Bally Island and Rathlin Island off the coast of Northern Ireland. Recognizing the importance of his discoveries, Lloyd's of London asked Marconi to study the possibility of using radiotelegraph transmissions to signal steamboat arrivals. For some time, all of Marconi's experiments had been crowned with immediate success, and on the very first day, despite a thick fog, Marconi's instruments were able to signal the arrival of at least ten ships. Unfortunately, these tests were overshadowed by a tragic episode. As the experiments were being conducted, one of Marconi's men, Glanville, fell from a rock in the fog and died.

In response to Marconi's latest demonstrations, Lloyd's decided to install radiotelegraphy in all of the Company's signaling stations. This was the first business coup of the Wireless Telegraph and Signal Co.

By this time, the experiments had involved even the House of Commons. The Speaker had been able to transmit messages to and receive perfect answers from the members of the House. Intrigued by Marconi's string of success, an English shipping company offered to have Marconi's transmitter and receiver apparatus installed on board one of their ships. With the vessel thus equipped, Carisbrooke Castle received the first telegram transmitted from a commercial ship, as the vessel sailed past Bournemouth. It was another sensational success for the inventor.

Marconi realized that radiotelegraphy would have a limited future unless it became possible to prevent the signals from one receiving station to be picked up by another station. This problem was commonly known as syntony, or "tuning".

To grasp the seriousness of this problem, one has only to imagine the chaos that would occur if, when switching on the radio, listeners were given no means of selecting among classical programming, rock music or sporting events, but were compelled to receive all signals at the same time.

Marconi's goal was to create transmitters and receivers capable of sending and receiving rhythmic impulses of a specific period—that could place the transmitters's oscillations in "phase-coincidence" with the receiver's "capacity of resonance." In order to deliver this, he first had to eliminate the negative effects of continuous waves.

## The First Press Service

Both problems were resolved simultaneously with two different, but equally valid solutions. The first dealt only with the dimensions of the aerial, which had the shape of a vertical metal cylinder coaxially inserted in another cylinder. Syntony was achieved by providing both the receiver and the antenna with an identical receiver.

The second solution consisted of inserting a double-coil battery (with one variable coil) in the circuit of the transmitter. The primary coil of the battery was connected to the oscillating circuit, the secondary one to the antenna—with an identical set up in the receiver. By varying the coil number, Marconi could tune in on as many stations as he wanted. This was another monumental discovery for Marconi, since it enabled simultaneous communications by several neighboring stations. The invention was duly covered by a patent, for which the English number was 7777. This was the famous "four sevens" patent.

Marconi was now ready to install the first experimental commercial radiotelegraphy station for public use, between Bournemouth and the Isle of Wight. The station was officially inaugurated on 3 June, and Lord Kelvin, who was there to inspect the equipment, had the honor of sending the first radiotelegram. The famous physicist insisted on paying his shilling. "Though this station is still experimental," Kelvin told Marconi, "I wish to be the first to pay for the message as an acknowledgement that your system is both practical and commercial."

Lord Kelvin's radiotelegraph message, sent to one of his collaborators in Scotland, read: "To Maclean, Physical Laboratory, University, Glasgow. Tell Blyth this is transmitted commercially through ether from Alum Bay to Bournemouth and by postal telegraph thence to Glasgow—Kelvin."

In a lecture delivered in Rome in 1903, Marconi explained how his selective syntony actually worked:

> It was while observing the way the sound of a peal of bells produced by men at the end of their respective bell-ropes that I found a suggestive analogy.
>
> To ring a large bell, it is necessary for the bell ringer to give a series of jerks to the rope at regular intervals until the width of the oscillation reached is sufficient to have the clappers hitting the side of the bell. The necessary frequency of the jerks on the rope, that is of the impulses given to the bell, varies according to its size and is less frequent the larger the bell.
>
> The frequency of the jerks which makes a certain bell ring once it is swinging will never make a bell of very different dimensions ring so well.
>
> The same thing happens in an infinitely shorter time in trying to produce electric oscillations in a good electric resonator by means of waves through space.
>
> Consequently, in order to affect the resonator the radiator must emit a series of impulses or oscillations in electrical accordance with the oscillations of the receiver. Electric resonance, like

mechanical resonance, depends on the cumulative effect of a great number of small impulses transmitted with a certain rhythm.

Thus agreement between the two radiotelegraph stations can be reached only when the transmitting station radiates a sufficient number of these electric impulses in a measured rhythm and these impulses reach a receiver able to vibrate electrically in time with the oscillations of the impulses themselves."

Between 20 and 22 July 1898, Marconi was also organizing the first radio-bulletin. The famous sailing regatta at Kingstown, organized by the Royal Yacht Club, was then in progress. The event was always followed with great interest by both sailing enthusiasts and the members of English high society. Dublin's *Daily Express* had asked Marconi whether it was possible to broadcast information on the progress of the competition to land from a ship following the regatta. Realizing that this was a priceless opportunity to demonstrate thecommercial applications of his invention; Marconi immediately, accepted the offer.

A fast tug-boat, the Flying Huntress, was hired. Guglielmo installed a transmitter on board, and a receiver was set up at Kingstown. Connection with the offices of the Dublin newspaper was handled through the normal telephone service. To the amazement of its readers, the "Daily Express" published reports of the races even before the boats were in sight of the shore. The story caused a sensation throughout the British Isles.

Even the Royal Family were impressed by the event, and by the end of July, Queen Victoria had radiotelegraph stations installed both at Osborne House, on the Isle of Wight, and on the royal yacht of the heir to the throne, the future Edward VII, who was confined to bed in his cabin with an injured knee. In sixteen days, not less than one hundred and fifty messages were transmitted, always with perfect results.

Here is how Marconi reported his achievements, during a lecture presented to the Institution of Electrical Engineers in London on 2 March 1899:

Following this, in July we were requested by a Dublin paper, the *Daily Express*, to report from the high seas the results and incidents of the Kingstown Regatta. In order to do this, we erected a land station, by the kind permission of the harbor-master at Kingstown, in his grounds, where a pole 110 feet. high was placed. A steamer, the "Flying Huntress", was chartered to follow the racing yachts, the instruments being placed in the cabin. The height of the vertical wire attainable by the mast was 75 feet. A telephone was fixed from our land station at Kingstown to the Express office in Dublin, and as the messages came from the ship, they were telephoned to Dublin and published in succeeding editions of the evening papers. The relative positions of the various yachts were thus wirelessly signalled while the races were in progress, sometimes over a distance of ten miles and were published long before the yachts had returned to harbor. During the several days the system was [in operation, several messages were] sent and received, none requiring to be repeated. On trying longer distances, it was found that with a height of 80 feet on the ship and the same height as already stated on land, it was possible to communicate up to a distance of 25 miles, and it is worthy of note in this case that the curvature of the earth intervened very considerably at such a distance between the two positions. On one occasion, on a regatta day, I had the pleasure of the company of Prof. G.F. Fitzgerald of Trinity College, Dublin, on the ship, who, as would be expected, took a very great interest in the proceedings.

Immediately after finishing at Kingstown I had the honor of being asked to install wireless telegraph communication between the Royal yacht "Osborne" and Osborne House, Isle of Wight, in order that her Majesty might communicate with H.R.H. the Prince of

Wales, from Osborne House, to the Royal yacht in Cowes Bay, and during the trips His Royal Highness frequently took. The working of this installation was a very pleasant experience for me, and it afforded, also, an opportunity of more thoroughly studying the effect of intervening hills. In this installation induction coils capable of giving a 10 inch spark were used at both stations. The height of the pole supporting the vertical conductor was 100 feet at Osborne House. On the Royal yacht, "Osborne," the top of our conductor was suspended to the main mast at a height of 83 feet from the deck, the conductor being very near one of the funnels and in the proximity of a great number of wire stays. The vertical conductor consisted of a 7/20 stranded wire at each station. The Royal yacht was moored in Cowes Bay at a distance of 1 and 3/4 miles from Osborne House, the two positions not being in sight of each other, the hills behind East Cowes intervening. This circumstance would have rendered direct signalling between the two positions impossible by means of any flag, semaphore or heliograph system. Constant and uninterrupted communication was maintained between the Royal yacht and Osborne House during the 16 days the system was in use, no hitch whatever occurring. One hundred and fifty messages were sent, being chiefly private communications between the Queen and the Prince. Many of these messages contained over 150 words and the average speed of transmission was about 15 words per minute. By kind permission of the Prince of Wales, I will now read to you some of the telegrams which passed between the Royal yacht and Osborne House:

*August 4th*
*From Dr. Fripp to Sir James Reid*

*H.R.H. the Prince of Wales has passed another excellent night, and he is in very good spirits and health. The knee is most satisfactory.*

*August 5th*
*From Dr. Fripp to Sir James Reid*

*H.R.H. the Prince of Wales has passed another excellent night, and the knee is in good condition.*

The following telegram was sent during a cruise, and while the Royal yacht was under way, as you will see from the context:

*August 10th*
*From H.R.H. the Prince of Wales to Duke of Connaught*

*Will be very pleased to see you on board any time this afternoon when the 'Osborne' returns.*

This telegram was sent when the yacht was off [the coast of] Bembridge, at a distance of about seven or eight miles from Osborne. On August 12th the "Osborne" steamed to the Needles and communication was kept up with Osborne House until off Newton Bay, at a distance of seven miles, the two positions being completely screened from each other (even to the tops of the masts) by the hills lying between. At the same position, we found it quite possible to speak with our station at Alum Bay, although Headon Hill, Golden Hill and over five miles of land lay directly between. The positions were eight and a half miles apart. Headon Hill was 45 feet higher than the top of our conductor at Alum Bay station, and 314 feet higher than the vertical wire on the "Osborne". The yacht on the same trip proceeded till about three miles past the Needles, communication having been maintained during the whole trip. Another day, when I did not happen to be on board, the yacht went on a cruise round Bembridge and Sandown, communication being maintained with Osborne House, although more than eight miles of land lay between the two positions. The Prince of Wales and other members of the Royal Family, especially the Duke, were highly satisfied with its practicability. I consider these results rather interesting, as doubts have been expressed by some as to whether it would be possible by this system to telegraph over long stretches of land. Results across hills were also obtained near Spezia by officers of the Italian Navy, using my system."

## An Invitation from Overseas

Three points in this speech deserve particular attention: one, Marconi's illustration of the waves capacity to overcome the curvature of the earth; two, the proof that regular communication could be made even over obstacles as high as the Headon Hill; and three, the mention of the important work done at La Spezia, which Marconi generously—though perhaps also with an eye on maintaining good public relations—attributed to the officers of the Italian Navy. In the same lecture, Marconi was also able to give a demonstration of the possibility of transmitting very short waves in a specific direction, an achievement that will receive further attention later in this study.

Newspapers all over the world reported Marconi's achievement. From New York, the director of the *Herald*, James Gorgon Bennett, who had sent one of his correspondents, Milton Snyder, to the Kingstown regatta, now arranged an invitation for Marconi to visit the United States to set up a communication apparatus for the 1899 American Cup, similar to the one used for the English regatta. Guglielmo declined the invitation, despite heavy pressure from some of the executives of his own company, who viewed the affair as a fabulous opportunity to promote the proposed launching of an American Marconi Wireless Company. At the time, Marconi had something else in mind. He was determinated to have wireless telegraphy cross the Channel for a broadcast between the English and the French coasts. Marconi had already talked with his father about the possibility of approaching the Paris Government. The chance finally came through a request from the association of English seamen, Trinity House, which controlled the lighthouses. The Wireless Telegraphy Company was asked to make transmissionsbetween the South Foreland lighthouse and one of the lightships deployed to inspect the sea in the dangerous straits of Dover.

In the previously quoted lecture to the Engineer's Institution of London, Marconi described these events:

> The officials of Trinity House offered us the opportunity of demonstrating to them the utility of the system between the South Foreland Lighthouse and one of the following light-vessels, viz., the "Gull", the "South Goodwin" and the "East Goodwin". We naturally chose the one furthest away—the "East Goodwin"—which is just 12 miles from the South Foreland Lighthouse. The apparatus was taken on board in an open boat and rigged up in one afternoon. The installation started working from the very first without the slightest difficulty. The system has continued to work admirably through all the storms, which during this year have been remarkable for their continuance and severity. On one occasion, during a big gala in January, a very heavy sea struck the ship, carrying part of her bulwarks away. The report of this mishap was promptly telegraphed to the Superintendent of Trinity House, with all details of the damage sustained. The height of the wire on board the ship is 80 feet, the mast being for 60 feet of its length of iron, and the remainder of wood. The aerial wire is let down among a great number of metal stays and chains, which do not appear to have any detrimental effect on the strength of the signals. The instruments are placed in the aft-cabin, and the aerial wire comes through the framework of a sky-light from which it is insulated by means of a rubber pipe. As usual,

a 10-inch coil is used, worked by a battery of dry cells, the current taken being about 6 to 8 amperes at 14 volts. Various members of the crew learned in two days how to send and receive, and in fact how to run the station, and owing to the assistant on board not being as good a sailor as the instruments have proved to be, nearly all the messages during very bad weather are sent and received by these men, who, previous to our visit to the ship, had probably scarcely heard of wireless telegraphy, and were certainly unacquainted with even the rudiments of electricity. It is remarkable that wireless telegraphy, which had been considered by some as rather uncertain, or that might work one day and not the next, has proved in this case to be more reliable, even under such unfavorable conditions, than the ordinary land wires, very many of which were broken down in the storms of last month. The instruments at the South Foreland Lighthouse are similar to those used on the ship, but as we contemplate making some long distance tests from the South Foreland to the coast of France, the height of the pole is much greater than would be necessary for the lightship installation. We found that 80 feet of height is quite sufficient for speaking to the ship, but I am of opinion that the height available on the ship and on shore would be ample even if the distance to which messages had to be sent were more than double what it is at present. Service messages are constantly passing between the ship and the lighthouse, and the officials of Trinity House have been good enough to give expression of their entire satisfaction with the result of this installation. The men on board send numerous messages almost daily on their own private affairs; and this naturally tends to make their isolated life less irksome.

My company has been anxious for some time to establish wireless communication between England and France across the Channel, in order that our French neighbors might also have the opportunity of testing for themselves the practicability of the system, but the promised official consent of the French Government has only been received this evening. Otherwise this communication would have been established long ago. The positions for the stations chosen were situated at Folkestone and Boulogne, the distance between them being 32 miles. I prefer these positions to Calais and Dover, as the latter are only separated by a distance of about 20 miles, which is only slightly more than we are doing every day at Poole and Alum Bay, and as we find that distance so easy, we would naturally prefer further tests to be made at much greater distances. We did ask for permission to erect a station at Cherbourg, the corresponding station to be at the Isle of Wight, but the French authorities stated that they would prefer us to have our station in that country in some other position on the north coast.

My system has been in use in the Italian Navy for more than a year, but I am not at liberty to give many details of what is done there. Various installations have been erected and are working along the coast, two of these being at Spezia. Distances of 19 miles have been bridged over in communicating with war vessels, although 10 miles have been found quite sufficient for the ordinary fleet requirements. Other installations are now contemplated in this country for commercial and military purposes, and I am confident that in a few months many more wireless telegraph stations will be established both here and abroad.

## Across the Channel

In this lengthy quotation, Marconi's reference to the experiments by the Italian Navy were clearly aimed at inciting the English and French admirals to action, by way of hinting to the secret, and therefore important, results already achieved by the Italians.

The other subtle observation concerns the simplicity of the instruments of wireless telegraphy—so simple, in fact, that even "the crew" could learn to transmit and receive the signals in a matter of days. This was another factor which made Marconi's invention even more feasible. The famous English physicist, John Ambrose Fleming, had also been present at the experiments at South Foreland. Years later, Fleming would invent the thermionic tube, of fundamental importance for the subsequent development of radio.

"A touch of a key on board the lightship," Fleming, who was a great admirer of Marconi, would later report, "suffices to ring an electric bell in the room at the South Foreland, twelve miles away, with the same ease and certainty with which one can summon the servant to one's bedroom at a hotel. An attendant now sleeps hard by the instrument at South Foreland. If at any moment he is awakened by a bell rung from the lightship, he is able to ring up in turn the Ramsgate lifeboat."

Fleming's statements were not made casually. In that same stretch of sea, that very winter, several rescue operations had been successfully completed, thanks to Marconi's device. In one spectacular rescue, a boat carrying a cargo worth 52,858 Lira had been towed safe and sound to harbor—earning Marconi and his invention the astonishment and admiration of the English Admiralty Court.

On the same evening that Guglielmo delivered his speech at the Institution of Electrical Engineers in London, news arrived that the French Government had accepted the inventor's proposals to connect England and France by radiotelegraph. Marconi was delighted. The first international radiotelegraph connection—something he had dreamed of for years—had finally arrived. On the English coast at South Foreland, the equipment was ready and waiting; all that remained was to set up the corresponding equipment on the French coast. The French station was also installed at record speed.

On 27 March, in front of a small crowd of politicians and military personal, officers and scientists, the first messages by means of wireless telegraphy covered the thirty-two miles between South Foreland and Wimereux, linking England and France across the Channel.

Guglielmo sent the following message to the Faculty of Physics at the Catholic University of Paris:

> Marconi sends his respectful compliments to Mr. Branly across the Channel by means of wireless telegraphy, and this fine achievement is due in part to Mr. Branly's remarkable researchers.

Sitting at the transmitter in Wimereux, Marconi did not choose the recipient of his first greetings on the French land at random. He could have easily addressed it to the President of the Republic or to the Ministry of Postal Services or to the Admiralty. But the French political world was in turmoil at the time, and paying homage to one political figure rather than another could have created resentment. The scientist Branly, on the other hand, was above the conflict.

In the international scientific world, where Calzecchi-Onesti's prior invention continued to be ignored, Branly was still considered to be the originator of the coherer. In his message, Marconi also acknolwedged Branly as the instrument's originator. Still, it seems odd, considering all that Marconi had read and studied about Hertzian waves, that he had not seen the most important Italian review of physics, *Il Nuovo Cimento*, which carefully described Calzecchi-Onesti's achievement. In fact, years later Marconi made amends for the telegram to Branly, admitting that he had been in the dark about his fellow countryman's work. But it is possible that this later apology—coming at a moment in history when Fascism was promoting past Italian glories and when Marconi was at the height of his popularity in Italy—was inspired by primarily political reasons.

After the experiments on 27 March, the work of Marconi and his team progressed rapidly throughout the month of April. A number of important tests were conducted successfully on behalf of the French Navy. Receivers and transmitters were set up on the gunboat Ibis and the cargo boat Vienne. Guglielmo was accumulating important experimental data and demonstrating the value of his communication system to as large a circle as the French authorities would permit. On one occasion, the group even included the Chinese ambassador—a meeting that was, of course, not left to chance.

## In the Service of the British Navy

In addition to its numerous successes, the Marconi station of Wimereux was also the scene of an odd and disconcerting episode. During a particularly stormy night, a madman with a pistol burst into the chalet d'Artois, where one of Guglielmo's assistants was working at the transmitter. Pointing the weapon at the operator—a young technician named Bradfield—the intruder shouted that electric waves were responsible for his stomach pains. A typical Englishman, Bradfield did not lose his self-control. He calmly told the intruder that the pains had already been reported by other people. He added, however, that he could make the man immune from any further consequences of the waves. All the man needed to do was simply to touch two conductors and get a very light, harmless "immunizing" shock. Bradfield even showed him how. The madman was persuaded to remove all metal objects on his person, including coins and the gun. After receiving the electric shock, the Frenchman picked up his things and left quite happily.

Meanwhile Marconi was busy travelling back and forth between England and France. Each test presented a precious opportunity to improve his old equipment and manufacture new devices. Toward the end of April, he again sought peace in the solitude of Poole, at the comfortable Haven Hotel. Here, he was engaged, as he wrote in a letter to Preece, "in interesting experiments on syntony." In the letter, Marconi added that he, "had been able to show the French commission some positive results," and that he hoped, "to be soon able to set up a station demonstrating this innovation." As it would later be revealed, he was working on the creation of a four circuit tuner. The patent number 763772 was issued for the new invention on 28 June 1904. However, the interest and the requirements of the French did not leave him much time for his laboratory research. In June he was in France once again, where on the 17th, he was the victim of an accident. The coach which was taking him to the Chalet d'Artois overturned, and Marconi suffered severe contusions to the knee that confined him to bed for a week. Fully recovered by the beginning of July, Guglielmo began a new series of experiments between sea and land, and between ships in movement during maneuvres organized by the English Navy. The radiotelegraph connections operated at a distance of one hundred and forty kilometers. Here is how Marconi reported these exercises to the Royal Institution in London:

The most interesting and complete tests of the system at sea were, however, made during the British naval manoeuvres. Three ships of the 'B' fleet were fitted up—the flagship "Alexandra" and the cruisers "Juno" and "Europa." I do not consider myself quite at liberty to describe all the various tests to which the system was put, but I believe that never before were Hertzian waves given a more difficult or responsible task. During these manoeuvres, I had the pleasure of being on board the 'Juno', with my friend Captain

Jackson, R.N., who had done some very good work on the subject
of wireless telegraphy before I had the pleasure of meeting him,
being in command. With the 'Juno', there was usually a small
squadron of cruisers, and all orders and communications were
transmitted to the 'Juno' from the flagship, the 'Juno' repeating
them to the ships around her. This enabled evolutions to be carried
out even when the flagship was out of sight. This would have been
impossible by means of flags or semaphores. The wireless installations on these battleships were kept going night and day, with
important manoeuvres being carried out and valuable information
telegraphed to the admiral when necessary.

The greatest distance at which service messages were sent was 60
nautical miles between the "Europa" and the "Juno," and 45 miles
between the "Juno" and the "Alexandra." This was not the maximum distance actually obtained, but the distance at which, under
all circumstances and conditions, the system could be relied upon
for certain and regular transmission of service messages. During
tests, messages were obtained no less than 74 nautical miles (85
land miles).

As to the opinion which naval experts have arrived at concerning
this new method of communication I only refer to the letters published by naval officers and experts in the columns of The Times
during and after the period of the autumn manoeuvres and to the
fact that the Admiralty are taking steps to introduce the system
into general use in the navy. As you will probably remember, victory was gained by the "B" fleet; and perhaps I may venture to suggest that the facility which Admiral Sir Compton Domville had of
using the wireless telegraph in all weathers, both by day and night,
contributed to the success of his operations. Commander Statham,
R.N., has published a very concise description of the results
obtained in the Army and Navy Illustrated.

The most important results from a technical point of view
obtained during the manoeuvres were the proof of the great

increase of distance obtainable by employing the transformer in the receiver as shown in Figs. 1, 2,and 3 and also that the curvature of the earth which intervened, however great the distance attained, was apparently no obstacle to the transmission. The maximum height of the top of the wire attached to the instruments above the water did not on any occasion exceed 170 feet, but it would have been geometrically necessary to have had masts 700 feet high on each ship in order that a straight line between their tops should clear the curved surface of the sea when the ships were 60 nautical miles apart. This shows that the Hertzian waves had either to go over or round the dome of water 530 feet higher than the tops of the masts, or to pass through it, which latter course I believe would be impossible.

Some time after the naval manoeuvres, with a view of showing the feasibility of communicating over considerable distances on land, it was decided to erect two stations, one at Chelmsford and another at Harwich, the distance between them being 40 miles. These installations have been working regularly since last September, and my experiments and improvements are continually being carried out at Chelmsford, Harwich, Alum Bay and North Haven Poole.

Marconi's account continued:

On the month of September last, during the meetings of the British Association in Dover, and of the Association Française pour l'avancement de Science in Boulogne, messages were exchanged with ease between Wimereux, near Boulogne, and Dover Town Hall, a distance of 30 miles. An interesting point was that it was demonstrated that the great masses of the Castle rock and South Foreland cliffs, lying between the town hall, Dover, and the lighthouse, did not in the least degree interfere with the transmission of signals. This result was, however, by no means new. It only confirmed the results of many previous experiments, all of them showing that rock masses of very considerable size intervening between two stations do not in the least affect the freedom of communication by ether-wave telegraphy.

It was during these tests that it was found possible to communicate direct from Wimereux to Harwich or Chelmsford. This result was published in a letter from Professor Fleming addressed to The Electrician on September 29th. The distance from Wimereux to Harwich is approximately 85 miles, and from Wimereux to Chelsford also 85 miles, of which 30 miles are over sea and 55 over land. The height of the poles at these stations was 150 feet, but if it had been necessary for a line drawn between the tops of the masts to clear the curvature of the earth, they would have had to have been over 1,000 feet high."

With all these successes behind him, while Governments and Ministries from all over Europe were intensifying their offers and setting up their own laboratories and experimental stations, Guglielmo decided to accept the earlier invitation to America from the "New York Herald" to organize a newspaper telegraph service during the international regattas for the America's Cup. The "Evening Telegraph" had also extended a similar invitation.

He sailed from Liverpool on 11 September 1899, on the liner Aurania bound for New York, accompanied by one of the directors of his company, William Goodbody, and by three technicians, William Bradfield, Charles Rickard and William Densham. Some of his most sophisticated instruments were also on board. Curiously, it was also reported that the inventor was sporting a moustache at the time—perhaps to disguise his extremely youthful, almost boyish appearance from the press.

6

## The American Fiancee

### No Bigger than a Frenchman

As expected, Marconi received a warm welcome upon his arrival in New York. Anticipating the fervent interest of the American media, Guglielmo, who was always an expert in public relations, prepared a statement which was distributed to all press representatives when he landed. Among other things, the press release boasted:

> We shall be able to transmit details of the regatta off New York as accurately and rapidly as by telephone. Distance does not matter, and mountains will be no obstacle to our transmission.

Not every journalist, however, limited himself to the description of technical details; one reporter described a "serious, somewhat self-centered young man who spoke little but then always to the point." Another newsman provided the following colorful, if somewhat inaccurate, description of the inventor:

No bigger than a Frenchman and not older than a quarter century, he is a mere boy, with a boy's happy temperament and enthusiasm, and a man's nervous view of his life work. His manner is a little nervous and his eyes dreamy. He acts with the modesty of a man who merely shrugs his shoulders when accused of discovering a new continent. When you meet Marconi you're bound to notice that he's a for'ner. This information is written all over him. His suit of clothes is English. In stature he is French. His boot heels are Spanish military. His hair and moustache are German. His mother is Irish. His father is Italian. And altogether, there's little doubt that Marconi is a thorough cosmopolitan.

The first days Marconi spent in New York were rather agitated. If reports are true, even before he was able to unpack his suitcases at the Hoffmann House Hotel in Broadway, the building was shaken by the explosion of a heating boiler. One over-reactive client immediately accused Marconi of being responsible for the incident with the mysterious instruments hidden in his cases. Marconi's assistants opened the containers to allow the hotel's staff and the hysterical client to verify the absurdity of the charge for themselves. During this operation, however, it was discovered—to everyone's great dismay—that the precious little box containing the coherers was missing. Without the coherers, all of his experiments would be impossible, and to build new ones away from the Wireless Company's well-equipped workshop would have required too much time and energy.

This was one of the few occasions when Marconi lost his legendary coolness. He was so upset by the incident that he threatened to catch the first boat back to England. During the search for the instruments, Bradfield—who already demonstrated his great resourcefulness in the previously described episode with the French madman—checked to see if the box had been misplaced during the loading operations in Liverpool. It was discovered that another ship had left Liverpool the same day, bound for Boston. The publisher of the "Herald", who had no intention of forfeiting his radiotelegraph reports, immediately sent one of his reporters, Robert Livingston, to Boston. The case with the coherers was quickly located; and by the following day, the instruments were safely in Marconi's hands.

Radio telegraph instruments were installed on the liner Ponce of the Puerto Rico Line, and on the yacht Grande Duchesse, which was appointed to follow the regatta.

On the arranged date, Marconi and his men were ready, but the competition was postponed to avoid clashing with another important event—the triumphant arrival in New York of Admiral Dewey, after the dazzling victory of the U.S. Navy against the Spaniards in Manila Bay.

The regatta officially started on 5 October. On the second day of the competition, Marconi succeeded in broadcasting four thousand words to the editorial office of the Herald, which were subsequently printed in several editions and announced by an army of newsboys all over New York.

Guglielmo and his invention were greeted with the same enthusiasm in the United States that had marked his achievement at Kingstown. The U.S. Navy had already reached an agreement, by which Marconi would carry out experiments on U.S. war ships, and the U.S. Army followed by asking for a practical demonstration of radiotelegraphy between a post on Fire Island and one of its lightships.

## The "Four Sevens" Patent

In Marconi's experiments for the U.S. Navy, several tests were conducted between the ironclad Massachussets and the cruiser New York; communications were sent between the two ships and between the ships and a station at the Highlands. Distances of over 60 miles were easily reached, but in many cases the signals were illegible because of interference. These handicaps had been foreseen by Marconi, who was able to overcome them using his syntonization instruments. However, these instruments were not yet covered by a patent. Therefore, despite repeated requests from the U.S. Navy, Marconi never went beyond a series of general explanations of the instrument that did not satisfy the American authorities. The official report of the U.S. Navy reads:

> During the tests, the instruments were open to the naval board, except certain parts which were never dismantled, and these mechanics were explained in a general way. The exact dimensions of the parts were not divulged. Marconi, although he stated to the Board before these attempts were made that he could prevent interference, never explained how, nor made any attempts to demonstrate that it could be done.

This passage fully reflects Marconi's personal technique in business; confident of his own ability, he simply stated that he could eliminate the interference, but made no attempt to provide proof of his assertions in advance. He would not risk divulging any of his secrets before they had been protected with a patent.

At that stage, the situation of his patents was as follows: In England he was covered, as we have seen, from the moment of his application on 2June 1896. On 30 November of that same year, he also obtained a patent in Italy, awarded by the Turin office of the Ministry of Agriculture, Industry and Commerce, and registered with the number 43193. The first American patent (number 586193) had been issued on 13 July 1897. At the bottom of the request, the inventor had signed, "The student Guglielmo Marconi, subject of the King of Italy." The patent—the lack of which had compelled Marconi to be reticent in his dealings with the U.S. Navy—was filed in America only in 1901, with the number 11913. This was the American equivalent of the previously cited English patent 7777.

As with Marconi's first patent, the novelty was not in the discovery of a new scientific principle, but in the utilization of an old principle for radiotelegraph purposes. The method by which the natural frequency of oscillations could be controlled had been known for some time. It was realized that, if a circuit was built to be a good energy radiator (an open aerial circuit, for instance), spark-produced oscillations would transform themselves rapidly into radio energy.

Years later, Marconi wrote the following description of his American experiments: "Some tests were carried out for the United States Navy; but owing to insufficient apparatus and to the fact that all the last improvements had not been protected in the United States at that time, it was impossible to give the authorities there such a complete demonstration as was given to the British authorities during the naval manoeuvres."

In a word, the inventor did not want to compromise his exclusive rights to the ownership of his work—a concern that would prove well-founded only two years later. In 1901, an American physics professor, Amos Emerson Dolbear, sued Marconi for claiming priority in the invention of radiotelegraphy. Guglielmo finally won the case, with the American Supreme Court passing an exemplary sentence, but one can only imagine what would have happened if Marconi had not been exercised the extreme caution that he had earlier displayed in his dealings with the U.S. Navy. In addition to bringing its inventor fame, radiotelegraphy was also proving to be a sound business proposition for Marconi—one that required him always to be on guard in protecting his rights.

## On the Atlantic Waves

In November 1899, after the tests with the U.S. Navy, Marconi and his three collaborators embarked on the ship Saint Paul and returned to England. Goodbody remained in America to promote the creation of the America Marconi Company.

On the voyage across the Atlantic, Guglielmo was at the center of two interesting episodes: the first concerning his private life; the second the continuing triumph of wireless telegraphy.

For the latter, we can leave the account to Marconi himself:

A few days previous to my departure from America the war in South Africa broke out. Some of the officials of the America line suggested that, as a permanent installation existed at the Needles, Isle of Wight, it would be a great thing, if possible, to obtain the latest war news before our arrival on the St. Paul at Southampton. I readily consented to fit up my instruments on the St. Paul and succeeded in calling up the Needles station at a distance of 66 nautical miles. All the important news was transmitted to the St. Paul while she was under way, steaming 20 knots. The news was collected and printed in a small paper, called the *Transatlantic Times*, several hours before our arrival at Southampton.

This was the first time when passengers of a ship far out at sea were able to get news and I think that we may consider the day quite close when passengers will be able to remain in direct and regular contact with the country they are leaving and with the one they are bound for, by means of wireless telegraphy."

Marconi's account amounts to a candid confession of the advertising campaign for which the whole operation had been organized. The transmission's success opened the doors of the world's major shipping companies to Marconi and his radiotelegraphy system.

On board the Saint Paul, Marconi was at the center of most activities, not only because he was well-known, but also because of the continuous work going on under his direction. In spite of his busy schedule, the inventor managed to make friends with two of the ship's passengers—the well-known publisher, H.H. McClure, and a wealthy and attractive young woman from Indianapolis, Josephine B. Holman. McClure became one of Marconi's most fervent admirers, promoting the latter's discoveries in all his publications, while Holman was the first of a long series of amorous adventures which, from that day on, were to crowd Marconi's private life.

Josephine was beautiful and carefree, and Guglielmo, despite his formal manners and the technical and commercial interests which occupied him, had lost little of his youthful ardor. Immediately attracted to one another, the two became friends and quickly fell in love. Even before the couple disembarked at Southampton, their engagement had been announced and the girl had been appointed treasurer of the *Transatlantic Times*. The paper's director was Bradfield, while McClure was the administrator. Marconi signed all copies of the first newspaper, composed strictly of news received by wireless telegraphy. Copies were sold at a dollar each, and the money was given to charity.

Meanwhile, Marconi's love affair with Josephine Holman proved to be more than a flash in the pan. The relationship lasted for more than two years, and almost ended in marriage, with both families giving their consent to the union.

Annie Marconi, however, was less than enthusiastic about this wedding; as a mother, she did not look favorably on the possibility of "losing" her favorite son, particularly to the first girl with whom he had become intimate.

Annie made the best of a bad situation, however, and established a friendly relationship both with her prospective daughter-in-law and her family. In a letter of 4 July 1901, she wrote to her son:

My dearest Guglielmo,
    I wrote you yesterday, but must send you a few lines today too, to tell you I have just received a very kind and sweet letter from Miss Holman thanking me for my letter and saying they all hope very much I will come to America with you and that they may have the pleasure of seeing me at Craigmor. I wish I had received this letter before and I should not have said anything to you about her not writing. Now it is all right and I feel much happier and shall write to her soon. I intend to go to Porretta next week. Alfonso remains here with Papa, so when you send him his shares, address him here. He is now looking forward to hearing from you soon. Our friends here think it is only right I should be at your wedding".

But the wedding never took place.

## In South Africa with the Army

At the beginning of 1902, the relationship between the two young people was broken off. In another letter, Annie reports that it was Miss Holman who decided to call off the wedding. The truth was that Guglielmo did not seem to Josephine to be a promising husband—both because of his work, which kept him away most of the time, and his temperament in affairs of the heart. Her practical American nature advised her to end the relationship. The young Italian, however, did not take it too much to heart. Since he was no longer deeply involved with Josephine, he consoled himself with another affair—a habit he would follow throughout his life.

Upon his arrival at Southampton, Marconi was faced with two important tasks. In the scientific field, he was determined to carry out a whole series of tests to finish the preparations for his syntonization system and to increase his capacity for transmitting enough power to cross the Atlantic with wireless telegraphy. In addition to his purely scientific interests, the inventor also wanted to follow the constant economic and financial development of his company more closely.

In the meantime war had broken out in South Africa. From America, Marconi had already sent orders to his men at the Wireless Co. Ltd. to offer their services to the English military authorities. In the following report, Marconi described the campaign:

> At the tardy request of the War Office, we sent out Mr. Bullock and five of our assistants to South Africa. It was the intention of the War Office that the wireless telegraph should only be used at the base and on the railways, but the officers on the spot realized that it could only be of any practical use at the front. They therefore asked Mr. Bullock whether he was willing to go to the front.

As the whole of the assistants volunteered to go anywhere with Mr. Bullock, their services were accepted, and on the 11th of December they moved up to the camp at De Aar. But when they arrived at De Aar, they found that the arrangements had been made to supply poles, kites or balloons, which, as you all know, are an essential part of the apparatus, and none could be obtained on the spot. To get over the difficulty they manufactured some kites, and in this they had the hearty assistance of two officers—viz. Major Baden Powell and Captain Kennedy , R.E., who have often helped me in my experiments in England.

The results which they obtained were not at first altogether satisfactory, but this is accounted for by the fact that the working was attempted without poles or proper kites, and afterwards with poles of insufficient height, while the use of the kites was very difficult, the kites being manufactured on the spot with very deficient material. The wind being so variable, it often happened that when a kite was flying at one station there was not enough wind to fly a kite at the other station with which they were attempting to communicate. It is therefore manifest that their partial failure was due to the lack of proper preparation on the part of the local military authorities, and has no bearing on the practicability and utility of the system when carried out under normal conditions.

It was reported that the difficulty of getting through from one station to another was due to the iron in the hills. If this had not been cabled from South Africa, it would hardly be credible that anyone should have committed himself to such a very unscientific opinion. As a matter of fact, iron would have no greater destructive effect on these Hertzian waves than any other metal, the rays apparently getting very easily round or over such obstacles. A fleet of 30 ironclads did not affect the rays during the naval manuvres, and during the yacht race I was able to transmit my messages with absolute success across the high buildings of New York, the upper storeys of which are iron.

However, on getting the kites up, they easily communicated from De Aar to Orange River, over a distance of some 70 miles. I am glad to say that from later information received they have been able to obtain poles, which, although not quite high enough for long distances, are sufficiently useful. We have also sent a number of Major Baden Powell's kites, which are the only ones I have found to be of real service. Stations have been established at Modder River, Enslin, Belmont, Orange River, and De Aar, which work well and will be invaluable in case the field telegraph line connecting these positions should be cut by the enemy. It is also satisfactory to note that the military authorities have lately arranged to supply small balloons to my assistants for portable installations on service wagons.

While I admire the determination of Mr. Bullock and our assistants in their endeavour to do the very best they could with most imperfect local means, I think it only right to say that if I had been on the spot myself I should have refused to open any station until the officers had provided the means for elevating the wire, which, as you know, is essential to success.

Mr. Bullock, and another of our assistants in South Africa, has been transferred, with some of the apparatus, to Natal to join Gen. Buller's forces, and it is likely that before the campaign is ended wireless telegraphy will have proved its utility in actual warfare. Two of our assistants bravely volunteered to take an installation through the Boer lines into Kimberley, but the military authorities did not think fit to grant them permission, as it probably involved too great a risk. What the bearing on the campaign would have been if working installations had been established in Ladysmith, Kimberley, and Mafeking before they were besieged, I leave military strategists to state. I am sure you will agree with me that it is much to be regretted that the system could not be got into these towns prior to the commencement of hostilities.

I find it hard to believe that the Boers possess any workable instruments. Some instruments intended for them were seized by authorities at Cape Town. These instruments turned out to have been manufactured in Germany. Our assistants, however, found that these instruments were not workable. I need hardly [assure you] that [no] apparatus has been supplied by us to anyone from whom the Boers could possibly have obtained any of our instruments.

I have spoken at great length about the things which have been accomplished. I do not like to dwell upon what may or what will be done in the immediate or more distant future, but there is one thing of which I am confident—that the progress made this year will greatly surpass what has been accomplished during the last twelve months; and, speaking what I believe to be sober sense, I say that, by means of the wireless telegraph, telegrams will be as common and as much in daily use on the sea as at present on land.

## The Company Baptized

There are at least three significant points in this report. First of all, there is the detailed description of the operations on the battlefields and behind the lines—obviously intended to publicize the wide range of practical uses of radiotelegraphy in the military field. Then there is the charge that the responsible authorities did not fully comprehend how much the Marconi system had to offer, along with a warning against similar mistakes. Finally, Marconi's generous public acknowledgement of the importance of his collaborators demonstrates why those who worked with the inventor fell under his spell so easily, remaining faithful and devoted to him. Marconi was impatient with both dishonesty and incompetence, but he also knew how to recognize people's merits and how to praise them. Throughout his life, his assistants were ready to help him in even the most dangerous activities.

The first year of the century also marked the achievement of Marconi's (and his father's) oldest dreams, when the Wireless Telegraph and Signal Co. Ltd. finally changed its name to the Marconi Wireless Telegraph Co. Ltd. The inventor's name was finally merged with his company. The decision to rename the company was approved at the shareholders general meeting on 23 February 1900.

According to the Acts of the Company, Marconi did not object to the change of name, but he did request that it should be clearly recorded in the minutes that he had neither proposed nor favored the suggestion.

After his numerous experiments and demonstrations, requests for radiotelegraphy installations kept Marconi constantly busy. Ship installments seemed to be the most commercially desirable. Because of this, another society was founded on 25 April of that same year: the Marconi International Marine Communication Co. Ltd. The directors of the new company represented British, German, French, Italian and Spanish interests. Marconi himself and Major Flood Page (then general director of the parent company) were on the board. According to the deed of partnership, the company was to operate through exclusive building licenses with associated firms in various parts of the world, "except the United States, Hawaii, Chile and their respective colonies."

For Great Britain and Italy, licenses for the patents and the instruments were limited to mercantile marine and pleasure boats, and could not be extended to the ships of the Navy. This demonstrated that Marconi was also a far-sighted precursor in the field of multinational corporations.

Professor John Ambrose Fleming was appointed as scientific adviser to the Marconi Company. Professor Fleming was soon to provide radiocommunications with one of the most efficient instruments for the production and reception of electromagnetic waves:

the thermionic tube. This is yet another demonstration of Marconi's remarkable intuition in his choice of men with whom to collaborate.

At the time, Fleming was one of the most highly reputed physicists in England, particularly in the field of electricity. Marconi immediately realized how valuable Fleming's theoretical assistance could be in solving his own practical problems with radiotelegraphy. Marconi's working arrangement with Fleming recalls, in some ways, his earlier relationship with Professor Righi in Pontecchio. In one crucial way, however, the situations were completely different. Augusto Righi did not believe in radiotelegraphy, and he had no particular trust in his young protegé. Fleming, on the other hand, had appreciated Marconi from the time of their first meeting. Fleming eventually became one of the most passionate supporters of wireless telegraphy.

Under heavy pressure from the Kaiser's Government, German technicians and scientists were busy conducting experiments on radiotelgraphy in a desperate attempt to catch up with Marconi's achievements. The Germans now had the valuable support of Professor Slaby, who had left England after attending several experiments by Marconi and his team. This experience provided him with sufficient technical knowledge to organize his work on a much sounder basis than before. In his private comments, the distinguished German scientist always recognized the priority of Marconi's invention and its most significant successes. But the radiotelegraphic industry was a ruthless business that often exceeded the boundaries of normal commercial competition. Marconi was often accused by many of Slaby's colleagues of appropriating German scientific knowledge for his own experiments.

For his part, Professor Slaby openly and officially contradicted these accusations against Marconi on April 1898, when he wrote the following words in a magazine with a very wide circulation:

In January 1897, when the news of Marconi's first successes ran through the newspapers, I myself was earnestly occupied with similar problems. I had not been able to telegraph more than one hundred meters through the air. It was at once clear to me that Marconi must have added something else—something new—to what was already known, whereby he had been able to attain to lengths measured by kilometers. Quickly making up my mind, I traveled to England, where the Bureau of Telegraphs was undertaking experiments on a large scale. Mr. Preece, the celebrated engineer-in-chief of the General Post-Office, in the most courteous and hospitable way, permitted me to take part in these; and, in truth, what I saw there was something quite new. Marconi had made a discovery. He was working with means the entire meaning of which no one before him had recognized. Only in that way can we explain the secret of his success. In the English professional journals, an attempt has been made to deny novelty to the method of Marconi. It was urged that the production of Hertz rays, their radiation through space, the construction of his electrical eye—all this was known before. True, all this had been known to me also, and yet I never was able to exceed one hundred meters.

In the first place, Marconi has worked out a clever arrangement for the apparatus which by the use of the simplest means produces a sure technical result. Then he has shown that such telegraphy (writing from afar) was to be made possible only through, on the one hand, earth connection between the apparatuses and, on the other, the use of long extended upright wires. By this simple but extraordinarily effective method, he raised the power of radiation in the electric forces a hundredfold.

## Ten Cents a Word

Despite all this, Marconi was compelled to fight tooth and nail against the German claims, even in the field of syntonic instruments which were exclusively the result of his experimental work and had the support of Professor Fleming's theories.

By 1900, Germany had bought a Marconi system to link Riff with the light-ship Borkum, where they had established a regular commercial service for messages coming from ships. Another apparatus had been set up on the mail boat of the Norddeutscher Lloyd Line, the Kaiser Wilhelm der Grosse, and according to an official report of the Imperial Postal Service of Oldenburg, the number of commercial radiograms sent and received by the light-ship between 15 May and the end of October 1900 totalled five hundred and sixty-five. But the Kaiser's scientists were throwing all their energies into the task on their own account—particularly Slaby, who had invented a syntonic system which was said to be superior to Marconi's.

Guglielmo questioned this claim, both in theory and practice. Piece by piece, he invalidated the technical and scientific arguments put forward by Professor Slaby, and in the lecture of 1901, he presented his conclusions:

> I have also tried connections similar to Slaby's extension wire in the receiver, but I find that the real sifting out of waves is done in the oscillation transformer, although sometimes it may be desirable to increase the period of oscillation of the serial conductor by adding inductance to it, or at other times to decrease its period by placing a suitable condenser in series with it.

At the end, he added with his usual sense of fair play:

I trust it will not be thought that I wish in any way to minimize the importance of Slaby's work. I only wish to get at the facts and to draw a discussion on a very interesting subject.

In fact, the German radio scientist, because of his constant rejections of foreign contributions and in particular because of the campaign his country had launched against the Marconi Company, was left many years behind.

1900 was a vintage year for Marconi. Apart from tidying up the administration of his company and improving the instruments used in his radiotelegraph systems, Marconi achieved a number of striking successes in the field. He connected Saint Catherines in the Isle of Wight and the Lizard in Cornwall over a distance which seemed prodigious at the time—three hundred kilometers. The success was especially valuable for Marconi because it delivered another crushing blow to the theory that the earth's curvature prevented the transmission of Hertzian waves. To create an optical line between the Lizard and the Isle of Wight, Marconi would have had to lift his antennae to an altitude of two kilometers, while in fact the instruments were only a few dozen meters above sea level. This experiment provided the evidence that Guglielmo needed before tackling the "big thing"—connecting Europe and the States by wireless.

Without the results at the Lizard and Saint Catherine's, Marconi would have found it much more difficult to convince his financiers to invest in the imposing radiotelegraph apparatus at Poldhu in Cornwall. Marconi knew that the station was indispensable, and he gave himself body and soul to the task of financing and installing it. In the midst of this endeavor, Marconi was also simultaneous following other radiotelegraph events around the world. Having extended his "four sevens" patent to America, Marconi informed the

U.S. Navy that, not only could he explain in detail the interference recorded the previous November on the ships New York and Massachusetts; he could also eliminate it, using a new apparatus that was no longer subject to interference.

This was the best way to open the path to profitable contracts between the U.S. Navy and the Marconi Company. Despite the drawbacks of the previous experiments in the U.S., the nation had widely acknowledged and praised Marconi's work. The Navy Minister had written officially to him from Washington:

> This Ministry wishes to thank you and to express its gratitude for the experiments with the Marconi radiotelegraphy system which you have recently carried out before a Naval commission. This Ministry also wishes to congratulate you for the excellent results achieved. The certainty that signals can be transmitted in conditions where no other system is practicable makes your method invaluable.

Despite all this, Guglielmo's offer was not accepted. The American Marconi Company had asked for royalties of ten cents a word for each message sent between ships on maneuvres. In Washington it sounded like an unacceptable proposal, and the first long-awaited contracts came to nothing. Other contracts, apart from those with Germany, were signed with Belgium, however. The mail boat, Princess Clementine, sailing between Dover and Ostend, received a radiotelegraph after a station was set up at La Panne, on the Belgian coast.

For overseas transmissions, Marconi still needed to produce radiations of a power never reached before, and he consequently had to study the site with great care. In the solitude of Poole, he devoted himself to research and technical experiments, while back in London, he took care of the commercial and financial transactions of his companies. Guglielmo then began considering those parts of the English coast which seemed to him most suitable for his experiments. He finally decided on Cornwall, at the point where the promontory juts out into the sea. In July 1900, the inventor and two collaborators made a final reconnaissance at Poldhu, near the village of Mullion.

## Fleming's Genius

For solutions to the technical problems involved in the set-up, Marconi relied completely on Fleming. Here is the report of one of the inventor's collaborators, Richard Norman Vyvyan, who had accompanied Marconi on his journey to Cornwall:

The Wireless Company in 1899 had appointed Professor J.A. Fleming F.R.S., of University College, London, as Scientific Adviser to the Company, and knowing the experience that Dr. Fleming had gained in dealing with extra high tension alternating currents in electric lightning work, Marconi consulted him in regard to the nature of the electrical plant it would be necessary to install to generate and control the powerful electromagnetic waves he required. They decided that it would be necessary to employ an alternator, driven by an engine, and actuating high tension transformers in order to charge a bank of condensers, which would discharge through an oscillation transformer across a spark gap, and they further agreed that the alternator should have an output of 25 kilowatts. Marconi entrusted Dr. Fleming with the working out of the details of this plant, and to devise some method of interrupting the primary circuit of the transformers to allow signalling at will. It was decided that the station for the transatlantic experiments should be built on the west coast of Cornwall in some isolated place, to avoid the possibility that the powerful electrical oscillations might affect electric circuits used for lighting or other purposes in the neighboring district, and also in order that there should be no obstacle to the clear passage of these waves over the ocean in the immediate vicinity of the station.

Owing to the experience that I had had, previous to joining the Wireless Company, it was my good fortune to be selected to take charge of the construction of this station and to assist Dr. Fleming in obtaining the necessary machinery and plant. In July 1900 I accompanied Marconi and the Managing Director of the Wireless Company, Major Flood Page, to Cornwall, where a site was selected at Poldhu, near Mullion, on the West Coast of the Lizard.

Meanwhile, Dr. Fleming had been busy working out the details of the high tension plant and designing the power condensers for the installation, and I was employed in assisting him, until possession of the site was obtained early in October 1900, whereupon I returned to Poldhu to supervise the work.

To get signals across the Atlantic, Marconi had calculated that he would require a capacity of 1/50th of a microfarad discharging across a two-inch spark gap. One of the many problems was to obtain this by the single action of a transformer on a condenser without raising the transformer voltage to an unworkable value. Dr. Fleming thereupon devised a method of double transformation, whereby the current from a transformer was employed to charge a condenser, discharging through an oscillation transformer across a spark gap. The secondary of the transformer, consisting of more turns than the primary, was connected to a second spark gap, a second condenser and the primary winding of a second oscillation transformer being also across this spark gap. The secondary of the last transformer was in series with the aerial.

The effective working of this arrangement depends of course on the proper syntonization of each circuit. But the principles of syntonization were by this time thoroughly understood, largely as a result of Marconi's work on Syntonic Wireless Telegraphy.

Another important problem requiring solution was to devise a satisfactory method of signalling. It must be remembered that to design a transmitter one hundred times more powerful than the type used up to this date involved the careful consideration of every detail of the plant. Syntonic wireless entails resonance between circuits, and great care had to be taken to prevent voltage peaks due to resonance from getting back into the transformers and alternator, causing surges which might break down the insulation. Any method of signalling by which the transformer is suddenly connected to, or disconnected from, a condenser might give rise to this condition. Dr. Fleming devised several methods but the first practicable method, used in the first tests at Poldhu, was quite a simple one. It consisted in the insertion in one of the leads from the alternator to the transformer of the high tension winding of a 20 kw. 2000 to 200 volt transformer. The low tension winding was connected, through a large key, with a water resistance. The closing or opening of the key altered the impedance of the alternator transformer circuit, and thus slow signalling was possible.

## An Exceptional Structure

The construction of the Poldhu station was completed in time to begin experiments in January 1901. The power of the signals was to be at least one hundred times greater than that reached in all the other stations. The first tests, however, were essentially designed to check the efficiency of the new methods and the new apparatus.

Fleming, Marconi and their assistants devoted a lot of time to this work.

The station was actually finished by Spring, but it took Marconi, Fleming and Vyvyan several more months to prepare the equipment for the experiments. Tests were carried out between Poldhu and the station on the Isle of Wight and had to be made with special care because Marconi did not want to interfere with the broadcasts regularly taking place between ships and the coastal stations already set up at Crookhaven, Cork, Rosslare, Wexford, Holyhead, Yarmouth, and North Foreland. The station at Poldhu had an unusual structure. The antenna (or rather a system of aerials) was formed by twenty wooden masts sixty meters high, in a circle sixty-six meters in diameter. These long poles supported a series of electric cables, insulated at the top of the mast and connected to the transmitting circuit which was placed in a single-storey building, right at the center of the ring. Together, the wires formed an inverted cone. Two other small buildings had been erected by Marconi's men near the transmitter to serve as energy generators, as well as a work-shop and storehouses. Marconi was absolutely convinced that wireless telegraphy was possible not only at an experimental level, but also from a commercial point of view. Thus in March 1901, he sailed, together with Vyvyan, for the United States in search of a site for a station identical with the one at Poldhu.

A suitable place was soon spotted in South Wellfleet, Massachusetts, near Cape Cod. Vyvyan was given the task of preparing the necessary contracts and supervising the construction. He wrote back to England, advising that the mast arrangement, as designed, was unstable from an engineering viewpoint. His warning was ignored, however, and he was forced to comply with the original plan again at Cape Cod. Vyvyan's observations were correct. On 17 September 1901, a storm wrecked several of the masts supporting the cone of the Poldhu antenna. A few weeks later, the same fate struck the apparatus at Cape Cod, which had been built at record speed. After the disaster, Marconi and Fleming decided to resort to a more simple system of fan-shaped antennas. For the new design, two robust wooden masts, placed fifty meters apart and anchored to the ground with a series of tie-rods, supported a heavy insulated cable. From the cable, no less than sixty wires were hung and then gathered together at a single point on the ground, thus forming a gigantic fan against the sky.

While the work was in progress, Marconi and his team had noticeably increased the number of stations on board ships. In May 1901, the motorship Lake Champlain of the Beaver Line, on its maiden voyage between Liverpool and Halifax, had become the first British ship equipped with Marconi instruments for commercial public telegraphy. The corresponding stations on land were those at Holyhead and Rosslare. In Canada the Company began the construction of two stations at Belle Isle and Chateau Bay. By the end of the same month, the Lucania of the Cunard Line had radiotelegraphy on board, and when the Lake Champlain returned from her first voyage to Canada, she was able to contact the Lucania in mid-ocean. Contracts now poured in from everywhere. Within four months, three other ships of the Cunard Shipping Company had been eqiupped: the Campania, the Umbria and the Etruria.

Marconi was now presented with another tricky problem. As the number of installations grew and the network of radiotelegraph instruments proliferated, the company needed trained staff. To address this need, he decided to set up a training school at Frinton, to be completely financed by the Marconi Company. This was the first school in the world for engineers and technicians of wireless telegraphy. At the end of the courses, which covered all the new technological fields not yet offered by the universities, students were employed by the company. The courses included instruction on antenna construction and building methods for the erection of wooden masts on every kind of ground.

## Victory over Distance

Simultaneous with the opening of the Radiotelegraphy Institute at Frinton, another school was opened at Chelmsford for the education of foreign staff and associate partners. This second school remained at Chelmsford until 1903, when it was moved to Seaforth Sands near the service depot at the Marine Company, where sea services and equipment maintenance were planned for the Company's worldwide operation. On 26 September 1901, an agreement was reached between the Marconi Company and Lloyd's of London to set up at least ten radiotelegraph stations for sea signalling—not only for the public service of traffic control on English seas but also as a private service for investigations required for the payment of insurance policies. The agreement included a clause that the service would be supervised by one of the directors of the Marconi Company. Colonel Hozier was listed as the first director.

In Corsica, two important stations were built at the request of the French Government, fully equipped with syntonic transmitters. Similar equipment had also been installed on board a number of French ships.

The first long distance test had been successfully conducted from Poldhu with a transmission to the new station at Crookhaven, on the west coast of Ireland, three hundred and sixty kilometers away. These results confirmed for Marconi that he would soon be able to increase the distance tenfold—assuring him the capacity to cross the

Atlantic. The Crookhaven results were not made public, however, and Marconi continued to wait for the right moment to conduct his greatest experiment.

After the construction of the fan antenna at Poldhu, Marconi became impatient and decided not to wait there until work was completed at Cape Cod. On 27 November, with the consent of the other executives of the Marconi Company, he crossed the Atlantic on the Sardinian. Two of his closest collaborators, Kemp and Paget, accompanied him. Two caves had been loaded on the Sardinian, which was docked at Liverpool, with Marconi's most advanced receiver, complete with a syntonic circuit connected to the usual Morse machine. Among the supply of coherers, there was also an automatic coherer involving mercury which had been manufactured by the Italian Navy. As an alternative reception system, Marconi had also taken telephone headphones. A large wicker basket contained the covering and the ropes of two balloons and six kites; another three boxes contained electric wires and other material.

Guglielmo landed at Newfoundland on 6 December. At the time, Newfoundland had not yet become a Canadian province and was still a colony of Great Britain. Marconi's arrival was not announced to either the public or the press; with the exception of the *New York Herald*, who sent a single reporter. The journalist was led to believe, however, that he had come to observe transmission experiments only between the land and ships passing close to the coast. Marconi presented himself to the governor of the island and also met with other important people of the Newfoundland establishment. In each case, however, he took great care not to disclose his real intentions. Marconi informed everyone with whom he met that his intention was to carry out experiments with ships passing near the coast. In this way, he obtained full cooperation and was given free use of the open space necessary for the installation of his station.

To corroborate this official version Guglielmo cabled to Liverpool asking the Cunard Line and other shipping companies whose ships had radiotelegraph equipment on board to keep him informed of their positions and the time of their voyages in the vicinity of Newfoundland. The reports of the "Herald" correspondent offer convincing evidence that Marconi was completely successful in keeping up this facade.

After a quick survey of the island coastline, Marconi chose Signal Hill, an isolated height overlooking Saint John's harbor. According to the *Herald* report, Marconi observed:

On top of the hill there is a small plateau of some two acres in area which I thought very suitable for the manipulation of either the balloons or the kites. On the crag of this plateau rose the new Cabot Memorial Tower which was designed as a signal station and close to it there was an old military barracks which was then used as a hospital.

On Monday, December 9, barely three days after my arrival, I began work on Signal Hill, together with my assistants. I had decided to try one of the balloons first as a means of elevating the aerial, and by Wednesday we had inflated it and it made its first ascent in the morning. Its diameter was about fourteen feet and it contained 1,000 cubic feet of hydrogen gas, quite sufficient to hold up the aerial, which consisted of a wire weighing about ten pounds.

Although foggy, the weather did not look unfavorable for our work, and we continued [our] experiments. One of the balloons measuring fourteen feet in diameter was sent up. The wind freshened, quickly increasing to a gale, and when the balloon had gone up about one hundred feet we decide to take it down. Unfortunately, the rope broke and it disappeared out at sea.

Today's accident will delay us for a few days, and it will not be possible to communicate with a Cunarder this week. I hope, however, to do so next week, possibly with the steamer leaving New York on Saturday.

As usual, Marconi was a master at managing public relations. He realized that the longer he could conceal his real intentions from both the press and the scientific community, the greater the impact of his discovery would be around the world.

On December 9th, Marconi had sent a cablegram to Poldhu with a codified message asking his men to transmit at a certain time, every day, the signals of three dots of the letter "S" of the Morse's code.

When Marconi lost a balloon due to the bad weather, he started to work with the kites. Many years later, Paget described the events of those historical days for a special program of BBC.

That morning, we were able to fly a kite to four hundred feet. The kite flew over the stormy Atlantic, surged up and down by the gale tugging at its six-hundred foot aerial wire. The icy rain lashed my face as I watched it anxiously. The wind howled around the building where, in a small dark room furnished with a table, one chair and some packing-cases, Mr. Kemp sat at the receiving set while Mr. Marconi drank a cup of cocoa before taking his turn at listening for the signals which were being transmitted from Poldhu—at least we hoped so."

Also Marconi gave his own recollections of the events leading up to the historic transmission:

It was shortly after mid-day (local time) on 12 December 1901, that I placed a single ear-phone to my ear and started listening. The receiver on the table before me was very crude—a few coils and condensers and a coherer, no valves, no amplifier, not even a crystal. I was at last on the point of putting the correctness of all my beliefs to the test. The experiments has involved risking at least £50,000 to achieve a result which had been declared impossible by some of the principal mathematicians of the time. The chief question was whether wireless waves could be stopped by the curvature of the earth. All along I had been convinced that this was not so, but some eminent men held that the roundness of the earth would prevent communication over such a great distance as the Atlantic. The first and final answer to that question came at 12:30.

Suddenly, there sounded the sharp click of the 'tapper' as it struck the coherer, showing me that something was coming, and I listened intently. Unmistakably, the three sharp clicks corresponding to three dots sounded in my ear; but I would not be satisfied without corroboration. 'Can you hear anything, Mr. Kemp?' I said, handing the telephone to my assistant. Kemp heard the same thing as I—and I then knew that I had been absolutely right in my calculations. The electric waves which were being sent out from Poldhu had travelled the Atlantic, serenely ignoring the curvature of the earth which so many doubters considered would be a fatal obstacle, and they were now affecting my receiver in Newfoundland. I knew that the day on which I should be able to send full messages without wires or cables across the Atlantic was not far distant.

The distance had been overcome and further development of the sending and receiving apparatus was all that was required. After a short while the signals stopped, evidently owing to changes in the capacity of the aerial which in turn were due to the varying heights of the kite. But again at 1:10 and 1:20, the three sharp little clicks were distinctly and unmistakably heard, about twenty-five times altogether. On Saturday a further attempt was made to obtain a repetition of signals, but owing to difficulties with the kite, we had to give up the attempt. However, there was no further doubt possible that the experiment had succeeded, and that afternoon, 14 December, I sent a cablegram to Major Flood Page, managing director of the Marconi Company, informing him that the signals had been received, but that the weather made continuous tests extremely difficult. The same night I also gave the news to the Press at St. John's, whence it was telegraphed to all parts of the world.

## Thirty Thousand Watts

The echoes of Marconi's announcement reverberated worldwide, both throughout the press and the scientific community. "The most wonderful scientific development in modern times," reported *The New York Times* in a front-page story the following day. More or less the same words were echoed by the English, French, and Italians, along with the rest of the world's press. Sadly, the *Herald* journalist, who had actually been in Newfoundland for the experiment, missed the scoop altogether. Believing that Guglielmo and his aids were really doing what they had told him, he could find nothing better than the following to open his crucial, 14 December report:

> The weather on Signal Hill was extremely cold and unfavorable for wireless telegraphy experiments. The kite used yesterday fell into the water near the cliff, but was afterwards rescued by a passing tug-boat and returned.

The reporter would exact his revenge immediately afterwards, sticking to Marconi like a shadow and even registering his sighs.

For Marconi, the experiment was a real triumph. Thousands of telegrams and congratulations poured in from all over the world. On the island of Newfoundland a great celebration was organized in his honor. The governor and other leading figures at St. John's said they would be very happy if he could set up a permanent and powerful radiotelegraph station on the island. On 15 December he declared to the *Herald* correspondent:

> The success of these tests will alter my plans. I intend to suspend further tests with kites and balloons for a short time and erect a large station here at a cost of fifty thousand dollars, having towers or masts for supporting wires. This, of course, provided there is no governmental objection. This will necessitate my going back to England at the end of next week in order to have the necessary equipment sent here, with suitable transmitting machinery and other requirements.

Before leaving for Europe, Marconi made a quick survey of Spear Cape to see if the place was suitable for the installation he had in mind—the corresponding point, on the American continent, of the Poldhu station.

For the initial tests at Poldhu, Marconi had operated with thirty thousand watts, launching waves into space which were two thousand meters long. He was correct in his assumption that, with proper modifications after further trials, the transmission and reception of messages would become quicker and more efficient, making them much easier to use commercially.

Following the announcement of the victory over the Atlantic, one of the executives of the American Marconi Company, Cuthbert Hall, made a rash declaration at a press conference in New York. After observing that Marconi's latest achievement definitively disproved the theory that the earth's curve limited the number of messages that could be exchanged, he then mentioned the very low cost of radio installations when compared with the enormous expenses of laying the submarine cables that still required maintenance and replacement. This was more than sufficient to send the telegraph companies who operated with those cables into a towering rage. After all, the cables in question had been laid with great difficulty and huge investments of capital only forty-three years earlier. The American Commercial Cable Company immediately issued a statement declaring that Signor Marconi had mistaken lightning or the ground current for radiotelegraph signals. However, it was the Anglo-American Company, which was responsible for the first transatlantic cable, who understood the real meaning of Marconi's experiments.

On his return from Cape Spear to St. John's, Newfoundland, Marconi found an officer of the law waiting to inform him:

> Unless we receive an intimation from you during the day that you will not proceed further with the work you are engaged in and remove the appliances erected for the purpose of telegraphic communication, legal proceedings will be instituted to restrain you from further prosecution of your work and for any damages which our client may sustain or have sustained; and we further give you notice that our clients will hold you responsible for any loss or damage by reason of your trespass upon their rights.

As the sole agent for cable communications between Newfoundland and England for fifty years, the Anglo-American Company considered itself to have a monopoly on future wireless communications. Marconi did not take the intimidation tactics of the company's lawyers very seriously at the time. The cable company was very serious, however, not only because it genuinely believed Marconi's claims, but also for a more urgent and practical reason— the company's shares on the London Stock Exchange had dropped sharply following Marconi's announcement, and were continuing to fall.

Apart from the cable companies, however, everyone else was excited about Marconi's communications breakthrough. The government authorities in Newfoundland promised their support. The Governor, Sir Cavendish Boyle, obtained the approval of Edward VII, the King of England, and his Council unanimously adopted the following resolution: "The council are much gratified at Signor Marconi's success, marking, as it does, the dawn of a new era in transoceanic telegraphy, and deplores the action of the Anglo-American Company."

Despite all this, Marconi decided to turn his attention elsewhere. He left St. John's for Nova Scotia on his way to New York. Meanwhile, as controversy over the credibility of Marconi's success raged throughout the scientific world and in the newspapers, the inventor received dozens of offers from societies, local governments, and institutions throughout the world. Alexander Graham Bell, the great American inventor who was now the owner of the American Telephone Company, offered Marconi the use of a large stretch of land at Cape Breton.

## The Choice of Glace Bay

The inventor did not want to make any premature decisions. He was encouraged by the warmth of the public, though perhaps saddened by the doubts and dismissals of some representatives of the scientific and technical community.

The most persistent pressure on Marconi to set up a permanent transatlantic station in the New World had come from the Canadian authorities. Alec Johnston, a member of Parliament for Cape Breton and the owner of the Sydney "Record" in Nova Scotia, personally welcomed the inventor.

Johnston had been informed that Marconi would land at North Sydney from the liner Bruce and that he would take the train for New York. Many years later, he shared with Degna Marconi the following description of his encounter with the inventor:

> I was pacing up and down the pier when the steamer arrived. The passengers commenced to disembark with little delay. The train which was to carry them to their respective destinations would shortly arrive, and consequently there was no time to lose. I had no difficulty in picking out my man from the rest of the passengers. While his luggage was being assembled, I approached him, introduced myself and in a very few words explained to him the purpose I had in mind. This purpose was not merely to obtain a newspaper story but to point out, if he would listen to me, that in my opinion the experiments in which he was engaged could be carried out from points along the Cape Breton coast as well as from Newfoundalnd, and in so far as distance was concerned, the difference seemed of little consequence.
>
> At this stage I gathered that Signor Marconi was registering interest. But he raised the point that the same difficulties that confronted him in Newfoundland might similarly operate against him in Cape Breton. It was easy to set his mind at rest on that score. There were no communication companies that could or would set up any claim of monopoly.

At Sydney, Johnston introduced Marconi to the Governor of Nova Scotia, who persuaded the inventor to stay for a few days to inspect the coast between Sydney and Louisburg. To this purpose the Dominion Oil Company, which owned large areas of land, a railway and a shipping line, put a special carriage at Marconi's disposal. The Company took care to have some of their experts accompany Marconi on his surveying tour with orders to see to his every need.

When the train running along the coast reached the vicinity of Glace Bay, Marconi's attention was attracted by a strip of flat land surrounded by rocks and stretching towards the ocean. As soon as the inventor expressed his interest, one of the experts touring with Marconi pulled the bell cord and the train stopped. Marconi and the others got off and went to take a closer look at the place, which was called Table Head. The site was ideal for building the station he had in mind.

On his return to Sydney, Guglielmo and his supporters drew up the general outlines of the program they were to follow. First of all, it was decided that they would ask for the financial help of the Federal Government of Ottawa; in case of a refusal, the money would have to be found from some local source. The following day, Marconi, followed as always by the faithful Kemp and Paget, went to Ottawa and was introduced to the Prime Minister, Sir Wilfied Laurier who agreed on the spot to put up sixteen thousand pounds. The Canadian government also committed itself to further financial support to finish the station at Cape Cod, which after the destruction of the antennae had still to be completed. The success of the transmission of the three dots of the letter "S" had been turned into an excellent business.

After signing the documents of the agreement and drafting outlines of the contracts which would be completed in detail later, Marconi left for New York. But during the journey, he stopped at Cape Cod, not only to inspect the work in progress, but also to place Vyvyan in charge of the future station at Table Head. The schedule was as follows: after the compulsory stop in the American metropolis, Guglielmo would immediately leave for England to build the necessary equipment for the Canadian station in the Company's laboratories. Fleming, as usual, would take care of the electrical projects, since Marconi wanted this station to be more powerful than

Poldhu. By this time, Marconi was no longer carrying out experiments—he was starting the first commercial, overseas wireless service.

## Triumphs and Criticism

In New York, Marconi received a warm welcome from his admirers. The criticism of his work had not subsided, however, and were still reported in the press. Nevertheless, many of the reports were positive and enthusiastic. On 17 December, *The New York Times* had written:

> If Marconi succeeds in his experiments with intercontinental wireless telegraphy, his name will stand through the ages among the very first of the world's greatest inventors. The thing he is attempting to do would be almost transforming in its effect upon the special life, the business and political relations of the peoples of the earth. The animating spirit of modern invention is to overcome the obstacles of time and space, 'to associate all the races of mankind' by bringing them nearer together. Commerce, of course, has done more than any other agency to make that association intimate and lasting. The initial success of Marconi appeals powerfully to the imagination.
>
> It will be the fervent hope of all intelligent men that wireless ocean telegraphy will very soon prove to be not a mere 'scientific toy,' but a system for daily and common use. The men of science point out obstacles. They have commonly been deemed insuperable. The first triumph is an augury of future conquests.

The most famous American newspaper gave Marconi the credit he deserved, but could not be silent about the doubts expressed elsewhere. The most malicious of these attacks not only referred to the theoretical objections in some scientific circles (from those who still believed that the earth's curvature could not be overcome), but also implied that Marconi and his assistants had mistaken mere atmospheric discharges for Morse code signals. No one went so far as to suggest fraud, but, for Marconi, the mere suggestion that his announcement of victory over the Atlantic was to be considered too rash was already an offence.

Controversies spread from one newspaper to the next. In London, the 18 December issue of the *Daily Telegraph* had this to say:

> Not wistending the detailed signed statement by Signor Marconi appearing in the *Daily Telegraph* yesterday, there was an indisposition among the representatives of cable companies to accept as conclusive his evidence that the problem of wireless telegraphy across the Atlantic had been solved by the young inventor. Skepticism prevailed in the City. 'One swallow does not make a summer,' said one, 'and a series of S signals do not make the Morse code.' The view generally held was that 'electric strays' were responsible for actuating the delicate instrument recording the S's supposed to have been transmitted from near the Lizard to Newfoundland on Thursday and Friday. Some attributed these wandering currents to the old trouble—earth currents. Others to the presence of a Cunarder [a ship] fitted with the Marconi apparatus.

Doubts were uttered by men of undisputed authority in the scientific field, such as Oliver Lodge, who wrote in a letter to the *Times*:

> Sir, It is rash to express an opinion either way as to the probability of the correction of Mr. Marconi's evidently genuine impression that he obtained evidence on the other side of the Atlantic of electrical disturbances purposely made on this side, but I sincerely

trust that he is not deceived. . . . Proof is, of course, still absent, but, by making the announcement in an incautious and enthusiastic manner, Marconi has awakened sympathy and a hope that his energy and enterprise may not have been deceived by unwanted electrical dryness of what wintry shore.

The *Times*, however, always remained a supporter of Marconi. As late as 1935, on the occasion of the one hundred and fiftieth anniversary of the newspaper, the inventor sent the following note of gratitude along with his congratulations: "I cannot forget the invaluable help and support that the *Times* gave to me."

In America, the famous inventor Thomas Alva Edison, after overcoming some initial doubts of his own, declared himself completely convinced of the truth of Marconi's words. Michael Pupin, a well-known professor of electrology at Columbia University, agreed with Edison's assessment:

According to the newspaper reports I have read, the signals were very faint, but that has little to do with it. Marconi has proved conclusively that the curvature of the earth is no obstacle to wireless telegraphy.

In Italy, the weekly newspaper *La Critica*, under an eccentric editor who had sworn not to give in to Marconi, published a series of ferocious attacks, along with an insulting challenge: "Let the Atlantic alone! Why doesn't Marconi try to cross the Straits of Messina with electric waves?" Evidently the paper's editorial staff was as ignorant as it was presumptous, since Marconi had already proved that he was capable of meeting such a challenge, even before the Atlantic undertaking.

Nevertheless, *La Critica* would continue to hound the inventor with challenges and insults over the next few years. Even as late as

1914, when radiotelegraphy had established itself as a valid means of communication for people all over the world, the paper was still accusing Marconi of trickery and deception.


## Misunderstanding in Bologna

More subtle and malicious attacks were issued from some of Marconi's peers in the scientific community. One example came from the publication, *La telegrafia senza filo* ("Wireless telegraphy"), written by Augusto Righi and his assistant B. Dessau:

Mention has already been made of the news according to which Signor Marconi has received, in a station at St. John's in New-foundland, signals sent with his system from the station at Poldhu, in Cornwall, on the other side of the Atlantic.

Let's dispense with the debate about the truth of this piece of news, because if the signals had not come from the other side of the Atlantic, there would be no reason to doubt the possibility of a transmission at earth surface—both on account of subsequent reflections, as well as on account of diffraction—which does not prevent communications over very long distances; it is only a question of the power of the transmitting equipment and the sensitivity of the receiving ones.

Let's go back to the past, to the time when, with the inventions of Gauss, Weber, Steinheil and Morse, wire telegraphy had started to develop. Let's imagine that, instead of those inventions, [only] Marconi's had been announced and that the world, unaware of transmissions with wires and accustomed to use only the means that Marconi had made available, would have willingly put up with the inconvenience of two-way interference and the need for conventional signals. And finally, [let's imagine] that only today another Morse would come to teach us telegraphy with wires. It is likely that wire would be welcome today as a sign of progress.

To Marconi's satisfaction, many other scholars openly proclaimed more flattering opinions of his discoveries. A number of these were collected in a review of popular science, *L'Elettricista* ("The electrician"), in a special issue devoted to Marconi's achievement at Signal Hill. Sir William Preece's opinion was included among the entries.

"I have never doubted the possibility of signalling at great distances by means of Hertzian waves with the system of Guglielmo Marconi, nor have I disputed his great experimental ability," wrote Preece.

Lord Kelvin's contribution to the magazine was even more enthusiastic: "I can tell you," he wrote, "that Marconi has obtained one of the most splendid successes with his wireless telegraphy over great distances, with the complete transmission of the messages."

There were many other, equally glowing assessments of Marconi's work. "My admiration for Marconi's great success in transmitting intelligible signals across the Atlantic, with the help of the new and improved apparatus, is profound and sincere," declared Professor Silvanus Thompson. "Marconi's pertinacity in developing its resources more fully and his great experimental ability have made him worthy of our admiration."

The final word was reserved for Professor Pietro Blaserna, who added:

Marconi had qualities not at first apparent, but which he was soon to show—initiative, invention and perseverance. To all this he added great experimental ability. Many followed him in this path and among them there were also some distinguished scientists.

Some of them have even claimed that their systems were more rational than Marconi's. But we must recognize that our young inventor has always left them behind. I am asked for an opinion on his daring attempt to telegraph across the Atlantic. I have a great opinion of Marconi's ability and the seriousness of his purpose, I am strongly inclined to believe his word when he maintains he has heard, and several times, the three dots of the agreed signal.

## Radiotelegrams at Sea

After the first enthusiastic reception at the Waldorf Astoria in New York, Marconi held a meeting with the leading men of his American company to outline plans for the future and then left immediately for England to review his contracts and make additional arrangements for the Canadian station. Consequently, apart from his technical assistants Kemp and Paget, he brought with him Cuthbert Hall, one of the top technicians in his American Company. When the group landed in England, Marconi, having been thoroughly informed of the skepticism greeting his announcement from Newfoundland, tried to avoid the press. He had had all the publicity—good and bad—that he needed. His task now was to persuade the board of the Marconi Company to invest time and money in overseas telegraphy; he wanted, at all costs, to disprove his critics. The comments of Sir Oliver Lodge had caused him the deepest bitterness. In view of this, after giving strict orders to the officials of his company not to disturb him, the inventor took refuge once more with his mother, who was waiting for him at the London house in Talbot Road.

On 26 January, at the administrative meeting of the Marconi Wireless Telegraph Co., Guglielmo, with a simple, direct account of his intentions, effortlessly convinced his advisers, that they should give him the confidence and support he needed. He had met frequently with Professor Fleming, who made essential contributions to the plans for the American stations. Soon afterwards, in fact, both the stations in Nova Scotia and at Cape Cod would begin operation. Before proceeding with these plans, however, Marconi wanted to demonstrate for both his shareholders and the scientific community that the three dots of the letter "S" he had picked up on the headphones at Signal Hill had been neither a dream nor wishful thinking.

On 22 February, embarking on the ship Philadelphia to go back to Canada and sign the stipulated agreement, Marconi took with him his most sophisticated equipment and a crowd of collaborators. The liner had not yet left port when an antenna fifty meters high was fixed among its masts.

Among the pseudoscientific follies with which Marconi had to contend was the view that the earth's rotation on its axis presented an obstacle to radiotelegraph transmission from West to East. As soon as they set sail, Marconi and his men set to work to disprove the mistaken concept; as the ship advanced out into the Atlantic, the men maintained their contacts with the stations both at the Lizard and at Poldhu, up to a distance of 3,378 kilometers. Determined not to leave any room for doubt this time, Marconi substituted a normal Morse machine for the headphones.

The radiotelegrams he received were recorded in black and white. Guglielmo asked the ship's captain, the officers and a number of passengers to join in the experiments, persuading them to sign the paper strips given out by the Morse machine with each message. The white pieces of tape, with their dots and dashes, were then shown by Marconi to the press on his arrival on the other side of the Ocean.

MARCONI

With these new experiments, Guglielmo had thus exceeded the distance reached with the experiments at Signal Hill, and even his most skeptical critics had to bow to his results.

The messages were registered on board the Philadelphia in front of witnesses in these terms:

Messages received on board from Marconi station at Poldhu (Cornwall) as follows: No. 1—250.2 miles; No. 2—464.5 miles; No. 3—1,032.3 miles; No. 4—1,163.5 miles; No. 5—1,551.5 miles. Signals 2,099 miles from Poldhu when we were in Latitude 42.01 N., and Longitude 47.23.

Upon his arrival in New York, Marconi improvised a press conference for the large crowd of journalists who had assembled to welcome him on the quay. Displaying the paper tapes with the messages and the passenger's signatures, he proudly declared: "There is no longer any question about the ability of wireless telegraphy to transmit messages across the Atlantic."

During the voyage on the Philadelphia, Marconi observed the negative effect of the sun's rays on radioelectric transmissions. "The bright light of the sun and the blue sky," he noted, "though transparent, are a kind of fog for powerful Hertzian waves." To overcome this new obstacle, he decided that the new station which was going to build at Glace Bay would have to be at least twice as powerful as that at Poldhu. He went over his plans at length with Vyvyan, while the two men were on their way to Table Head. Luckily they found a large, second-hand alternator which allowed him to continue with his plan. Vyvyan remained at Table Head to supervise the work, while Marconi went to Ottawa to finalize his agreement with the Canadian Government. Before awarding Marconi with the money, the Ottawa government obtained his promise not to ask more than ten-cents-a-word for each message which was broadcast.

For the construction of the Canadian station, Vyvyan could use as cheap labor a group of unemployed miners, among whom there were not only Americans but quite a number of Italians, Indians and immigrants from other countries.

Vyvyan would later write:

On arrival in Canada, after a brief visit to Ottawa to discuss details of the Contract with the Government, Marconi proceeded to Cape Breton Island, on the east coast of Canada, to find a suitable site for the Canadian station. Many districts were inspected, including Louisburg, Morien and Glace Bay. Eventually a site was chosen near the town of Glace Bay at Table Head. Marconi then returned to England, leaving me to make the necessary arrangements and construct the station. I was appointed Managing Engineer of the Marconi Company in Canada and remained in Canada for the next six years until 1908.

Table Head is in the great coal mining district of Eastern Canada, and the site of the station was actually directly above one of the important mines. The coal mines had attracted workers from every European country and the labor for building the wireless station was a curious mixture. We had Canadians, Indians, Poles, Italians, Americans, and others from southeastern Europe, all employed at the same time.

Marconi left it to my discretion to determine the size of the buildings, and the details of the plant which would be purchased in Canada, stipulating that the alternator should be of 50 kw. output, instead of 25 kw. as at Poldhu. As it was decided that the station should be built as rapidly as possible, I bought a second-hand alternator, but of 75 kw. capacity instead of 50 kw., and a suitable steam engine and boilers. I made the building for housing the wireless plant nearly four times the size of the Poldhu building, which was a fortunate provision since all the extra available room was occupied before we were successful in getting messages across the Atlantic. Meanwhile it had been decided to erect four wooden towers, 210 feet high, both at Glace Bay and Poldhu, to support the aerial. The designs of the towers were prepared in England and sent out to Glace Bay. They were erected in the form of a square with the building so placed that the aerial insulator leading into the building came exactly in the centre of the square. The aerial as first designed consisted of a square cone upheld by stays stretched between the four towers.

After settling the contract in Canada, Marconi traveled to Cape Cod to supervise the work that was being done there before returning to England. In addition to the experimental and administrative work he had done, he was now ready to obtain a patent for a formidable new invention: the magnetic detector.

7

## Peace with Italy

### Naval Manoeuvres

Since the demonstrations carried out in Italy in 1897, including the important experiments on behalf of the Navy at La Spezia, Marconi had not been back across the Alps, and his relations with the Italian authorities had cooled almost to the point of hostility. But Marconi had always waived his right to any financial reward or royalties for the use of his apparatus by his native country.

In view of such conduct—which he maintained even against the charge of some of the Company's financiers that he was putting his devotion to Italy before the interests of the firm—Marconi expected better treatment from the Italian authorities than he received during the years between 1897 and 1901.

At La Spezia, he had already completed experiments thoroughly demonstrating the value of radiotelegraphy at sea, and he had made his findings available to the officers and technicians of the Italian Navy. He had even offered them the ongoing use of his equipment and made such preparations for further contact and supplies as might be mutually convenient. In return, he had received fine words and promises, but communications between Marconi and the Italian authorities had ended there.

What really angered the inventor, however, was an attitude that became increasingly prevalent in Italian government circles, especially those involving the Navy, with which he had once been on the closest terms. After the positive results at La Spezia, many of the Italian "brass-hats" began to behave cynically and ruthlessly toward Marconi—in spite of the generosity and good will he had shown them in the past. "We already have Marconi's apparatus," reasoned the Italian authorities, who still had an attache in London in charge of monitoring the inventor's recent work. "We already have all the information we can get from him. We are now in a position to discover any new advances he may make in the future. Why then spend time and money applying to Marconi when we can do it all ourselves? In this way, we can remain protected by military secrecy and at the same time demonstrate the scientific and technical preparedness of our officers."

It should be remembered, however, that technicians of the Italian Navy had already achieved a number of successes on their own account. In 1899-1900, the naval semaphorist, Paolo Castelli, for example, had invented and made fully operational a new type of self-restoring coherer based on mercury and powdered carbon. By means of this device—as one of Marconi's detractors, Admiral Ernesto Simion, wrote with considerable self-satisfaction—the Italian Navy had succeeded in obtaining adequate radio links between the island of Palmaria and Leghorn and between Palmaria and Portoferraio, at distances of seventy-three and one hundred forty-three kilometers, respectively.

Marconi knew all this and was naturally offended to see his trust and patriotism repaid in this fashion. Even his once-cordial relations with the Italian ambassador in London (where in 1898 Carignani had succeeded General Ferrero) had become practically nonexistent. Then, in the spring of 1901, something happened which caused the Italian authorities to review their position toward the inventor.

It was April, and Lieutenant Luigi Solari was carrying out radio-telegraphic tests on the island of San Bartolomeo, across from La Spezia. Solari's goal was to install a number of wireless telegraph links, using descriptions of new syntonic systems demonstrated by Marconi himself to the Royal Society. The Italian Navy, having learned as much as Marconi had made public, had decided to produce its own devices, without so much as a thank you to the inventor. But they had underestimated Marconi, who knew how to describe the results of his experiments and the function of his apparatus with the greatest clarity, while at the same time concealing technical details of construction, especially when they were covered by patent.

For this reason it was always difficult to copy Marconi's instruments without his help—a fact that Solari was to discover at great cost. He later wrote:

I picked up a radio transmission on a telephone connected to a rudimentary receiving apparatus, and the signal was clear, rhythmical, constant and rapid. From then on I had no peace. I knew it was coming from a foreign station much more advanced than our own. After several days of patient and continuous listening, in which I was personally involved, I realized it was a French installation in Corsica. It was the Clavi station in contact with another of the same system situated at Biot in Southern France, both of them set up by the Marconi Company for the French government. In spite of the encouraging results of the Navy's recent experiments, I saw at once our clear inferiority in relation to the French, who had resorted to Marconi himself. And I reported as much to the Admiralty through the official channels.

Solari was right; during that period Marconi's inventions had made remarkable progress. He had completely superseded wave-detection by coherer (self-restoring or otherwise); while in Italy scientitists were still working, at least in theory, with the primitive systems first outlined by the inventor. Solari continued:

> Minister Morin came to La Spezia for the launching of the R.N. Regina Margherita, and I asked for an official audience with him. Admiral Morin, who had known me as a cadet at the Academy, welcomed me affably, and when he heard my proposal to reopen discussions with Marconi, he said "I will appoint a commission." And a few days later, on June 24th, 1901, the commission met at La Spezia presided over by Admiral Grillo, to whom I made my report. The commission concluded by proposing to send me to see Marconi, who was informed through the ambassador in London.

## The Marchese Solari Is Kept Waiting

In London, Solari requested a meeting with Marconi, but the inventor did not reply. After waiting for some days, the officer finally presented himself at the company headquarters. However, as Marconi's assistants explained to the Italian scientist, Marconi was simply too busy to meet with him at the time. Among other things, the inventor was completing the installation of the stations at Poldhu and the Lizard; carrying out complicated experiments in preparation for the great leap across the Atlantic, and directing the installation of his radio telegraphy for commercial and military use by land and sea. Above all, he was occupied in his laboratory at Poole where he preferred to shut himself away for his most demanding research, far from prying eyes and tiresome questions.

Back in Rome, meanwhile, the Ministry of the Navy was eager for news of the outcome of the mission. Poor Solari was kept waiting for a month. With nowhere else to turn, Solari managed to ingratiate himself with one of the doorkeepers of the Marconi Company, a man named Holloway, who finally—perhaps encouraged by a bribe—revealed the names of three places where Marconi might be found. The officer immediately telegraphed all three, announcing his impending arrival. From the answer he received—Marconi requested the messenger from the Italian navy to wait for him in London—Solari understood that the quarry lay in Poole, at the Haven Hotel, and he departed for Poole at once. Upon Solari's arrival, Marconi at last agreed to meet him.

Many years later, Solari related:

He began by telling me that he was most grieved by the attitude of the Italian government towards him over "the last four years." I told him that the Ministry of the Navy recognized their mistake and that I had been sent to appeal to him as a man of principle for a service to his country. As soon as I mentioned Italy he looked at me intently and his manner changed. I plucked up courage and gave him the report of my experiments at La Spezia, which had confirmed the efficacy of the Marconi stations set up in France. Marconi read my account closely then spoke: "It's clear that you believe in my work. I will authorize you to visit my laboratory; I will trust you." Then he said: "When it comes down to it, whatever they may do or say in Italy to my discredit, I am an Italian and shall always love my country."

Solari's report continued

Signor Marconi, with the greatest generosity and goodwill, has not only agreed to present his instruments to His Majesty's

Government and H.M. Navy together with all the necessary information, but has also renounced the payment of 100,000 lira due to him on ceding the use of his patents in the kingdom to the society set up for the purpose (Wireless Telegraph and Signal Co.), wishing to grant his country especially favorable conditions. And he continues to demonstrate his devotion to his homeland, unselfishly providing details of new experiments and technical improvements with the same goodwill [that he had shown] only a few days ago in an interesting report directed to the naval attache at the embassy in London."

Solari had finally achieved his aim. Taking advantage of Marconi's patriotism, he had managed to restore the relationship that, foolishly broken by the Italian authorities, was not to be broken again. Indeed Marconi was subsequently to receive every honor that his country and full recognition of the value of his work. Solari stayed another month in Poole. There, he was able to see the inventor's work first-hand and get to know how his apparatus worked and how to use it. Solari intended to use Marconi's apparatus to set up a radio link between Rome and the island of La Maddalena. Marconi gave his fellow countryman free access to the station at the Lizard but not, at first, to the station at Poldhu. Marconi was still suspicious and he made Solari wait for another month before allowing him to visit the more sophisticated facility. When the inventor was suddenly called away to Newfoundland for the installation of six new stations, he generously invited Solari to take whatever he needed for his experiments and to copy what he wanted for only the cost of the materials.

"It could happen," Marconi said at the time, "that in case of war Italy might need to be self-sufficient; I wish the army and navy to be able to reproduce my apparatus without having to rely on any foreign company."

On his return to England, Marconi recorded his past conversations with Solari in a personal letter to Morin, Minister for the Admiralty:

> I thank your excellency for the mission entrusted to ship's lieutenant Luigi Solari. He is taking the most recent developments of my system back to Italy with him. I hope that the collaboration now reestablished between myself and the Navy will continue to develop. To this end I have the honour to inform you that my patents are freely at the disposal of the Army and the Navy without payment and that my apparatus may be reproduced in the Royal Arsenals, provided they are not divulged to outsiders.

Quite naturally, the inventor did not wish to tie his hands for the future, remembering how the authorities had treated him over the last four years. At the same time, he wanted to test the "change of heart" of which Solari had assured him. It is interesting to note that Marconi attributes the composition of the letter—including the glowing description of Solari—to Solari himself. Marconi only took credit for the signature. After sharing a dinner with his mother and the Italian officer, the inventor had said to Solari: "You write easily; come into my study and set down clearly what I've just been saying." Soon after Marconi was signing his declaration to the Minister of the Navy.

In this way, the peace between Marconi and Italy was signed and sealed. Solari finally returned to Italy at the end of February 1902, with Marconi sailing for Canada on board the Philadelphia. At Rome, the young officer's report met with success. He was received by the King and charged with supervising new installations at Montemario, the island of La Maddalena, Caprera, and on the warships Morosini, Sicilia, Carlo Alberto and Garibaldi. After these tasks had been completed, Solari was once more despatched to La

Spezia, where, soon after, an episode occurred which, according to Solari's account, gave rise to the first historic radio telegraphic campaign of the cruiser Carlo Alberto.

The Hon. Battelli, Professor of Physics at the University of Pisa, gave a lecture at La Spezia on wireless telegraphy. He conceded to Marconi the honor of being first in the field but praised the so-called "Slaby system" as more highly developed and capable of yielding better results. Immediately, in a letter to the daily, *Secolo XIX*, of Genoa, Solari took issue with Battelli. It seems the affair displeased Admiral Carlo Mirabello, commander of the naval squadron at La Spezia, as Solari later recalled:

> He called me in and asked how it was that I, a young ship's lieutenant, felt free to contradict an eminent professor of physics on a scientific question. "I know I'm right, sir." "Then prove it. Sail with me to England on the Carlo Alberto. If it turns out as you say, I'll be one of Marconi's greatest supporters; if not, you will be posted to Africa."

## The Magnetic Detector

Before sending off his famous declaration granting free use of his patents, Marconi expressed a desire to carry out a series of tests on board an Italian naval vessel. On the one hand, the arrangement would allow the Italian navy the chance for glory in a scientific undertaking of great importance as well as the benefit of all the innovations and developments to come from the projected experiments; at the same time, Marconi would be able to carry out, without any expense to his company, tests over great distances at sea and in the most diverse climates—tests which the inventor judged essential before setting in motion the transatlantic stations at Table Head and Cape Cod.

In Italy, Solari had referred Marconi's request both to the Minister of the Navy and to the King. The request was immediately granted, and the Carlo Alberto was placed at his disposal. The Carlo Alberto was an ideal choice for two reasons: first, because the cruiser had already been outfitted with one of the stations provided by Marconi for Solari; and second, because it was one of the finest ships in the navy, chosen to take part in the international naval review that was planned as part of the celebrations for the coronation of England's King Edward VII. After taking part in the festivities in England, the ship would be placed entirely at the disposal of Marconi. The attitude of the Italian government towards the father of radio had certainly changed.

Another sign of this change occurred on 31 May of that same year, when the Accademia dei Lincei decided to award Marconi a prize of ten thousand lira from the Sartorio foundation. After years of hostility and neglect by his countrymen, Marconi was thrilled to receive the award, just as he was pleased to learn that the government had welcomed his request to carry out long-range experiments at sea with the greatest freedom.

Meanwhile the inventor had not been resting on his laurels. After completing the contracts in Canada and the United States— which involved constructing the stations which would soon begin permanent radio contact with Poldhu, drawing plans for and instructing the engineers in the operating arrangements—he had found time to shut himself away in his laboratory at Poole and resume his experiments. There, he created a new and remarkable device—the magnetic detector—which superseded the old coherer once and for all.

The old coherer had been an essential element for detecting and receiving electromagnetic waves, but it had also been the most precarious device in the whole radiotelegraph system. This was because the device was based on the optimal contact of metal particles, and the performance of the particles varied according to the position and to any sudden movement to which the instrument was subjected. It was difficult, for instance, to operate accurately with such an instrument on board ship when the sea was very rough. Realizing that this was the weak point of his system, Marconi decided to create something more reliable. He needed a device which would free wireless telegraphy from bondage to the delicate, often unreliable, tiny glass tubes. The inadequacy of the coherer had been revealed to the inventor most convincingly during the experiments on board the Philadelphia, when he had also noticed the negative influence of the sun's rays on transmission with very long waves. During these experiments, it became increasingly apparent to Marconi that—whatever technical improvements he might devise—the instrument would never be reliable enough for a regular communication system over great distances. Something new was desperately needed—something based on a different principle than that of the contact of metal particles.

Marconi had studied the results obtained by the physicists Rutherford and Raylegh in their work on the effects of electric oscillations on iron subjected to a constant magnetic force. Convinced by their results that he was on the right track, he began work in the laboratory at Poole to see what would happen if magnetic bodies with varied magnetism were subjected to the action of "electric waves."

Here is the inventor's own account of the results:

The magnetic detector which I have described possesses . . . a practically uniform and constant resistance . . . As employed by me up to the present, it has been constructed in the following manner: On a core or rod consisting of thin iron wires are wound one or two layers of thin, insulated copper wire. Over this winding insulating material is placed, and over this again, another longer winding of thin copper wire contained in a narrow bobbin. The ends of the winding nearest the iron core are connected to the plates or wires of the resonator, or, as is the usual practice in long-distance space telegraphy, to earth and to an elevated conductor; or they may be connected to the secondary of a suitable receiving transformer or intensifying coil, such as are now employed for syntonic wireless telegraphy. The ends of the other winding are connected to the terminals of a telephone or other suitable receiving instrument. Near the ends of the core, or in close proximity to it, is placed a magnet, preferably a horseshoe magnet, which by a clockwork arrangement, is so moved or revolved as to cause a slow and constant change, or successive reversals, in the magnetization of the iron core. I have noticed that if electrical oscillations of suitable period be sent from a transmitter according to the now well-known methods, rapid changes are affected in the magnetization of the iron wires, and these changes necessarily cause induced currents in the windings, which induced currents in their turn reproduce on the telephone with great clearness and distinctness the telegraphic signals which may be sent from the transmitting station... The tests to which I have referred above confirm my belief that the magnetic detector can be substituted for the coherer for the purposes of long-distance space telegraphy.

In 1903, at a time when the connections between Europe and America were already an everyday occurrence, Marconi added these reflections on the discovery and operation of the magnetic detector:

All the best results obtained were in fact mostly due to the use of this new receiver, which, I am convinced, has left the tube of metal filings behind and has rather disappointed all those who thought that wireless telegraphy was exclusively dependent on the coherer. The magnetic receiver which I am talking about is based, in my opinion, on the magnetic hysteresis [a term describing the phenomenon by which the instantaneous value of a body's magnetic field varies] taking place in the iron, when in certain conditions this is subjected to the action of high frequency electric waves.

The instrument was formally introduced to the scientific public on 12 June 1902, at a historic lecture to the Royal Society in London by John Ambrose Fleming and was patented thirteen days later as number 10245. For the next ten years, the device would prove to be the world's most efficient radiotelegraph receiver.

## A Cigar Box

After days of reflection and sleepless nights in the laboratory in Poole, Marconi had completed the plan for the magnetic detector in his head, but he did not have access to wire thin enough to use in his experiments. One morning, he jumped on his bicycle and peddled from the Haven Hotel to nearby Bournmouth where he went from shop to shop looking for what he wanted—without success.

Marconi was about to give up when he remembered a florist's shop he frequently visited. The shopkeeper, as he recalled, sometimes used fine metal wire to support the stems of flowers. As he walked through the shop door, Guglielmo greeted the woman with the broadest of smiles, asking not, as he usually did, flowers for his lady friends, but simply a long spool of wire. The shopkeeper was both amused by his unusual request and happy to supply him with all the wire he could use.

Back at the laboratory, Marconi asked Kemp to get him a wooden case for his experiment, and the faithful assistant immediately produced a cigar-box. Using the box, the florist's wire and a few other materials from the laboratory, Marconi's cunning fingers began to construct the first magnetic detector. As Kemp later recalled, the entire operation took less than fifteen minutes.

Meanwhile, the cruiser Carlo Alberto, with Admiral Mirabello and Luigi Solari on board, sailed from Naples on 10 June 1902. The two men were scheduled to make their way to England, where they would join the coronation celebrations, and then take Marconi on board for the return to Italy. The experiments would be carried out en route under Marconi's guidance and with the participation of the large station at Poldhu and the one at the Lizard.

Solari later recalled:

At dawn on July 18th," wrote Solari, "we were in direct radio contact with Marconi who was at the Lizard [Solari's mistake, since, as we see below, Marconi was in fact at Poole]. Mirabello was able to read Marconi's cordial greetings to our ship on the Morse tape while the ship was still hundreds of miles from land. Whenever the apparatus stuck, I licked my fingers and pressed the ends of the coherer to close the circuit as Marconi had shown me. The reception was then resumed in a regular manner. Admiral Mirabello, who had observed this, while attentively following the emergence of Marconi's message, whenever the apparatus stopped would shout, "Lick! Lick!" At last the message could be read in its entirety: "Greetings to our fine ship. Guglielmo Marconi."

We reached Poole in the afternoon. The sea was rough, but Mirabello wanted me to take a sailing boat to fetch Marconi. I brought him straight back. Marconi was welcomed on board the Carlo Alberto with all the sailors waving from the rigging."

## The Radiotelegraphic Campaign with the Carlo Alberto

One of the other passengers on the Carlo Alberto was a young friend of Marconi's from Bologna, Ranieri Biscia. Ranieri, who was then only a midshipman but would later rise to the rank of admiral. He kept a careful diary of the voyage, which was less rhetorical but more accurate then Solari's, and embellished with numerous drawings. In his account, Biscia notes the exchange of "telegrammed" greetings between the Carlo Alberto and Marconi's station on land when the high masts of the station at Poldhu appeared on the horizon. After the greetings came news that would disrupt the celebration. Edward VII had suddenly developed appendicitis, and the doctors advised an immediate operation. The naval review was postponed until further notice. There was nothing for the crew and passengers of the Carlo Alberto to do but to turn around and head back to Italy—with Marconi on board. Mirabello steered the ship straight for Poole, where the inventor was waiting; by late afternoon, the inventor was safely on board, cheered by both officers and men.

That evening, a dinner was held in the inventor's honor, and the following morning, the crew began the task of loading the equipment and other materials needed for the experiments. In the meantime, thinking it would be some days before the ship sailed, Marconi had left for London to give final instructions to his men at the Company before leaving on a voyage of indeterminate duration. But Admiral Mirabello now received new orders from the Ministry of the Navy. The king of Italy, Victor Emmanuel, had decided to pay a visit to the Czar of Russia. The meeting was to take place in Kronstadt, Russia's largest naval base. The king had asked that the Carlo Alberto be present to lend greater importance to the occasion. Mirabello telegraphed the news to Marconi, who was pleased by the

*Fototeca storica nazionale* 1

3

*<<Ill. Ital. >>, 1912* 2

*Archivio de Cesare* 4

1. Marconi at five with his mother.

2. Augusto Righi in 1912.

3. Marconi in 1894.

4. Marconi's first transmitter.

*Degna Marconi* 5

*Fototeca storica nazionale* 6

*The Marconi Company Ldt.* 7

5. At Villa Griffone with his father and mother, and, standing, his brother Alfonso.

6. With his assistant, Kemp, at Signal Hill.

7. On board a tug boat of the Italian Navy (Gulf of La Spezia, 1897).

*The Marconi Comapny Ldt.*

8

9

10

8. The radio station at Glace Bay.

9. Marconi and assistants at Glace Bay.

10. Marconi in America in 1901.

11

*Fototeca storica nazionale*

12

<< *Ill. Ital.* >>, *1912*

13

11. With Inez Millholland on board the *SS Lucania*.

12. Marconi at Tobruk (Libya).

13. In Madrid with Alphonse XIII, king of Spain.

14. An early field radio station.

15. Marconi at Fiume (today's Slovenia) in 1919.

16. The cruising yacht *Elettra*.

14

15

16

17

Fototeca storica nazionale 18

19

17. The wedding of
Marconi with Cristina
Bezzi Scali.

18. Marconi and Benito
Mussolini.

19. With pope Pius XII
at the official opening of
the Vatican radio sta-
tion.

20. With Marie Curie in
Rome (1931).

Fototeca storica nazionale 20

Fototeca storica nazionale

21

Fototeca storica nazionale

22

23

21. With Ambassador Dino Grandi and members of the Italian National soccer team in London in 1934.

22. A special broadcast from Rome to the United States: Marconi defends the Italian invasion of Ethopia.

23. Marconi's funeral.

24. Guglielmo Marconi.

change of itinerary, since it gave him the chance to experiment at longer range and in waters he had not previously visited. Marconi's assistant Kemp also boarded the ship at Poole, after the loading was complete. Marconi, who had other business to conduct before the departure for Italy, made arrangements to join the others at Dover. On the short trip between Poole and Dover, after only one night's sailing, Kemp and Biscia, with the help of the sailors, had already rigged a high mast on the deck and set up a four-wire antenna between it and the mainmast.

## Choice Episodes

Marconi had instructed the Poldhu station to transmit, at regular intervals, the call sign in code for the Carlo Alberto, as well as more important news. While the ship headed at full steam for Kronstadt, the reception remained perfect, even as the miles separating transmitter and receiver continued to increase. At seven hundred miles, the Poldhu signals were perfectly clear. In the North Sea, the ship opened communications with the twelve stations already built on the old continent. Contact with Poldhu was good until the ship passed Gotland, where, as Marconi had anticipated, the transmissions ran into the negative effects of the sun's rays on the wave bands they were using. After this, the workers at Poldhu were instructed to transmit only at night, and the ship's antenna was modified into fan-shaped device. To achieve this adjustment, wires were attached to a cable strung between the radio mast and the main mast, then pulled down with the lower ends gathered into a single bunch that was then strung to the radio cabin for connection with the transmitter.

The experimental work of Marconi and his assistants did not stop once they arrived in Kronstadt, even when, for several days, the ship became a kind of stage on which the Italian and Russian authorities exchanged visits in full dress. It was an elaborate spectacle, complete with the presentation of arms, boatswains piping, flags waving, bands playing, and lavish lunches and dinners. All these activities were conducted according to European custom, to demonstrate the cordial relations between the two countries in the presence of their respective sovereigns.

During these exchanges, Marconi and his radio telegraph were naturally the object of much curiosity, not only because the inventor was now internationally famous but, above all, because wireless telegraphy had become the most desirable means of communication for navies around the world. Moreover, Admiral Mirabello, Solari and the other Italian officers were proud to have Marconi and his instruments on board. And Marconi was happy to play the role of national hero, as long as it did not interfere with his experiments.

As Marconi told a journalist on his return to La Spezia, there were a number of entertaining incidents during the trip. One evening in Kronstadt, at a reception preceding the official presentations, the daughter of the Russian admiral asked Marconi what he was doing on board the Carlo Alberto. "I'm a soldier," the inventor answered. "Why are you not in uniform?" she replied. "What is your rank?" "I am his orderly," answered Marconi, pointing to Solari in his resplendent uniform. He then slipped quietly away, enjoying the joke.

Marconi was frequently amused by Solari's extroverted and exhibitionist character, and often pulled pranks, like the one described above, on his good-natured colleague. For the shy and reserved Marconi, a few well-placed and well-timed words were enough; Solari provided the rest of amusement. For instance, it was more than just chance that led a journalist from the *Saturday Review*, on board the Carlo Alberto when it put in at Kiel on the return voyage, to attribute the invention of wireless telegraphy to Solari in the magazine's issue of 1 August 1902.

Another incident was later recounted by Solari himself:

> One night during a storm in the Baltic, the Carlo Alberto was pitching and rolling in a fashion disconcerting for anyone beginning to feel the symptoms of sea-sickness. Mirabello, Marconi and I were in the radio cabin. I was sitting at the receiver, summoning all my concentration to overcome the nausea caused by the movement of the ship in that confined space. Marconi had noticed my pallor and cast anxious glances at his apparatus in front of me. Mirabello was smoking a cigar, puffing out great mouthful of smoke. Marconi recognized my distress: 'Admiral,' he suddenly began, 'don't you know that a German professor has declared that a pillar of smoke can act as a screen to electric waves?' 'Really?' said Mirabello. Without pausing to reflect, he opened the door and threw away the offending cigar. I heaved a sigh; Marconi burst out laughing; Mirabello saw the joke and joined in the laughter too.

## The Meeting with Popov

While at Kronstadt, Marconi was less concerned with the visits of the Russian notables (though these led to the sale of two ship's radio stations) than with the solution of a distressing technical problem. Since entering port, the Carlo Alberto had been unable to receive the signals from Poldhu, even at night. With their usual tirelessness, the inventor and Kemp made scores of tests, modifying some components and replacing others until, at last, on the night of 15 July , the messages from Cornwall were once more clearly audible—over a distance of more than 1,600 miles of sea and land.

On 16 July, Victor Emmanuel and Czar Nicholas came aboard, and the interest of the sovereigns and their retinues naturally focused on Marconi and his apparatus. According to Luigi Barzini, who was present at the scene, Marconi gave a detailed demonstration of his devices and showed the strips of paper with the Morse signals from Poldhu. He also explained how radiotelegraphy and the magnetic detector worked, concluding with a radiogram which read: "Long live the Czar of Russia, long live the King of Italy."

The Czar asked where the message had originated, and Marconi, both amused and somewhat embarrassed, explained that it was the result of a special transmission organized by Luigi Solari from the prow of the ship, since it had not been possible to get the signals from Poldhu for several days. The Czar asked to meet the author of the transmission in order to thank him personally.

Marconi had another sympathetic visitor during his stay at Kronstadt. Admiral Makarov, a noted technologist in the field of underwater weapons, arranged for Marconi to meet the noted Russian scientist Alexander Stefanovic Popov. Some years earlier, Popov had produced a device that used a coherer to reveal the electrical waves in the atmosphere, and he was eager to meet the Italian inventor and see his apparatus for himself.

"I come to pay homage to the father of radio," said Popov upon meeting Marconi.

"But I could be your son," Guglielmo answered with a smile, referring to Popov's work rather than his age. The Russian was, in fact, only 43 at the time, though he looked ten years older. The conversation was a lengthy and friendly one, and Marconi was happy to provide answers to all Popov's questions.

## At Kiel and Portsmouth

During the voyage back to England, Marconi resumed his experiments full scale until the Carlo Alberto was docked again. The ship finally harbored at Kiel, Germany, where things did not go smoothly with the German press or authorities because of the rivalry between Marconi's Company and that of Professor Slaby.

On 3 August 1902, the Kiel correspondent of *Il Corriere della Sera* wrote the following:

Unhappily accustomed to the land of the uniform—where dress is everything—I expected to see the great inventor appear in dark suit and spats. Instead, thanks to Italian good sense "Guglielmo Marconi, the electrician" was wearing his beach outfit with white cap and—the height of bourgeois elegance—a green tie.

One can see that he is highly delighted with the recent results of his triumphant endeavors. He has the outward calm which might make him seem a Northerner, if you did not notice his great burning eyes, his almost British manner of speaking. But he is full of humor and stories, and enthusiastic about the Czar as, by all accounts, the Czar has presented Marconi with the order of St. Ann.

"Really," he told me, "I have never seen a ruler who after the first impression is less awe-inspiring. You think, whatever will he be like, the Czar of all the Russians, the supreme autocrat! And instead, how easy-going he is! So much so that when going from one room to the next he goes through the usual ceremony: 'After you!'—'But no, after you!'"

Not even the name Slaby, which I raised to see what Marconi thought of the famous "invention" of the professor from Charlottenburg, so much admired in Germany, could disturb the holiday mood of the young Italian scientist.

"What do you want me to say? These things happen. Professor Slaby came to see me in England with nothing less than a letter from the Emperor. I saw in him only a man recommended by his sovereign, our ally, and then a professor, a man of pure science, to boot. I showed him everything, explained everything. But when he got back home, he turned into an industrialist! And, thanks to some modifications, managed to take out a patent, a German one. It taught me a lesson. From now on everything is secret, apparatus under lock and key, no matter who comes, even if he was recommended by God Almighty"

"But in the meantime you will get handsome damages?"

"Oh no, first of all, the damages wouldn't all be for me, because my patents throughout the world, with the exception of Italy, which I reserved for myself, belong to the Marconi Wireless Telegraph Company of London and New York. And then the Germans with their Slaby cannot communicate outside a range of 70 or 80 kilometers, while we already claim 2,600, so that there was a great to-do when a Marconi station didn't respond to aerograms Slaby sent from a German boat. For our part, not only have we 30 stations in England already, 4 or 5 in America, several in Italy and on the steamers of the main lines, and soon we shall have the central exchange for the continent, perhaps for the whole of Europe, on Monte Mario in Rome. Even the largest German steamers, with one or two exceptions, are fitted with Marconi equipment. Even officers of German warships when you ask them what apparatus they have, at first answer, 'Slaby, of course,' but then admit, 'It's a Marconi!'"

"It will be an old Marconi and won't be much use," he laughs, "and I don't know how they got hold of it, since, as far as I know, they've never paid a penny for patent rights. But this is my Company's business," he concludes philosophically, "now let's go and have lunch!'"

After Kiel, the ship sailed on towards England. The ship exchanged messages with the royal yacht, Victoria and Albert, also fitted with Marconi apparatus. According to plan, King Edward was on board, convalescing after his operation for appendicitis.

On the first day the royal yacht sailed, all the foreign vessels gathered at Portsmouth for the naval review in the King's honor, anchoring in front of the Carlo Alberto. The Italian ship was scheduled to lead the procession the following day, since Admiral Mirabello proved to be the foreign officer with the highest ranking. But when the ships began to move, either because of the wind or some probable handling error, the Carlo Alberto had difficulty getting under way, and, instead of leading the fleet, had to bring up the rear. Even so, the presence of Marconi lined up on deck with Mirabello and the other officers—along with the unusual rigging set up to carry a huge, fan-shaped aerial of metal wires suspended from a stay between the two mastheads—aroused the largest share of the crowd's attention for the Italian vessel.

Marconi took advantage of the stay in English waters, first to visit Poole and then to London to follow the work of his Company. After a brief stay in London, he had further suppliers loaded on board the Carlo Alberto, and then took his place in the radio cabin as the cruiser sailed for Italy.

## Signals in the Fog

The inventor's primary concern was now the possibility of establishing a radio link between the English transmitters and the ship, once it had passed the straits of Gibraltar and entered the Mediterranean.

He wanted to determine with certainty if, as he thought, it was possible for electromagnetic waves to pass through a land mass as mountainous as France or Spain. At two o'clock in the morning, on 4 September, the cruiser had already passed through the straits. A thick fog surrounded the ship. Marconi positioned the vessel so that the line between it and Poldhu was completely obstructed by the Iberian mainland. Unfortunately, no signal could be received. After some fruitless and nerve-wracking efforts using the headphones, Marconi left the cabin for a breath of air. Mirabello was on deck. "We shall have to wait for the three-o'clock signals," Guglielmo told him. "Perhaps there's been a breakdown which explains the silence at two o'clock. If at three there's still nothing, I'm afraid that the continent of Europe may be an obstacle to the propagation of electric waves." Everything was at stake in Marconi's attempt to prove, once and for all, that radio waves could cross a great barrier of rocks just as they had crossed the Atlantic.

At precisely three o'clock, the Morse key attached to the radio receiver began to print out the dots and dashes of a series of "V's," the call sign from Poldhu. Marconi, who had stayed up all night waiting anxiously, could now go to bed happy. The signals from the station in Cornwall had overcome the mountains of Spain, including the promontory of Gibraltar. The transmissions continued while the Carlo Alberto sailed across the Mediterranean to Kegler and then La Spezia. Marconi had ordered the men in England to transmit a message of greeting to the king of Italy. He had arranged to record it on board—the first message to cross Europe—to present to the King upon his arrival. Unfortunately, however, when the appointed time arrived, something happened, which Marconi had not foreseen and which greatly annoyed him. The operator in Poldhu must have been a novice in the use of the telegraph key, and after the first series of letters had been transmitted and received normally, the marks on the paper strip began to show one error after another—finally deteriorating into a meaningless succession of dots and dashes. The operator had apparently noticed his mistakes after the transmission had started, and then begun to send the letters again, piling them one on top of the other.

This was one of the few times that Marconi, who was also suffering from a fever at the time, lost his proverbial composure. Suddenly overcome with exasperation, he seized the receiver and slammed it violently on the table. The outburst relieved his feelings, and a moment later, he was at work resetting the apparatus; then he patiently sent instructions to Poldhu. The previous operator was replaced, and at last the message to the King began to come through. This time the message began to arrive perfectly, but in the middle of the transmission, there was another mishap. The transmitter suddenly shifted to a different waveband and could no longer syntonize with the Carlo Alberto.

## The Coil on a Candle

Not having a spare syntonic coil on hand, Marconi immediately improvised another by winding copper wire round a candle. When the new inductor was put into place, the reception of the message was at last perfect. It was the night of 9 September. The radiotelegram read: "Admiral Mirabello—Carlo Alberto—the Directors of the Marconi Wireless Telegraph Company beg your excellency to present their most devoted and respectful compliments to His Majesty the King on the occasion of the first message from England to Italy."

The radiotelegraphic campaign of the Italian cruiser had shown definitively that distance posed no limit to the propagation of electric waves provided that the available power was proportional to the distance to be overcome. While the experiment confirmed the negative effects of solar rays on the waves, it also provided Marconi with a richer understanding of phenomena connected with atmospheric disturbances, demonstrating that, the less sensitive the receiver, the fewer negative effects on the radio link. Finally, the experiment showed that the magnetic detector functioned better in every way than the coherer, no matter how well-developed.

The ship finally reached La Spezia, after a brief stop at Forte dei Marmi to salute the Minister of the Navy, Admiral Morin, who was in Versilia. Marconi was radiant with the successes on the Carlo Alberto, and communicated his enthusiasm to the journalist Belcredi of the *Tribuna* in an interview subsequently carried by *Il Corriere della Sera* on 14 September 1902.

Marconi explained:

"The experiments have shown that land masses, even if complicated by high mountains like the Alps or Pyrenees, are no obstacle to communications. Just imagine that at Gibraltar, rounding the gulf right under the rock with its cannon, I received the dispatch announcing the Czarina's miscarriage. The station at Poldhu in Corwall, knowing that the Carlo Alberto had been in Kronstadt, thought it appropriate to send us the news as soon as it was known in England. So we have proof that two squadrons—one posted, for example, in the Mediterranean and the other in the Indian Ocean—can communicate independent of land, just as England can communicate with Malta. Each night, and as far as Lisbon each day, we received lengthy dispatches, making four copies, one for the non-commissioned officers and one for the men. And so on board, in mid-ocean, without wishing to compete with the press," he smiled, "I published a kind of newspaper, eagerly devoured. If you had seen the sailors' joy on the morning when they learned that

Admiral Palumbo at the head of a powerful squadron had sailed for Tripoli! Then came the news that it was a simple courtesy visit. But some persisted in believing there was more to it. When we heard of a light bombardment at Haiti, many of them felt there was a mistake about the location and that the bombardment had been somewhere else!"

"What speed is your telegraph's aerial transmission?" asked then Belcredi. "Aerial is perhaps not quite accurate," Marconi replied. "Let's say speed through the ether. This transmission is equal to the speed of light, about 300,000 kilometers a second."

"Can you send a telegram around the world and back to its starting point?" "Certainly," Marconi replied with almost frightening tranquillity. "It's simply a question of increasing the power of the transmitting station. The principle is absolute and knows no obstacles."

"But in circling the globe, your telegram would have to pass through regions exposed to the sun, and then the light would obstruct the course of the electric wave."

For all his politeness, Marconi could not suppress a smile. "It's true" he said, "that at the moment, daylight is less favorable to transmission than darkness, but before long you'll see that this slight difficulty will be overcome . . . I could say that I have already overcome it. . . ."

To conclude, Belcredi asked Marconi about the stations already set up and their commercial success. Marconi replied with a smile: "I see you have doubts about it. Yet there it is, even though the stations may cost half a million each. And the submarine cable companies know it; that's why they campaign against me in the newspapers. Sixty English warships have installed my system and pay an annual rent to the Company. Then there are another 26 commercial steamers paying to use it. In the British Empire, there are 41 stations belonging to Lloyds of London, connected with lighthouses, who have undertaken not to adopt any other system for the next fourteen years."

"Since the campaign against me can't destroy my invention," continued the inventor, "they are trying to cast doubts on its practicability, but that hasn't stopped me from starting a company in Brussels with a capital of half a million, another in the United States with 25 million and another in England with five million, and their activities have already tripled."

"Your enemies have also talked of possible interception of the radiograms," interposed Belcredi. Let them prove it," Marconi smiled. "It isn't possible without a special installation and without guessing the frequency."

"And you won't be setting up a station in Italy?"

"I am at the government's disposal. All the contracts made abroad leave me free in relation to Italy. I love and admire England, not only because my mother is English, but for the strength and energy of the people, and because I owe a great deal to the English; but my heart is still Italian. Tomorrow I am having discussions with the Admiralty on the installation of a large station, but the site hasn't yet been decided."

The article ended with the following account of the inventor's forthcoming activities:

Marconi said he was indebted to the Admiralty for their help and encouragement. He told how Minister Morin agreed that the Carlo Alberto should go to the United States and Canada to take part in further experiments. Marconi will go on board, then to Cape Breton in Nova Scotia and afterwards to Cape Cod in Massachusetts, where two powerful stations are ready and waiting to be inaugurated by Marconi.

## Reporting to the King

From La Spezia, Marconi and Solari took the train to Racconigi, where Victor Emmanuel III was on holiday. Solari provided the King with an account of the work completed on the Carlo Alberto. His report was accompanied by the following brief preface from Admiral Mirabello:

> Together with the account, I have pleasure in sending an example of the magnetic detector constructed on board, a most ingenious instrument just invented by Marconi. Extremely simple as it is, it is self-regulating and never gets out of order. A faithful recorder of every signal, it has never failed in its object, as I can personally testify.
>
> The splendid results of this campaign, which will go down in the annals of radio telegraphy, carried out under the aegis of our flag, with exclusively Italian personnel, mark a triumph for our Country and for our Navy.

The wording of this report might suggest that the magnetic detector was invented on the Carlo Albert. But, as we have seen, Marconi had already made and patented the device before the voyage, after a series of preliminary tests. On board the ship, he had made another detector—not only to honor the Italian navy and the king, but also to use in conducting tests under actual conditions at sea.

In his country residence in Piedmont, the king warmly welcomed Marconi and Solari. He read the report carefully and asked about a number of details; he also entertained Marconi with lunch and dinner, and before bidding the inventor goodnight, asked what he would be working on next. Marconi explained that he would be leaving soon for Canada to complete the first permanent link between the American continent and Europe:

> The Canadian government by voting in a special law after my experiments in Newfoundland, wanted to give me proof of their faith in me and also material assistance. My big station at Table Head near Sydney in Nova Scotia is almost ready. From there I hope to transmit a complete message across the Atlantic for the first time. No one has ever tried, and hardly any scientists believe that my project will succeed. My first message across the Atlantic, with your permission, will be to your Majesty.

The king, who was certainly not immune to flattery, smiled with satisfaction, and Marconi took the opportunity to add: "Just one thing saddens me—that the event won't take place under the Italian flag." The sentence had the desired effect. "We'll send you a ship!" Victor Emmanuel replied. "The Carlo Alberto can remain at your disposal and go to Canada." This was more than Marconi had dared hope for; it was proof that the Italian administration had finally changed its attitude toward him.

Marconi stayed a few days longer in Italy. In Turin, he had a long conversation with Galimberti, the minister responsible for Posts and Telegraph. The inventor proposed a plan for the creation of a large station in Italy. After talking with various other authorities in the government, he was able to retire to Bologna and the Villa Griffone from the 19 to the 24 of September. In the town hall of the Emilian capital, Marconi was the object of clamorous attention.

On 30 September, the Carlo Alberto sailed for England. In view of the decisive test awaiting him, Marconi returned to the English capitol by train to give final instructions to his men and to prepare the apparatus for the experiment. The meeting of Marconi, Solari and

Kemp was scheduled for the 20 of October at Plymouth. Admiral Mirabello, who had been posted to command the Italian fleet in the Far East, was not there.

By the second night of the voyage across the Atlantic, Marconi had again resumed his experiments. A summary of the most important European news was transmitted from Poldhu each night. These messages were received regularly—in spite of the sea and the foul weather—up to a distance of four thousand miles. Marconi was delighted.

The ship entered the Bay of Sydney, Nova Scotia, on 31 October. Marconi, Kemp and Solari disembarked with their equipment and went to Table Head. It would take another nineteen days to set up the apparatus and begin the transmissions.

8

VICTORY OVER THE ATLANTIC


## In the Cold of Glace Bay

At Table Head, Marconi, Kemp, and Solari were given a warm welcome by Richard Norman Vyvyan. This friendly welcome did not disguise the serious difficulties that the group would have to overcome in order to establish the first radiotelegraph service across the Atlantic. According to a number of accounts, Vyvyan was a capable engineer, as well as a great admirer of Marconi and his work. Marconi had shown his usual flair for choosing the right man at the right time; Vyvyan had already provided the inventor with helpful advice on changes to the radio antennae and their supports. When Marconi arrived at Glace Bay, the construction of the station had already been completed according to his instructions. Four huge towers of wooden beams, almost seventy meters high, had transformed the landscape, with its rocky desert stretching out into a sea of ice; at the foot of these towers were built the storage rooms for the equipment, the living quarters and the actual transmitting station.

According to the preliminary program, Marconi and Vyvyan had decided to duplicate the power of the Poldhu transmitter; they were to operate another generator with an output of fifty watts instead of the one with twenty-five watts back in Cornwall. Since Marconi had given Vyvyan considerable freedom in decision-making, in the course of the construction Vyvyan found it more convenient to buy a second-hand generator producing seventy-five watts, more than three times the power of the Poldhu station.

The electric generator was run by a steam boiler. The antennae at Glace Bay (like those at Poldhu) took the shape of a double cone turned upside down, with the wide part on the ground narrowing to a point at the top. The base was formed by cables suspended from the tops of the four towers. From these electrically insulated cables hung a series of wires that joined together at the bottom. This was connected to the transmitter. It was obviously not a regular cone, since it had four distinct corners, marked by the four towers. At the time, the form and dimensions of the antennae were a necessary factor in radiotelegraph broadcasting. Marconi and his technicians had devoted substantial research to the matter, determining that the inverted-cone antenna was the best possible one, given the technology of the time.

The team's difficulties at Glace Bay were due to both the precariousness of the instruments and the appalling weather conditions, including bitter cold and constant snow storms; which left snow and icicles on the most delicate parts of the instruments. After a hard day's work getting the machinery started, another part would malfunction—or another instrument would break—on the following day. The facilities were extremely uncomfortable, with the men eating all their meals together and sleeping in tiny, cramped rooms. Although Marconi had complete faith in his men, he was also aware that under such conditions people could easily become irritable, and he did not want to take any unncessary risks. From the moment he arrived at Table Head, he established a rigorous code of discipline which was very like that on board ship. All the men at Table Head called each other only by their last names; they had a rigid work schedule and a similarly rigorous timetable for their meals, their periods on and off duty, and so on. At eight o'clock they all had their evening meal; Marconi sat at the head of the table and the other men took their seats according to rank.

## Yellow Time

From the existing records, we know that Marconi was the only man in the group to be addressed as "Sir". As a good seaman, Luigi Solari also abided by the disciplinary structure imposed at Table Head, but on more than one occasion, his outgoing behavior stood out in sharp contrast to the typically reserved nature of the other British members of the team. With a great deal of tact, Marconi asked Solari to try to be less talkative. As we shall see, Marconi's careful handling of Solari was only one example of the inventor's exceptional gifts as an organizer and leader.

At last everything was ready for the experiment to begin, but to the immense disappointment of everyone, the long-awaited signal from Poldhu did not come. It was therefore decided to conduct the experiment in reverse, with the signals now being sent from Glace Bay, and Poldhu acting as a receiving station. Through a cablegram in conventional code, Poldhu was to transmit one of the following words: "standard," "green time," or "yellow time," meaning respectively: "We have not received any signal;" "We have detected barely intelligible signals;" and "We have received the signals very clearly."

In a statement that would later be released by *The Times*, Vyvyan left a vivid record of those days of hope and disappointment at the Glace Bay station:

The first transmitting experiment was started from Glace Bay on 19 November 1902, using a single cone aerial of 200 wires, tuning to a capacity, with the jigger used, of 2/27th mfd., the spark length being 50 mms., but no signals were received at Poldhu. Various changes were made, day by day, and transmission effected every night without success until the 28th, when Podhu reported signals received for the first time, though they were not readable. The aerial was then changed and only one side, consisting of 50 wires of the cone aerial, was used and a further series of experiments carried out, with practically no results at Poldhu. On 5th December the secondary spark was increased to 100 mm., and for the first time some readable signals got through. The actual result of this two-hour program was: "weak readable signals for first half-hour; nothing doing during the next three-quarters; last three-quarters readable and recordable on tape." This was by far the best result obtained as yet. The next night during the same hours the programme was repeated with exactly the same arrangements but nothing was received, and again on the following night. It became evident that the great variation in reception must be due to extraneous causes, probably variations in the conductive quality of the medium. It was very difficult to determine whether one transmitting arrangement was better than another under these constantly varying conditions. Changes in arrangement were made every day up to the 14 December, when Poldhu reported, "Readable signals thorough the two-hour program." This result was much the best yet received and, owing to financial pressure and to quiet the adverse press criticism that was making itself noticeable, Marconi decided to attempt to send the first message from Canada the following night using the same arrangement. Dr. Parkin [later Sir

George Parkin, K.C.M.G.] was watching the experiments, as Correspondent of *The Times*, and the message he sent addressed to *The Times* was actually the first message to go by wireless across the Atlantic. It was transmitted for the first time on 15 December at 1:00 to 3:00 a.m., but conditions were unfavourable and it failed to get through. It was again sent between 6:00 and 7:00 p.m. with no better results and repeated during a further program from 10:00 p.m. to midnight. On this occasion the result was excellent, "Readable signals throughout," and the first message was therefore received on 15 December. The text of the message was as follows:

"*Times*, London. Being present at transmission in Marconi's Canadian Station have honour send through *Times* inventor's first wireless transatlantic message of greeting to England and Italy, Parkin."

Instructions had however been given to Poldhu that the message was not to be forwarded to its destination until further instructions, since Marconi desired that the Kings of England and Italy should each receive a message before anyone else.

### First *The Times*, then the Kings

When the cable from Podhu arrived with confirmation of the first success, everybody—engineers, technicians, manual workers— rushed outside into the deep snow, heedless of the ten degrees below zero. They jumped, danced and shouted their "hurrahs" to the surrounding emptiness. Next, they all met in the large dining room, which was nothing but a large wooden hut where a huge fire blazed in the fireplace. Marconi called a meeting for he had a clear plan of action in mind. For reasons of patriotism and publicity, Marconi desperately wanted to ensure that the first two official messages that crossed the Atlantic went directly to the King of Italy and the King of England before news of his achievement reached the public.

Remarkably, Marconi was successful in his attempt to withhold the news of his success. He also managed, through Parkin's newspaper reports, to reserve the news for the world's most prestigious newspaper, *The London Times*. In the same press release that included Vyvyan's previously quoted statement, Parkin added a few comments of his own, which read as follows:

A little after midnight the whole party sat down to a light supper. Behind the cheerful table talk of the young men on the staff, one could feel the tension of an unusual anxiety as the moment approached for which they had worked, and to which they had looked forward so long. It was about ten minutes to one when we left the cottage to proceed to the operating room. I believe I was the first outsider to inspect the building and the machinery.

It was a beautiful night—the moon shone brightly on the snow-covered ground. A wind, which all day had driven heavy breakers on the shore, had died away. The air was cold and clear. All the conditions seemed favourable.

Inside the building, and among its somewhat complicated appliances, the untechnical observer's first impression was that he was among men who understood their work. The machinery was carefully inspected, some adjustments made, and various orders carried out with trained alertness. All put cotton wool in their ears to lessen the force of the electric concussion, which was not unlike the successive explosions of a Maxim gun.

The journalist's remark was perfectly accurate. In those days the spark transmitter made a deafening noise. Parkin's report continued:

As the current was one of most dangerous strength, those not engaged in the operations were assigned to places free of risk.

It had been agreed that, at the last moment before transmission, I should make some verbal change in the message agreed on, for the purpose of identification. This was now done and the message thus changed was handed to the inventor, who placed it on a table where his eye could follow it readily. A brief order for the lights over the battery to be put out, another for the current to be turned on, and the operating work began.

I was struck by the instant change from nervousness to complete confidence which passed over Mr. Marconi's face the moment his hand was on the transmitting apparatus—in this case a long, wooden lever or key.

He explained that it would first be necessary to transmit the letter 'S', in order to fix the attention of the operators at Poldhu and enable them to adjust their instruments. This continued for a minute or more and then, with one hand on the paper from which he read and with the other on the instrument, the inventor began to send across the Atlantic a continuous sentence.

Outside there was no sign, of course, on the transverse wire from which the electric wave projected of what was going on, but inside the operating room the words seemed to be spelled out in short flashes of lightning. It was done slowly, since there was no wish on this occasion to test the speed. But as it was done, one remembered with a feeling of awe, what he had been told—that only the ninetieth part of a second elapses from the moment when he sees the flash till the time when the record is made at Poldhu."

On the night of 16 December, three messages were sent out from Glace Bay to Poldhu: one to the King of Italy, personally composed and signed by Marconi, and two to the King of England, with one signed by Marconi and the other by the Governor of Canada. Unfortunately, the messages were not received that night nor on the following evening because of the breakdown of an alternator during the transmission. The faulty device was quickly repaired, however, and the transmission of the messages from Glace Bay to Poldhu was finally completed on 20 December. Marconi's team, however, had orders to hold the transatlantic radiograms until the 21st of December. Making intelligent use of the difference between time zones, the inventor arranged for the messages to arrive in London and Rome at the same time. Here are the texts of the messages to the English King:

His Majesty the King.
May I be permitted by means of first wireless message to congratulate your Majesty on success of Marconi's great invention connecting Canada and England—Minto.

Lord Knollys—Buckingham Palace—Upon occasion of first wireless telegraphic communication across Atlantic Ocean may I be permitted to present by means of this wireless telegram transmitted from Canada to England my respectful homage to His Majesty the King—G. Marconi—Glace Bay.

The radiotelegram for the King of Italy was sent to the King's aide-de-camp, General Brusati. The message read:

On the occasion of the first Transatlantic radiotelegraphic transmission with this message through the air from the old world to the new I send my most heart-felt homage to his Majesty the King.

This Italian message is slightly more rhetorical than the previous two English messages: the former clearly an example of Marconi's dry, laconic style; the latter of the flowery prose of Luigi Solari.

The news of Marconi's triumph over the Atlantic traveled quickly throughout Europe, arousing public emotion, particularly after

Parkin's press coverage was picked up by the other newspapers. The responses of the British and Italian kings were equally enthusiastic. Edward of England sent the following telegram by way of his aide, Knollys:

> Guglielmo Marconi, Glace Bay
> I have had the honor of submitting your telegram to the King and I have received an order to congratulate you sincerely in the name of His Majesty for the great success of your efforts in the development of your very important invention. The King is always interested in your experiments and wishes to recall to you that your first tests were begun on board the royal yacht Osborne in 1898. Knollys.

The king of England also sent a personal telegram to the Governor General of Canada:

> I am very grateful for the radio message that you sent me and I am happy about the success of Guglielmo Marconi and his great invention which establishes an even stronger tie between Great Britian and Canada. Edward.

Among the many congratulatory telegrams from Italy, there were two from the Royal House:

> I hear with the greatest pleasure the wonderful result achieved which constitutes a new triumph for you to the glory of Italian science. Victor Emmanuel.

The second telegram was from Queen Margherita, who had also received a radio message from Marconi. The inventor had remembered her help with the first wireless radio experiments in Rome in 1897. The queen responded:

I wish to thank you for your kind message. If the genius of our ancestors was given to guide our ships to the discovery of far-away lands, to you and the recently united Italy is now reserved the glory freely to transmit mankind's thoughts across the sea. Margherita.

## Thirty-Eight Transmissions

After the special treatment given to *The Times*, Marconi turned his attention to the Italian press, dispatching the following message via Poldhu to the Stefani agency in Rome:

I am pleased to inform you and the press that I have attained a radiotelegraphy communication between Cape Breton (Canada) and Cornwall (England) with complete success. The inaugural dispatches included one from the Governor General of Canada to his Majesty, King Edward VII, and have already been transmitted to the King of Italy and the King of England. In the presence of its special correspondent and a Canadian member of Parliament, Dr. Parkin, one dispatch was also broadcast to the London "Times." Guglielmo Marconi.

At this stage Marconi needed a great deal of publicity to overcome enormous technical and financial difficulties and carry out his research operations. As usual, he proved that his instincts were perfect when it came to public relations gestures. The transmission of these messages, however, required a great deal of trouble and effort, since they could only operate in one direction. Each dispatch needed to be broadcast several times to ensure success, and setting up a regular radiotelegraph service operating between Europe and America was still a remote prospect.

Vyvyan left a vivid report of the tireless struggle in which Marconi's team was engaged:

The nights were therefore spent in sending messages and the days in trying out various modifications of circuits or apparatus. During the period from the transmission of the first message on 15 December up to 20 January, 38 messages were sent with varying results. Some were repeated 24 times before they were received; whereas others were repeated six times and received correctly on each occasion. It may be of interest to give the text of one of these messages, since it was the first message sent not of a congratulatory character, and because of an amusing incident in its reception. The message read:--

*"Times," London—by transatlantic wireless. Please insert in birth column Jan 3rd wife of R. N. Vyvyan Chief Engineer Marconi's Canadian Station of a daughter. Marconi.*

This message was received on tape, but atmospherics were present and one atmospheric converted the Jan into Jane, so the telegram as received read "Jane 3rd wife of" etc.

On 14 January 1903, Marconi left Table Head for the United States. Work on the second transatlantic station at Cape Cod was almost at an end. All that remained was to build the instruments and to organize the official inauguration. After three relentless days and nights of work, Glace Bay and Cape Cod were connected by wireless telegraphy. As usual, Marconi made sure to send the first message to the King of England, signed this time by the President of the United States, Theodore Roosevelt. The radiotelegram read as follows:

His Majesty King Edward the Seventh London (By Marconi's transatlantic wireless telegraphy).

In taking advantage of the wonderful triumph of scientific research and ingenuity which has been achieved in perfecting a system of wireless telegraphy, I extend on behalf of the American people most cordial greetings and good wishes to you and all the people of the British Empire. Theodore Roosevelt—White House, Washington."

The message had been sent on 18 January between 9:00 and 11:00 p.m., and the operator at Glace Bay was given the order to forward it to Poldhu between eleven o'clock and midnight. To Marconi's pleasant surprise, however, the Cornwall station received the message directly from Cape Cod. It was the first Marconigramme to reach England directly from the United States.

## A Mountain of Telegrams

Within a few hours, Marconi had received official acknowledgment for his new achievement from King Edward. The inventor's fame was now at its zenith. He had impressed even his fiercest critics and the most stubborn skeptics in the press and the scientific community. The two places closest to the Marconi station at Cape Cod—the Post Offices in Well Fleet and Provincetown, in Massachusetts— were forced to hire new staff to deal with the incredible number of telegrams and telephone calls sent to Marconi from all over the world. The king of Italy himself sent no less than half a page of enthusiastic congratulations.

Yet, despite joy over his success, Marconi realized that his beautiful and costly stations could not bear the burden of regular commercial service. Though his instruments were the most powerful in existence at that time, they were inadequate for Marconi's purposes. He needed to make his instruments more effective and by carrying out further tests. All this was to be done in the shortest possible time for very simple and cogent reasons. First of all, Marconi had to pay the vast expenses that his company had incurred in promoting his research programs. Secondly, the inventor was afraid to rest on his laurels, since there was always the threat that his competitors might surpass him, even with their inferior expertise. With these concerns in mind, the inventor soon left for London. He also wanted to report the status of his experiments to the senior executives of his company and to outline for them the technical instruments which were still needed for regular transmissions across the Atlantic.

Before going back to Europe, Marconi stopped briefly in New York, where he received a warm and enthusiastic welcome. He received one of many invitations from Thomas Alva Edison, the greatest American inventor of the day. Marconi arrived at the inventor's house in Orange, New Jersey, about an hour train ride from New York City, around lunch time. The encounter was very friendly and the two men immediately began talking about wireless radiotelegraphy and other problems in physics. They became so engrossed in their favorite subjects that they totally forgot about their lunch. Finally, the aching void in their stomachs became unbearable and Marconi reminded the inventor of the reason for the invitation. Remembering that it was Saturday and his housekeeper had gone home for the weekend; Edison offered Marconi the only refreshments that he had in the house at the time: some bread and cheese and a glass of water. Marconi never forgot this humorous episode, which he cherished as one of the dearest moments of his life.

## The Germans Are Too Inquisitive

Before leaving the States, Marconi gave precise instructions to his men at Glace Bay and Cape Cod to carry on with experimental transmissions and to improve the various pieces of equipment—starting with the antenna itself. Vyvyan, who was appointed technical coordinator for the whole program, found that life at Glace Bay suited him. Here is how he described his days in the Canadian wilderness:

> During the years that elapsed from the start of the construction of the original station at Table Head in Glace Bay until nearly five years later when the Transatlantic Service was opened, there were times when no experiments were being carried out at Glace Bay, while constructional work was in progress at Poldhu or Clifden, and the staff of the station had ample leisure for amusements. Life at Glace Bay was on the whole quite pleasant. The fishing was superlatively good; we had a lake about 100 yards from the site, and a trout brook ran through the site past the house where we lived; there were plenty of brown trout in the lake but when time allowed, we used to go to a river about 17 miles away, where the sea trout came in in vast quantities and running to large weights. Other amusements we had were riding, tennis, canoeing on the lake, and bathing; there was a little shooting, though this was poor, except for the duck and wild geese in the late autumn.
>
> The winter was trying at times, when the country was covered with snow several feet deep for months on end, but there was always sleighing, skating and ice hockey. The stillness of winter in the country in Canada is extraordinary, when there is no wind. All the birds have left, except a few crows, and although the tracks of countless rabbits are to be seen they themselves are invisible. Not a

sound can be heard but one's own breathing, beyond the occasional sharp crack of frost in a tree. The winter air is intensely exhilarating and the climate is wonderfully healthy.

The people in Glace Bay and Sydney were most kind and hospitable to us, and we were therefore not thrown entirely on our own resources. We had frequent visitors to the station. All important visitors arriving at the Eastern Canadian coast made a point of coming to see the station if they could obtain permission. One of the first of these to come to Table Head was Lord Dundonald, shortly after the South African war. He was received, as the hero of the relief of Ladysmith, with decorated streets; he spent a day with us. Dr. Parkin, the well-known Imperialist, stayed with us during the first experiments until his message was sent to *The Times*, while on other occasions we had visits from Mr. Fielding, Sir Frederick Borden, Sir Robert Borden, and the Prime Ministers of Nova Scotia and New Brunswick. The British Atlantic fleet visited nearby Sydney on several occasions and we saw a good deal of Admiral Douglas and of other officers of the fleet. On one occasion Prince Louis of Battenberg came to the station and while there a telegram came for him; I remember well his remarking to himself on reading it, "Dear dear, fancy little Ena going to be a Queen." It was the announcement to him of the betrothal of Princess Ena to the King of Spain. We also had visits from officers of the French squadron, and of course saw many officers from the Italian cruiser the Carlo Alberto.

Reporters were, however, not welcome visitors; they would come without warning and were very difficult to frustrate. We had strict instructions that no interviews were to be granted, but Directors in England had no knowledge of the pertinacity of the American Reporter. I well remember on one occasion the arrival of a reporter from one of the great New York newspapers. He came with a story that Marconi had confessed that he was not the inventor of wireless, but that it had been invented by an officer of the Italian Navy.

On my refusing to discuss the matter with him and stating the suggestion was absurd, he stated that he was not going back without a story, and if I did not grant him an interview he would invent one.

On another occasion the Society of American Reporters from the Middle West was touring Eastern Canada and had arranged without permission or notice to visit the station. About 300 suddenly arrived in a special train; I had all doors locked and gave them an impromptu lecture under the aerials. Luckily their time was all mapped out, and after an hour's talk to them, which must have bored them as much as it bored me, they departed. The cuttings describing the visit were sent to me, and one of these alluding to the lecture I gave them, said, "but as the Professor was a Frenchman and spoke very little English, we couldn't understand him."

On a later date we had a visit from the German fleet. The fleet anchored off Glace Bay, a dangerous roadstead, and the wireless stations could be the only object of the visit. In due course the German Admiral and about thirty officers arrived at the gates of the station, where I met them and offered refreshments after their long and hot walk. These were declined and the Admiral stated that they had come to see over the station. I informed him I should be delighted to show them over. Doubtless he had a letter of authority from Marconi or the Directors of the Marconi company authorizing me to do so. He said he had not; I expressed my regrets that without authority it was impossible for me to admit him. He became very brusque and informed me that His Imperial Majesty would be much annoyed. Again I expressed my regrets and he and his staff went off, again declining any refreshment. The fleet stayed at anchor and I kept a watchman on one of the towers to report. Next day boats put off from the fleet and in due course a crowd of about 150 sailors arrived at the gates. Apparently there were no officers with them: they pushed past me in an unruly mob. I informed them [that] admission was forbidden and, if they persisted, I would use force to prevent them from entering the station.

At the time we had a considerable body of workmen employed on certain construction work, and when they saw these men it appeared to strike them there might be trouble. A whistle was blown and they all went out, a disciplined force, and no longer an unruly crowd of men. I was severely attacked in the local papers afterwards for my apparent lack of courtesy."

## At the Service of the Press

Apart from their value as anecdotes, Vyvyan's reports give a valuable account of the serious technical difficulties and others hardships that Marconi and his team had to overcome. After his departure for England towards the end of January 1903, experiments had to be stopped in order to allow for the fine-tuning of the equipment. The transmission of messages between the United States and Europe was resumed on 20 March for four consecutive nights. Each night Poldhu successfully received two-hour long transmissions from the other side of the Atlantic.

The results were so encouraging that Marconi agreed to start up a trial broadcast service for *The London Times*. The first was sent on 28 March; others followed for a week, until April 6th, when the antennae at Glace Bay collapsed under the pressure of more than an inch of ice. The damage was very costly and completely unexpected, but it led to additional improvements in the equipment. For instance, the antennae cables used in particularly cold places would subsequently carry "thermic" wires that were warmed by the current and prevented the ice from coating the instrument.

At the beginning of summer, after the antennae had been rebuilt, experiments were resumed between Glace Bay, Poldhu and Cape

Cod. Although the signals sent from Glace Bay were received clearly in Cornwall, they were not received at Cape Cod, though the site was at at a distance shorter by one-third than the one between Table Head and Poldhu. The conclusion was that these phenomena were due to the "variability of the means" through which waves were passing.

Marconi had, by this time, realized that the antennae he had been using were too small to radiate the necessary energy, and that the distance beyond which it was possible to enlarge the range of the signals during the day grew with the increase of the wavelength. Marconi had proved that with a small antenna he could send radiotelegraph signals at a distance of two hundred miles with only a one-centimeter long spark; but if the antenna dimensions were sufficiently large, a two-millimeter spark was enough to reach distances of two hundred miles. Following these experiments, the inventor had an even bigger system of umbrella-shaped antennae built, then left on board the Lucania for new tests during the journey from Europe to America. Guglielmo had ordered both Poldhu and Glace Bay stations to broadcast continuous messages with the most important news from Europe and the United States.

## Germany Humiliated

On the technical front, an antenna in the shape of a fan was built at Glace Bay to match the umbrella-shaped device at Poldhu. Though much bigger, the new antenna was similar to the one used by Marconi on the cruiser Carlo Alberto during the first radiotelegraphic campaign. On 22 August 1903, Marconi embarked on the Lucania. From that day until his arrival in New York, Marconi published a daily newspaper that featured news received from both sides of the Atlantic. The first radiotelegraphic newspaper was called "Cunard Bulletin," after the shipping company to which the ship belonged. From that time forward, all the biggest liners en route from Europe to America and vice versa printed their own newspapers on board.

During the voyage of the Lucania, Guglielmo succeeded in receiving messages from Glace Bay as far as one thousand miles away in daytime and at a distance of 1,700 miles at night. This was an exceptional result, all the more significant in that it allowed him to overshadow the first international radiotelegraph congress, organized by Germany in Berlin, in August of the same year. Mainly to protect the interests of Slaby's radiotelegraph company, the German government decided to regulate radiotelegraph service with a series of international laws, which aimed, in effect, at limiting transmissions to a distance of 100,000 miles. The reason was very simple: at that time, the German system could not transmit any farther.

The congress—quite predictably—came to nothing. And it was all the more humiliating for Germany, in light of Marconi's New York success, which was reaffirmed by his presentation of the onboard newspaper. But Guglielmo was far from being satisfied. He wanted, at all costs, to transform transatlantic radiotelegraph service into a commercial venture. True, he accepted the honors given him by the American city. And he gave interviews in which he spoke confidently of the future developments of his communication system. But Marconi did not allow these factors to interfere with his work. As soon as he arrived in the States, he instructed Vyvyan to build a new antenna in order to increase the power radiating from Glace Bay; then he went to Cape Cod to start a new set of tests. After the first feverish work in Pontecchio and the exciting demonstrations in England, this was the most intense research period in the inventor's life. It was also a period during which Marconi's intelligence and determination were severely tested. Promising results were often followed by dubious ones, such as the loss of signals or the sudden and apparently unexplainable interruption in communication.

The truth was that, though the instruments were still rather rudimentary, they were still the best ones available at the time. The transmission system was still based on the production of sparks by means of the discharge of condensers activated by powerful generators of current. Something new was necessary—something which would allow rapid, but also reliable transmissions— and Marconi devoted all his efforts to this end. After weeks of tireless work, he finally engineered and built a new transmission system—the rotating disc oscillator—which completely revolutionized the old methods. The new oscillator was composed of a steel disc with special copper contact-makers pinned round the edge at regular intervals. When the disc rotated at very high speed between the electrodes of a generator, the contact-makers—shaped like studs—would cause a series of sparks at the desired frequencies and with a potential of fifteen thousand volts. This overcame the deficiencies of the previous spark system, which required big condensers to load the antenna circuit with high enough power for long-distance transmissions.

9

A DIFFICULT MARRIAGE

## A Happy Father

The years from 1901 to 1910 were among the most significant in Marconi's life. Italy was enjoying a moment of rapid economic and social development under the leadership of Giovanni Giolitti. The political scene was characterized by a series of more stable cabinets than in the past, thanks to a tacit agreement between the more progressive liberal groups and the socialists at the opposition. The same decade saw the definitive victory of wireless telegraphy. Marconi's system was no longer an experimental undertaking but a well-organized commercial activity, by now established as the quickest and safest means of communication over long distances and the only link between land and ships on the high seas.

On a technical level, wireless telegraphy moved from the skilled utilization of coherer electrophysical phenomena to the more efficient performance of the magnetic detector; and in the more powerful stations, rotating disc transmitters replaced spark generators.

In 1905 the scientific consultant for the Marconi Company, John Ambrose Fleming, invented the thermionic valve—still used for the transmission, detection, reception and amplification of radioelectric signals. This simple apparatus made possible for radiotelegraphy (transmission of the dots and dashes of Morse code) to develop into radio broadcasting (transmission and reception of human voices and music). This was the beginning of radio as we know it today and the first step toward the development of television.

It was also during this period that Marconi finally proved he was ready to set up a worldwide radiotelegraph network. He was now generally regarded as the most important inventor of his time: kings, princes, governments, scientific institutions, and academies competed for the privilege of receiving him and presenting him with awards. In 1909 he received the biggest honor of all when he became the first Italian to be awarded the Nobel Prize in physics

After Marconi had left Bologna for the first time in February 1896, the Marconi family had practically split apart, with Annie following her son to England, and Giuseppe and Alfonso remaining at Pontecchio. This forced separation had had a positive effect: it strengthened the love of the elderly farmer for his wife and sons.

Throughout the years, Giuseppe Marconi maintained a deep and constant affection for his brilliant son. After the founding of the Marconi Company in England, Giuseppe had devoted all his savings to buying as many company shares as he could afford. These he divided between his son Alfonso, Guglielmo himself, and various other relatives.

Of Giuseppe's life between 1896 and 1904, we know only what has been possible to piece together from his previously mentioned "almanac", and from what is left of the correspondence between father and son. Annie left again for England on 18 July 1897, after she had returned with Guglielmo at the time of his first wireless telegraph demonstrations in Rome and La Spezia. She did not return to Italy until the following year. On 19 May 1898, Giuseppe recorded her return in his diary, writing simply, "Annie is back." The two spent the summer of that year at Porretta and part of the autumn at the Villa Griffone, where he carefully read all the newspaper accounts about Guglielmo, marking down in his diary the dates when his son was mentioned. He cut out many of the lengthier articles and sent them to Guglielmo in England. Finally on 6 February 1899, one of his most cherished dreams came true when he left for London to see with his own eyes what his great son has been able to achieve in such a short time. While he was in England, Giuseppe traveled to Poole to visit Guglielmo's laboratory and see his equipment. There, he quickly made friends with his son's collaborators and inquired about every detail of their work.

Proud of his son's achievements he had seen, Giuseppe stopped in London a few extra days before returning to the Griffone on 22 March. On 7 February of the following year, he returned to London, lodging in a "seven-shilling-a-day" hotel—extremely extravagant for the time. His son's now exalted position did not allow for any less, however, and on 25 February Giuseppe hosted a meal in the hotel for the family's relatives and his son's closest friends.

Unfortunately, the fatigue of the journey, the excitement of the new experience and the harsh British weather made the seventy-seven-year-old man ill. He was eventually able to return to the Villa Griffone on 4 May. Annie followed him at the end of the month, and they spent the summer together at Porretta.

On 12 November, Giuseppe was alone again. Annie would not return to Italy until July 1901, when the couple spent several peaceful days at the Villa Griffone before traveling together to the thermal baths of Porretta and of San Pellegrino in the Alps

## Roman Triumphs

Unfortunately, the pages in Giuseppe's diary covering the years from 1901 to 1904 are missing, and there is no written record of this period in his life.

We know for certain that Giuseppe's health gradually deteriorated, and that Annie rarely left his side. When Guglielmo returned to Italy in the spring of 1903, after his first successful trans-Atlantic transmissions, Giuseppe Marconi—though full of aches and pains—did not want to miss the joy of sharing in the triumphant celebrations which greeted his son in Rome and Bologna. Together with Annie, he stood beside his son as Guglielmo was made an honorary citizen of Rome at a ceremony in the Italian capitol building on 3 May.

When Guglielmo arrived at the station, the crowd invaded the railway line and the train had to stop half a mile before the platform. An amusing incident occured when Guglielmo left the train at the same time as a young English couple on their honeymoon. The crowd, mistaking the young bride for the inventor's fiancée, led her triumphantly to the Grand Hotel, while the real husband struggled to elbow his way through the throng to explain the mistake.

Similar displays of enthusiasm took place after the ceremony at the capitol, as Marconi gave his first full report on the wireless telegraph and its development. As Guglielmo left the government building, boarding the carriage with his parents and Mayor Prospero Colonna, a group of adoring students unharnessed the horses and pulled the vehicle themselves through the streets of Rome.

Giuseppe must have been exceedingly proud at the sight of this triumphant welcome for his son. But what moved the old Bologna farmer most deeply was the welcome that his own native town reserved for Guglielmo. The ceremonies in Bologna were less spectacular than in Rome, but no less impressive—and certainly no less touching. The official speech in the great hall of the University was delivered by Augusto Righi, whose words were so warm and gratifying that both Guglielmo and Giuseppe were genuinely moved. Righi's homage—not only in front of a public audience but also from the university chair—was the best reward the Marconis could have imagined. The inventor himself was so overcome that when he got up to express his gratitude to Righi, he could not utter one word. Very pale, his eyes shining with emotion, Marconi stood speechless for what seemed like an eternity, until a thunderous round of applause ended his embarrassment.

During a meal at the court of Victor Emanuel III, Guglielmo was introduced to the German Emperor, Wilhelm II, who was visiting Rome at the time. Relations between the Marconi Company and the German rival, the Slaby Company—which was, in effect, owned by the German government—had recently become extremely tense. Things had been further complicated an incident involving Prince Heinrich, the Kaiser's brother, and some of Marconi's English staff. While the prince was traveling by sea from Hamburg to New York, he had signaled the Marconi stations off the British coast, asking them to forward five private messages for him. The British operators inquired as to whether anyone on board needed immediate assistance. Since the reply was negative, they declared they had no obligation to transmit any private communication from Prince Heinrich.

## At Dinner with the Kaiser

During the reception in Rome, the German Emperor spoke openly to Marconi regarding the event: "Dear sir," Wilhelm said to the inventor, "you must not think that I bear you any ill will, but I disapprove of the conduct of your Company." Reacting in the manner of a perfect English gentleman, Marconi replied: "Your Imperial Majesty, for me the mere thought of some personal animosity of Your Majesty against me would be a cause of distress. However, it is my responsibility to decide my company's conduct."

Marconi could behave with extreme adamance and pride when he felt he was in the right. Guglielmo had obviously inherited this trait from his father, about who he loved to tell the following anecdote. While serving as a town counselor many years earlier, Giuseppe received a message from the Prefect of Bologna, urgently requesting his presence. Instead of the compliant response that such a request would normally receive, the bearer of the message was shocked to hear the elder Marconi's reply: "If I am officially called as a citizen, I will hasten to the prefettura; but if it is a private matter, you can tell the Prefect I have no request to make: however, if he has a request, I am here ready to receive him." The Bologna Prefect was certainly not as powerful and important as the Kaiser, but the analogy between the two episodes is evident.

As old age and failing health finally prevailed over the strong constitution of Marconi's father, Giuseppe found it necessary to leave the solitude of the Villa Griffone for an apartment in the Albergati house in via Saragozza near the center of Bologna, in compliance with the wishes of his wife and son. In Bologna, he would have much easier access to the attention and care of physicians and the members of his family who lived in and near the city. The elder Marconi would stay in Bologna until his death, with Annie never leaving his side for an instant

## The Farmer's Will

Though he now spent most of his time in England or traveling from station to station to supervise his experiments, Guglielmo was able to enjoy one final, and providential, visit with his father.

During the second half of March 1904, Guglielmo was in Italy once again. He stopped briefly in Rome to discuss setting up—at the request of the Postmaster General, Galimberti, the Postmaster General—a large radiotelegraph station that would establish a direct communications link between Italy and Argentina. During this visit, Marconi spent the night of the 24th in Bologna with his family.

Urgent obligations with his company required his presence in London, but first he needed to stop at his home town in the capital of Emilia, both to see his parents and receive an honorary degree from the School of Applied Engineering of the University. This was to take place at a solemn ceremony on the 25th. Only Annie was able to join her son at the ceremony; Giuseppe could no longer leave his bed. Though the doctors agreed that Giuseppe was seriously ill, they did not consider his death to be imminent. Unfortunately, within only a few hours, his condition took a turn for the worse; soon after midnight, he died.

Guglielmo was deeply shaken by his father's sudden death and was overcome with fever. He attended the funeral service and was present when the will was opened. To everyone's great surprise, Giuseppe had left the large Villa Griffone and most of the land surrounding it not, in accordance with tradition, to his first-born, but to his youngest son, Guglielmo.

It was the old man's final sign of affection towards Guglielmo, and his last indication that he wished to be forgiven for his initial refusal to acknowledge his son's extraordinary gifts. Giuseppe had made his decision and consulted with his lawyer in the utmost secrecy. Perhaps he did his other children an injustice in leaving Guglielmo the best part of his property, but that was the only way he could put his heart to rest.

The demands of the Marconi Company gave Guglielmo little time to indulge in his grief; after the funeral, he had to leave his family almost immediately and return to London. Contrary to what has been reported in some biographies, however, the Marconi Company was not on the verge of bankruptcy at the time; according to the budget published on the 27th of that same month, the Company reported an income of £36,376, with a profit of £10,000. It was not a huge sum, but still a respectable figure which clearly showed the vitality of the firm. The biggest problem facing the Company at that moment was an ongoing conflict with the Ministry of Posts and Telecommunications.


## The Suffragette

The good old days on Salisbury Plain had passed. The British Telegraph Service, though acknowledging Marconi's merits, had adopted the attitude of a competitor towards his company—more for political motives than for technical reasons. Despite numerous applications, the Telegraph Service had continued to refuse to sign an agreement allowing post offices to receive and transmit messages for the Marconi Company. In cases where one party used wireless telegraph and the other had to be reached by post, there occurred an interruption between the sender and the receiver. This state of affairs seriously obstructed the expansion of the Company and prevented it from performing its activities with maximum efficiency.

Fortunately, after endless applications and meetings, the British Minister finally signed the eagerly awaited contract with Marconi in September 1904. From that moment on, every Post Office in the United Kingdom was authorized to receive, transmit and deliver any message from any part of the world broadcast through Marconi's wireless telegraph. To obtain the government's consent, Guglielmo actually threatened to remove all his stations from British territory and to install them only in those countries whose governments were ready to consent to a connection between the telegraph system inside their territory and the radio system.

During this same period, two other important events occurred in Marconi's life. In 1903, during the voyage from Europe to North America on board the Lucannia, Guglielmo met Inez Milholland, a pretty American girl; on the trip, he fell in love with her and proposed marriage. No wedding would follow, however. Given her background and personality, Inez was hardly the type of woman whom Guglielmo would have chosen as his companion for life.

Inez was an intellectual, as well as an unflinching supporter of equal rights between men and women in an age when these ideas could only arouse a complacent smile in a man like Guglielmo. On one occasion, she even rode a white horse down Fifth Avenue in New York to demonstrate against "male chauvinism." It was probably these very idiosyncracies, however, which first aroused Marconi's curiosity and interest. Perhaps it was the contrast between the young American suffragette and the inventor's devoted mother that so excited his imagination, otherwise totally occupied by radiotelegraphy.

One thing is certain: Guglielmo deeply admired and appreciated Inez Milholland, and they remained friends even after they parted. Years later, after Marconi became a father, he sought Inez's advice before choosing his children's school.

This fleeting love for the charming young American, along with a host of other, similarly brief flirtations throughout the inventor's life, reveal two essential traits of Marconi's personality. His Latin and Irish blood led him to fall in love with women swiftly and passionately. But then, with the same impulsive speed, he would suddenly abandon the affairs, his mind and heart taken up by more-pressing, career-related problems.

The tests carried out on board the Lucania and other technical improvements achieved at the Poldhu, Cape Breton and Cape Cod stations, contributed to another of the inventor's sensational exploits during the period. On board the Campania, which he boarded on 7 May 1904 bound for the United States, Marconi, in addition to maintaining simultaneous contact with both his English and American stations, obtained an uninterrupted link with three separate liners—The Etruria, the Aurania, and the Lucania—sailing more than one thousand miles away.

## The Saint Louis Congress

On 3 August 1904, Marconi inaugurated the first international commercial radiotelegraphy service in the Mediterranean, opening stations at Bari and Antivari, on the other side of the Adriatic. The Italian inventor was granted the use of the warship Sardegna for the occasion. He also built a station in Ancona on Monte Cappuccini, and in Venice at the Torre Piloti. Both stations were then linked with the master station at Poldhu.

In September Guglielmo was back in America, at the Saint Louis Exhibition, where scientists from all over the world met for a World Electricity Congress. The German representatives read a long paper vindicating Professor Slaby's claim to have invented radiotelegraphy. However, nothing was said about Marconi's work, however. Luigi Solari was present, representing Italy. Foreseeing contention with the Germans, Solari had gathered exhaustive documentary evidence on the subject, and as soon as the German delegate concluded his remarks, he asked for permission to speak. He then read verbatim, in both English and Italian, the speech that had earlier been presented by Professor Slaby at Charlottenburg University on 11 November 1897, in which the noted German scientist had publicly acknowledged the priority and superiority of Marconi's system over his own inventions.

"This is what Professor Slaby said and wrote in 1897," proclaimed Solari at the conclusion of his remarks. "How do you reconcile this explicit declaration with what you have just heard?" In reponse to Solari's remarks, all the delegates—except the Germans—stood up and applauded, enthusiastically shouting Marconi's name.

Later in the conference, Guglielmo, who rarely consumed alcoholic beverages, was involved in a minor, but embarrassing mishap. During an official banquet, he drank an excessive quantity of mint julep, a refreshing, but highly intoxicating summer drink composed of mint, sugar, crushed ice, and bourbon. Persuaded that the drink was to have a mild to affect on his behavior, Guglielmo rose to his feet at the end of his meal to say a few words to the assembled delegates. But the bourbon had worked its magic, and the inventor could barely maintain his balance—a fact that was apparent to everyone in the room. Reluctant to acknolwedge that he had, in fact, been intoxicated, Marconi insisted that someone had tried to poison him.

Meanwhile his company's business continued to expand at a remarkable rate. Marconi signed a contract with the Cunard Line which not only agreed to equip all its ships with Marconi stations, but also granted a £10 royalty for every hundred words transmitted or received by its ships. In addition, the Daily Telegraph subscribed to a regular radiotelegraph service for daily weather forecasts—an example that would soon be followed by a host of other newspapers and press agencies.

## The First Encounter

After Giuseppe's death in 1904, Annie had little to keep her in Bologna. When he was free from his obligations in other parts of the world, Guglielmo spent most of his time in London, where his elder brother, Alfonso, had also taken up residence some time before, assuming a position as an executive in the Company. For these reasons, Annie soon left Italy for good and settled in London.

During his stay in Poole, Guglielmo worked very hard but also allowed himself occasional diversions, such as boating and fishing, his favorite sport. Occasionally the inventor spent his afternoons and evenings in the splendid castle on Brownsea Island, a few miles from Poole harbor. The owners of the castle were the Van Raaltes, with whom Marconi had struck up a deep friendship and who, in turn, were happy to have such a famous celebrity among their guests.

It was during one of his visits to Brownsea castle that Marconi met his future wife, Beatrice O'Brien. She was nineteen years old at the time, regarded by everyone as a splendid girl. On her father's side, Beatrice was a descendant of the ancient Irish King Brian Boru (or Brian Borohime), who had reigned around the year 1000. On her mother's side, she came from the Scottish noble line of the Stuarts.

The thirty-year-old Marconi saw his future wife for the first time on the quayside at little Brownsea harbor. He had just sailed from Poole and was climbing the steps to meet Mrs. Van Raalte who had come to the harbor to meet him, accompanied by her daughter and Beatrice. Shortly before the meeting, Beatrice caught one of the heels of her silk shoes between two pebbles, snapping it completely off much to her embarrassment. Beatrice, on the other hand, found Guglielmo to be much too old for her, and even rather boring. Like any other eligible woman of her day, however, she was clearly flattered by the undisguised attentions of such a famous man, someone so sought after by leading society women of the time.

## Hunting for Gossip

The Inchiquin family owned a large castle at Dromoland, surrounded by wide and fertile fields, woods rich in game, and a superb park. Over the years, however, the financial solidity of the old house had been undermined, though the ancient splendor had not faded away. Beatrice's mother disliked the countryside and had bought a luxurious house in the heart of London, near Marble Arch. After the death of Beatrice's father, this house—which did not require the fifty servants of Dromoland castle—turned out to be the most economical solution to their problems.

Beatrice had heard of Marconi for the first time when she was fourteen years old, while she was walking one day with her favorite sister, Lilah, and her father in the nearby woods. Lord Inchiquin, who was interested in electrophysics, had told his daughters of the the remarkable wireless telegraph and its brilliant young inventor.

Lord Inchiquin died in 1900. According to the tradition of the day, the Dromoland property went to the first son, Lucius, who became head of the house. Beatrice then settled in London, along with her mother and seven sisters. Here Lady Inchiquin became a contributor to the "society columns" of a number of leading newspapers and magazines. Sketches of high-ranking people and gossip from the fashionable world flowed from her pen. Her stories reflected the idle drawing-room conversations taking place from the Court downward. She signed them with a variety of pseudonyms, though she did not publicly hide the fact that she was the author. Those who did not want to fall foul of her pen went out of their way to treat her as kindly as they could.

Like any serious professional, Lady Inchiquin did not confine her writing to exclusively what she saw and heard; in order to keep up to date and link together people and events, she had assembled a well-organized network of collaborators, conveniently composed of her eight charming and socially active daughters. The young women's task was to report to their mother everything they heard and saw at the fashionable parties and balls of London. Returning from an engagement late at night, the girls would write down every detail of their evening, then slip these notes under their mother's bedroom door before going to bed. It was mainly through her mother's columns that Beatrice knew of Marconi's importance and reputation, but it certainly had never crossed her mind that such a famous and influential man would one day propose to her.

## Bea's Refusal

After the first meeting between Guglielmo and Bea on the quay of Brownsea harbor, the inventor's visits to the Van Raaltes' castle became longer and more frequent. Forgetting his experiments, Marconi spoke frankly of his previous engagement to Inez Milholland, promising that he would immediately ask her to free him from his earlier commitment.

Beatrice listened patiently, amused and somewhat disconcerted by all his talk, but she apparently did nothing to encourage her exceptional suitor. Mrs. Van Raalte was also flattered by Marconi's interest in her daughter, and allowed him to continue the courtship. However, when Guglielmo offered to drive the girl back to London at the end of the holiday, her mother declined the invitation. As a society columnist, she, perhaps more than anyone else, realized the scandal the trip would have inevitably provoked in London society. So Beatrice went back to London by train accompanied by her maid. She later confessed, however, that she would have loved to have accompanied Marconi on the trip—not because of her affection for the inventor, but simply for the exciting prospect of the adventure itself.

Marconi remained in Poole only long enough to pack his things and instruct his staff. He then left for London. A few days later, Lady Inchiquin—who not only wrote about social events but also organized her own—gave a charity ball at Albert Hall. Guglielmo quickly purchased one of the expensive tickets and was among the first to arrive for the evening. Studying the gaily-colored crowd of damsels and their escorts, he had difficulty finding the Irish girl with the deep dark eyes.

Albert Hall is a large building with many parlors and lounges, staircases and balconies—all of which were packed that night with huge crowds of people. After an excruciating wait, the inventor finally spotted Beatrice at the top of a flight of stairs—sad and alone, watching the crowd. It was here that Marconi asked Beatrice to become his wife. Taken completely by surprise, Bea blushed at the proposal, only managing a mumbled request for a little more time to consider his offer. She needed a few days to be able to talk to her sister Lilah, she told Marconi. This was clearly an excuse, since Lilah was currently in Dresden, in Germany, attending a painting course. Every day Marconi sent Beatrice letters and flowers, hoping to sway her., but she remained uncertain. Finally, after a week had passed, she invited the inventor to tea, telling him flat out that she was not in love with him and could therefore not accept his offer.

It is easy to imagine how much Marconi must have been hurt by her response. For the first time, after so many romantic conquests in the past, his affection was gently, but firmly refused. And for the first time, Guglielmo found himself deeply and passionately in love.

For several months, Marconi and Miss O'Brien did not write or see one other. She spent time in London with her mother. When not conducting research in his laboratory, he toured the world organizing new radio stations. He traveled to Turkey, Bulgaria, and Rumania for the installation of powerful radiotelegraph units, briefly stopping in Italy to preside over the formation of the Marconi Company of Genoa.

## A Woman in Love

Turned down by Bea but unable to forget her, Marconi threw himself wholeheartedly into his job. Though he caught a malarial fever in the Balkans which was to torment him for many years, he still managed to complete a number of technical achievements during this period. The inventor's developments at this time included: the first receiving instrument employing Fleming thermionic valves; the directional antennae for long-wave transmissions, patented on 18 July 1905; new kinds of metallic plate condensers; and new oscillator circuits which would soon permit the transmission and detection of radio signals from Glace Bay to Poldhu, even during daytime. Marconi's company also obtained permission from the English government to establish a public radiotelegraph service between the British post offices via the Poldhu station and those in Canada connected to Glace Bay.

Marconi next saw Beatrice at the same place where he first met her, the Van Raaltes' castle at Brownsea. Invited once again for the holidays, Beatrice accepted on condition that she would not meet Marconi. Mrs. Van Raalte gave her solemn word that she would respect Bea's wish and not invite the inventor while Beatrice was staying with them. As soon as the hostesss knew for certain that the girl was coming to the island, however, she wrote to Marconi expressing her regrets over Bea's refusal to marry him and informing him, along with a warm invitation to visit, that Bea would soon be their guest again. Guglielmo immediately set off for Brownsea and a surprise reunion with the woman he intended to marry. When she realized that Marconi had arrived at the castle, Bea greeted him gracefully and without embarrassment. Feeling sorry that she had been unable to return Marconi's love, she accepted his declaration of friendship. During their stay at the castle, Marconi took Bea out on his boat on a number of occasions and lavished attention on her. Before long, their friendship turned into love.

Guglielmo asked her again to be his wife. This time Bea accepted, but only if the engagement was first approved by her beloved sister Lilah. Here is the letter that she wrote to her sister at the time:

It's so serious I don't know how to break it to you. I'm not crazy; it's only this, I've settled the most serious thing in my life. Can you guess it? I am engaged to be married to Marconi—on these conditions: only if he meets with your approval and when you come home in about three months' time. Only, only if you like him and, darling Luzz, you must try for my sake. I don't love him. I've told him so over and over again. He says he wants me anyhow and will make me love him. I do like him so much and enough to marry him. . . . I don't even know how Mamma or any of them will take it and as for you, my own darling Luzz, if you don't like him a little, I shall die. I told him this morning I was going to write and tell you; he realizes it depends on you. He says he is coming out to make love to you and bring you round, but I am afraid he would fall in love with you and I don't think I'd like that now. But seriously he has got to go to Italy for ten days sometime before Christmas, and I want him to go on the way to Dresden and see you. Do try to like him a little for my sake. I think he really does love me and would try to make me happy. We got engaged on the nineteenth and I never slept a wink till five in the morning. My feelings have been so extraordinary and wild I haven't been able to write, though I tried hard. He is not staying in the house now, as he had to spend most of the day at the Haven just opposite on business. It will be a funny Christmas, won't it, my last most likely as a spinster—and to think I never meant to marry! I had always arranged to be an old maid."

Lilah, along with the Van Raaltes, approved of the engagement; Beatrice's mother and brother, Lord Inchiquin, on the other hand, opposed it. Their objection was motivated primarily by the fact that Guglielmo was a foreigner—along with a disturbing report about the inventor's recent behavior in Rome.

While in the Italian capital, Marconi was often seen in public escorting an attractive young woman, Princess Giacinta Ruspoli. One newspaper reported that the two had been seen fondly gazing into each other's eyes in a box at the opera. The article even went so far as to announce their engagement. As soon as he saw the article, Marconi rushed back to London to appease Beatrice who, reacting against her mother and elder brother's vetos, had grown stubbornly determined to marry her man.

This time he was too seriously involved to pull out so easily. He decided to meet personally Lady Inchiquin and, in a short while, he won her over. The marriage took place on 16 March 1905, in the elegant church of Saint George in Hanover Square. The ceremony, which had been announced in the court bulletin, was lavishly sumptuous. The most outstanding names in the British nobility and representatives of the political and diplomatic world were present.


## A Well-To-Do Inventor

The world press was full of news of the wedding. Presents were sent to the couple from the most distant parts of the globe, so widely known was the inventor's name. *Vanity Fair* published a humorous caricature and sympathetic profile of the bridegroom. It is not unlikely that he bride's mother herself—who from the moment of her assent to the wedding had christened her son-in-law with the endearing nickname of Marky—had a hand in its composition. The article read:

> The true inventor labours in an attic, lives chiefly upon buns, sells his watch to obtain chemicals, and finally, after desperate privation, succeeds in making a gigantic fortune for other people. Guglielmo Marconi invented in comfort, retained any small articles of jewellery in his possession, and never starved for more than five hours at a time. Therefore he cannot expect our sympathy as an inventor, though he excites our wonder as an electrician.
>
> He is a quiet man with a slow, deliberate manner of speech, and a shape of head which suggests an unusual brain. He has Irish blood in his veins, for his maternal grandfather, Andrew Jameson, married a daughter to a Marconi of Bologna, from which union was born Guglielmo. Guglielmo, I may mention, is the Italian for Bill.
>
> Bill was educated at Leghorn under Professor Rosa, and afterwards at Bologna University. He first attempted to send wires without wires upon his father's land to the farm of neighbours. Chemistry was his earliest study, but from it to electricity was but a short step. From Italy he came to England, testing his instruments between Penarth and Weston. Returning home again, he obtained the loan of an Italian cruiser, and continued his experiments with success.
>
> What has been the result, the world knows. His system is used exclusively at Lloyd's and in the British and Italian Navies. It has made the Atlantic still less endurable for tired brains by providing liners with a daily paper. He has alarmed the Chinese with his devices at Pekin and Tien-Tsin, forcing them to compose special prayers against foreign devils and all their works. He has been the cause of a petition from the Cornish fisherfolk, who suggested that the Government should put him down before his electrical sparks ruined the weather. Lastly, to fill the cup of his sins, he has sent messages across the Atlantic, and created amongst shareholders in

cable companies a feeling which resembles the personal uncertainty of chickens under a hawk.

He is a hard worker, displaying the greatest resolution before unexpected difficulties. He rides, cycles, motors. Of music he is a sincere admirer. Being half an Irishman, his lack of more humour is prodigious."

The marriage began favorably, as one can judge from the follwoing letter written by Bea to her mother from Dromoland castle, where the newlyweds began their honeymoon:

Dearest Mamma:

Just a line to tell you we arrived here all right yesterday and to thank you ever so much for your dear letter. I was delighted to have a line from you. We are both so happy and Dromoland's just the same as ever, not changed one little bit. Except that the house seems so deadly quiet, one can't help feeling a bit lonely. We have been given no. 3 & 4; it's so strange being in the Visitor's part of the house. We didn't have such a very tiring journey, and today I feel as if we had never been travelling at all. The crossing was smooth as glass. I think it was better coming straight through, don't you think? The wedding went off very well, don't you think? It was too, too good of you taking all the trouble you did over it. We are both grateful and Marky sends his love and says he quite realizes how lucky he is!

So that's all right, isn't it! I can't get used a bit to being called Ma'am; it's too funny. Everyone has been too kind here and simply delighted to see us again. We were met at the station by old Mike, and Mrs. Simpson was at the top of the stairs, wildly pleased and excited at seeing us. We have had more than 350 telegrams of congratulations from all over the world. I can't write a longer letter now as the post is just going. Goodbye, dearest Mamma, with fondest love from us both and ever so many thanks for all you've done for us."

## A Jealous Man

The honeymoon lasted only a week; Guglielmo's engagements were so urgent that he had to go back to London at the request of his company's central offices. Husband and wife lived at first in a small hotel, then took up lodgings in one of the most expensive hotels in the city, the Carlton. Here they had their first disagreements.

Marconi was deeply in love with his wife but was also very jealous. Though she gave no real grounds for him to doubt her fidelity and was herself jealous of him, Beatrice seemed to Marconi to be overly pleased when someone paid a compliment to her beauty. Moreover, though Marconi was fully integrated and familiar with British habits and modes of thought, he still remained a nineteenth-century Italian who could hardly sympathize with Beatrice's typically independent Irish nature, strengthened by Lady Inchiquin's rigorous, yet free and open education.

Marconi skillfully masked his jealousy under the pretext that he was merely worried about his wife, but at times, his true feelings were too powerful to conceal. At one point, he persuaded Beatrice to promise that she would tell him in advance whenever she went out on her own the names of the streets and shops she would visit and the times of her walks—so that he would always be able to trace her immediately in case he returned to the hotel before she did.

Though the period was certainly one of the happiest of his life, according to the available records, Marconi still had more than his share of worries—from the pressures of setting up a family, to the technical challenges involved in his experiments, to the ceaseless demands of establishing a commercially profitable communications company.

In spite of the extraordinary achievements already described, regular transmissions between the two coasts of the Atlantic were still not possible. Even with the most scrupulous and painstaking arrangements, one could count on a guaranteed success only for broadcasts over a distance of two thousand kilometers during the day and three thousand at night. Marconi and his engineers were faced with a dilemma, realizing that they must either abandon the dream of a direct commercial service across the Atlantic and be content to expand the radiotelegraph network on the ships (a business in which they had no serious competition), or create a global system of relay stations whose installation costs were well beyond the means of the Marconi Company alone. For Marconi—who was always so careful to protect his inventions from opportunists—this would mean the sad prospect to share both the credit and the profits for his achievements.

## Dining with Roosevelt

Before making such a momentous decision, Marconi—who still had a profound faith in the possibility of a direct transatlantic connection—decided first to go to Table Head to improve the apparatus and press on with new experiments. Guglielmo and Bea embarked together on the Campania, and during the trip the inventor did not fail to conduct various tests with Poldhu, Table Head, and Cape Cod. It was Beatrice's first Atlantic crossing.

It was on this voyage that Beatrice first discovered her husband's preoccupation with time and time-keeping. Confronted with her astonishment at the sight of a small suitcase filled with a variety of timers, Guglielmo confessed to his young wife his life-long mania for watches. Marconia also explained that, because of his job, he needed to tell time with absolute precision, and that he also needed to be able to establish at any moment the correct time in New York, Rome, London, or Johannesburg.

As Beatrice would discover, time-keeping was not her husband's only peculiar habit. When Beatrice caught Guglielmo throwing his old socks out of a porthole, the inventor explained that he found it more convenient simply to buy new ones than to send them to the laundry and have them returned either unmended or with further holes in them. Before her son's marriage, it had been Annie Marconi Jameson who had taken care of her son's suitcases and personal belongings. Although amused and a bit perplexed by Guglielmo's behavior, Bea quickly assumed this role on behalf of her husband.

As the journey proceeded, Guglielmo became more and more involved with his experiments, leaving Beatrice to enjoy the brilliant social life organized on board. She was courted by everyone for her beauty and outgoing nature, and also because she was the wife of the brilliant inventor. Guglielmo rebuked her more than once for talking to an adoring passenger. He was so annoyed about it, in fact, that he even taught her Morse code to keep her occupied—and away from the admiring eyes of the other passengers. Beatrice was a diligent pupil. In a very short time she was able to understand the messages as they were received.

On their arrival in New York, the Marconis were fêted by the press and the most important celebrities. President Theodore Roosevelt invited them to dinner. They were caught up in a whirl of receptions, dances, dinners and press conferences.

## The Difficulties of Sharing a House

Soon, however, the brilliant soirées gave way to loneliness and silence. At the beginning of May 1905, the inventor decided to start his work at Table Head, where the Marconis shared a tiny house with Richard Vyvyan and his wife, Jane. Living with Jane Vyvyan, whom she initially disliked, along with the long hours waiting for her husband's return, brought Beatrice to the verge of despair.

"Marconi used to work harder than any of his men," Beatrice later recounted. "He used to sleep less than two hours each night. He was always first to get up to wake his collaborators. He was always very determined and precise in whatever he did; from this point of view he was not like an Italian, he was an extremely methodical man."

Marconi's daughter, Degna, later gave her own version of her mother's experience during this period:

To Beatrice's eye, accustomed to Dromoland and London, it looked cramped and indeed, as it had only two bedrooms, a minute bath, living-room, dining-room and kitchen, there was not room for them to keep out of each other's way. Marconi, of course, disappeared immediately into his world of men and machines, easy at the thought that Bea was not alone and that she was chaperoned.

"Beatrice had no idea what was expected of her. Jane rebuffed her fumbling efforts to pitch in and do her share. That she could not cook she well knew—Lilah and she had realized it at a tragic moment—but she adored babies and was as handy with them as any nanny. However, no offer she made of help was accepted by Mrs. Vyvyan and Bea thought she would never succeed in thawing her icy unfriendliness.

For a long time Bea kept her troubles to herself, but at last, in a flood of tears, she told her Marky about them. He was furious and all for having it out with the Vyvyans, which Bea had the wit to prevent, knowing it would be disastrous if anything came between him and his engineer. Instead she nerved herself to ask Mrs. Vyvyan bluntly what was the matter. That lady's reserve broke down and, while both girls wept, Jane admitted that she had been trying to forestall any superiority on Beatrice's part by getting her own in first. After that, they made up and dried their tears.

The two women became close friends after this episode, but life at Glace Bay was still very sad for Beatrice; who had always been so accustomed to and well-suited for an active social life. Glace Bay was not even connected to the rest of the country by a road, only by the railway to Sidney. One day Beatrice, who had taken to long solitary walks along the track, decided to walk to the center of town. Night fell before she could reach her destination, however, and she was forced to walk back in darkness. Understandably worried, Marconi sent the Company's locomotives along the tracks in search of her. Finally, when Bea arrived home well after nine o'clock, it was already pitch dark, and her husband's relief was temporarily overwhelmed by his anger. Years later, Bea remembered the moment as one of the sternest reproaches she ever received from her husband.

The results achieved at Table Head, along with the Company's increasing economic difficulties, persuaded Guglielmo to return to England without delay to reassure his financial supporters, and to find new funds to develop improved instruments. There was so much to do in so little time, in fact, that despite the inevitable objections from his wife, the inventor traveled to Europe alone.

## The Directional Antenna

During the voyage Marconi increased transmission distances but still could not exceed 2,900 kilometers in daytime. The same thing happened during the tests which he carried out immediately upon arrival at Poldhu. In spite of these disappointments, Guglielmo was in the process of making another exceptional discovery. Working at Poldhu, he found that an aerial, made of only one piece of wire lying horizontally on the ground, detected the signals more sharply when the free terminal of the aerial, far away from the receiver, was pointed in the direction of the receiving station.

Marconi finally settled on the idea of an aerial in the shape of an inverted L, with its horizontal arm much longer than the vertical one. Soon Marconi sent telegraph instructions to Glace Bay to build the new directional. As soon as the device was installed, the signals began reaching Poldhu more clearly and continuously than before. Licensed in July 1905, the direcctional antenna would, along with the installment of rotating disc transmission, ensure the ultimate success of worldwide wireless telegraphy

Marconi next decided to interrupt the work in progress at Poldhu and instead build a new station at Clifden, on the west coast of Ireland. Not only was there not enough land at Poldhu to accommodate a large directional antenna, it was also more costly and complicated to buy fields around the old installation than to start anew somewhere else. Marconi would continue working at Poldhu for many years, however, even settling there for a time with his wife.

For poor Bea, the little hotel near the radio station in Cornwall was no more comfortable than the Vyvyans' lodging; moreover, the inventor was desperately overworked from researching and attempting to save the Company from bankruptcy. Having to face the cost of the Clifden apparatus and the construction of new pieces of equipment, the Marconi Company was in dire straits. The Managing Director of the Company wrote the following letter to Marconi at the time:

> I am extremely busy. Half my time is taken up in very unsuccessful attempts to get money, and a great part of what is left in seeing how we can do without it.

When Richard Vyvyan was sent to South Africa with the task of selling and installing new radio stations, he had to leave without receiving a penny in advance for his expenses and with the agreement that he would be reimbursed once he returned—and only in proportion to the volume of deals successfully made. Luckily for both himself and the Company, Vyvyan came back with many orders. During this same period, H. J. Round, one of the other technical directors of the Company, wrote a letter to his parents complaining that he had not received his salary for two months.

This method of compensation could obviously not be applied with staff lower down the scale and Marconi was forced to fire one hundred and fifty workers and to put his own properties at the disposal of the Company.

Though he was under heavy strain, Guglielmo did not mention the situation to his wife. Beatrice was pregnant at the time and he did not want to upset her; he also viewed his home as a place to escape the distressing problems of running the Company. Knowing nothing of all this and tired of the "exile" at Poldhu, Bea decided to move to London where her mother rented a house at 34 Charles Street, right at the center of the City near Berkeley Square. If Beatrice chose to go back to London to be closer to her husband, she made a serious mistake, since the inventor was then engaged in important experiments and spending most of his time in Cornwall. Still, she was near her mother and her beloved sister Lilah. In February 1906, she gave birth to a girl who was named Lucia. Sadly, the infant lived for only three weeks.

Soon afterwards, the inventor finally informed his wife that business was going badly and that they could no longer consider themselves rich. Rather than complain or make a scene; Beatrice took the news calmly and tried to help her husband as much as possible. Unfortunately, Marconi also suffered a recurrence of malaria; for weeks he lay in bed with a violent fever, collapsing completely just when it seemed he had recovered. The long period of stress, the incessant journeys, and the intense activity had all contributed to his illness. He was in bed for a total of three months. When he finally recovered, he left for Nova Scotia along with his wife, her sister Eileen and her brother Barney, who was employed as an engineer in the Company.

### Everything Works Out Fine

In Canada, Vyvyan had settled everything; the station at Table Head was working well. In 1907, the new equipment at Clifden went into service too, with a three-hundred-kilowatt transmitter, unbelievably powerful for those times. Overlooking the station was a building one hundred meters long, in which the Company's scientists had installed the biggest electric condensers ever developed. These huge devices were composed of were metallic plates, measuring six by sixteen meters, which hung from special insulators attached to the roof and were isolated from one another by a suitable air space. These air condensers collected high quantities of electrical energy to be dis-charged through the antennae at the time of the transmission.

The two stations—Clifden and Table Head—secured a direct and constant contact, enabling Marconi to establish, during October 1907, the first authentic transatlantic radiotelegraph service. In that month alone, ten thousand words were broadcast. In February of the following year, official permission was granted for regular public ser-vice. Along with the official recognition by the government came even more violent campaigns from the cable companies. Since it could no longer be claimed that transatlantic transmissions were impossible, Marconi's competitors now complained that his mes-sages were unreliable and late in arriving.

In reponse to this, the Marconi Company promoted their own campaign to demonstrate that delays were due to poor functioning of telegraph lines inside the various countries. The Marconi Company quickly succeeded in overcoming these problems, however, and the worst moments in the controversy finally passed. Meanwhile, both the American Marconi Company and the Marine Company were overwhelmed with work, with requests for new installations arriving more and more frequently.

## The Nobel Prize

Marconi demonstrated his new-found prosperity by changing his residence from Charles Street to a more luxurious rental at the Ritz Hotel in London. On 11 September 1908, he was in America when a marconigram informed him of the birth of a second child, a girl named Degna. The inventor had become fascinated by the name while reading a history of Venice.

MARCONI

The following year marked two important episodes in Marconi's life: the first was the dramatic shipwreck of the liner Republic, rammed by the Italian steamer Florida off the island of Nantucket. The ship's 1,700 passengers were rescued by neighboring vessles who picked up the captain's radiotelegraph appeals for help. The dramatic rescue at sea was a clear example of the practical, and humanitarian, applications of Marconi's invention.

1909 was also the year that Marconi was finally awarded the highly coveted Nobel Prize for Physics. Marconi had to share the prize with Professor Karl Ferdinand Braun, one of the founders of the rival company Telfunken, but the prestigious award from the Swedish Royal Academy permanently silenced those critics who claimed that Marconi was only a businessman, that he had invented nothing but had only used other people's inventions on a commercial and industrial level, and that he had made no personal contribution to science.

Shortly before receiving the award, Marconi had traveled to America. A few days after his departure, Beatrice discovered that she was pregnant again. Overjoyed with the news, she embarked from Cork, Ireland on a steamer that would intercept her husband's ship at sea. On board, Marconi was having the time of his life, along with the famous singer, Caruso, and a group of beautiful actresses. When the inventor saw his wife climbing aboard the ship, he could barely conceal his disappointment. He quickly recovered after he heard her announcement and invited her to join the party. But Beatrice was inconsolable. She locked herself in her cabin for the entire night.

This was the first serious rift in the marriage. Soon enough, however, Marconi was able to persuade his wife to accompany him to Sweden for the Noble Prize ceremonies.

## Back to Villa Griffone

Beatrice was certain that her new child would be a son. Wishing his son to be of Italian nationality, Guglielmo persuaded Beatrice to move to Italy and the Villa Griffone. Together with Lilah and a small army of nannies, servants and cooks, Beatrice quickly reopened the old house. Apparently, none of the Italian members of the household knew how to prepare a cup of tea worth drinking.

Marconi's child was born on 21 May 1910. As everyone had expected, the child was a boy, baptized by a Waldensian minister with the names of Giulio, Giovanni, and Vittorio. Guglielmo was informed while on the way back from North America. The radiotelegraph was addressed simply: "Marconi—Atlantic."

A few days later, Guglielmo was at the Villa Griffone, where he spent the whole summer in a carefree and happy atmosphere—perhaps the most pleasant period of his married life with Beatrice.

In September, Marconi, his wife, and their two children were on their way back to England. The new house was a large and beautiful mansion in Richmond Park; there they were joined by Beatrice's two youngest sisters who had just made their debuts in society. She began to organize dinners and parties, inviting the high-society members of the time. Though eternally busy with his research and financial activities, Marconi did his best to adjust to his wife's lifestyle, but it was too much for him. It is understandable that the constant round of sisters-in-law, friends, and acquaintances annoyed Marconi more than it amused him. But Guglielmo was still very much in love with Beatrice, and still jealous. After several scenes and altercations, Marconi finally solved the intolerable situation by returning home from the stations at Clifden, Poldhu, and Poole as rarely as possible.

Meanwhile, business was running beautifully. Later in the same year, Godfrey Isaacs was named as the Company's Managing Director. Though he had no specific experiences with radiotelegraph problems, he was a financier and business man of the highest order. Even so, it was not smooth sailing, both because of the hard competition from Telefunken and because many others had begun to steal Marconi's ideas and inventions. A typical case involved the British Radio-Telegraph and Telephone Company, which surreptiously adopted the instruments described in patent number 7777 for syntonic transmissions. Isaacs sued the company in court, and obtained a sentence fully in favor of the Marconi Company, including damages and legal costs. Marconi's Company, however, was later forced by the same court to pay Sir Oliver Lodge £18,000 because some of his devices and ideas had been used as basic principles in the construction of some parts of Marconi's own equipment. Lodge would eventually be appointed as scientific adviser to the Company.

Now that Godfrey Isaacs had taken over the administrative responsibilities for the Company, Marconi returned to his position as technical director and resumed work on the many problems created by the many requests for new radiotelegraph networks all over the world. In 1909 a fire burned down the Glace Bay station and another station needed to be built at Cape Breton. On 8 April 1910, a radiotelegraph link between Australia and New Zealand was opened. On the 23rd of the same month, a new apparatus was inaugurated at Cape Breton. In June, new stations were installed at Durban station in South Africa and Coltano, near Pisa. A new Marconi Company was also founded in Spain—the Compañia Nacional de Telegrafia sin Milos.

With the pressures in his professional life now escalating, Marconi's relationship with Beatrice soon reached the breaking point. By 1912, things had gotten so bad between the couple that they planned to separate, but the intervention of some friends and Marconi's mother persuaded them to reconcile. Marconi's close friend, Fillipe Camperio, suggested that the inventor invite his wife to accompany him on a trip to Italy to supervise the work at Coltano station and other projects involving the Italian navy.

# DIFFICULT TIMES

## Business Is Booming

In 1912, the number of multi-national companies in Marconi's worldwide operation had increased to thirteen. Companies in several of the countries—including the United States, Canada, France, Argentina, Russia, Italy and Spain—had all registered significant stocks. The most successful operations were the British Marconi Wireless Telegraph Company, with a capital investment of 1,500,000 pounds, and the American Society, with a registered stock of 10 million dollars. Marconi's companies now had headquarters in London, Bruxelles, Paris, Buenos Aires, Madrid, Montreal, Petrograd, New York and Rome. A communication chart was published every month, providing a daily guide indicating the names and routes of every ship crossing the Atlantic with Marconi instruments on board, in order to facilitate the exchange of everyday communications and more timely responses to requests for help. Using the chart, each ship's captain could immediately determine which other liners were in the same area.

All these companies were run on the same corporate model: the English Marconi Company held most of the shares and appointed the managing and technical directors. Naturally they would all use the patents and apparatus devised by Marconi.

The network of stations around the world included Aden, Algeria, Australia, the Azores, Belgium, Brazil, French Guiana, Burma, China, France, Germany, Holland, India, Japan, Mexico, Morocco, Norway, four islands in the Pacific Ocean, Rumania, Senegal, South Africa, Sweden, Uruguay, the West Indies with Curacao, Jamaica, Trinidad and Tobago, Zanzibar. Stations in Italy included Asinara, Bari, Capo Mele, Capo Sperone, Maddalena, Forte Spurio, Monte Cappuccini, Monte San Giuliano, Ponza, Reggio, Santa Maria di Leuca, Venice, and Viesti.

Considering the fact that only a few months earlier the Marconi Wireless Company was on the brink of disaster, Guglielmo had accomplished a tremendous feat in a remarkably short period of time. Still, he was disappointed that Italian financiers had not been more generous in their support at the time when he most needed it. "If I had been listened to," Marconi later mused, "Italy would have had the chance of becoming the virtual owner of the large organization I had set up, freeing herself from the stranglehold of the foreign Cable Companies." But only the Banco di Roma had confidence in Marconi at the time, giving the inventor 500,000 Lira. Though the money was indispensable at the time, it was only a drop in the ocean.


### The "Marconi Scandal"

Apart from Marconi's ability as a scientist and organizer, the Marconi Company's fortune depended on the business skill of the managing director, Godfrey Isaacs. After increasing the firm's budget and making new and profitable contracts, he had promoted a series of legal actions, both in Europe and on the other side of the Atlantic, against several groups attempting to use Marconi's patents without permission or without paying royalties. Isaacs won each case in turn, obtaining appropriate compensation for damages and at the same time bringing great prestige to Marconi, his inventions and the Company. In the same period, Marconi, who had already maximized on a technological level his spark-transmission system, realized that, in order to go further in the field of radio waves, he needed a tough team of engineers and scientific researchers; he encouraged his colleagues to follow up on all possible innovations, particularly in relation to thermionic valves and their use. After the already mentioned invention of the diode by John Ambrose Fleming, the American Lee de Forest built the first triode. Once again, the first radio transmitting and receiving station would have Marconi's seal. Even when he was not working directly on the equipment, Marconi was and always would be a peerless supporter of every advance in the field of radiotechnology.

In spite of his numerous positive contributions to the Company, it was the so-called "Marconi scandal" which first brought Godfrey Isaac's name before the public. In 1909 the highest British authorities—convinced of the indisputable advantages that radiotelegraph transmission could offer in comparison with cable telegraphy—decided to set up a network of stations connecting England with the entire British commonwealth and worldwide territories. Among other advantages, radiotelegraphy could function under any condition. With the traditional cable telegraph, an individual could single-handedly interrupt communications simply by cutting the cables or pulling down a pylon. With Marconi's system, however, communications would remain secure—as long as the stations remained safe.

The Marconi Company presented to the government a project called "The Imperial Wireless Scheme," based on the creation of eighteen large installations to be built and operated by the inventor's team. This would enable the Royal Navy to set up a communications system for its ships throughout the world. The British Government was reluctant to grant Marconi such a monopoly on a commercial enterprise; but the Imperial Defense Committee exerted considerable pressure, insisting that Marconi's plans were the most economically convenient and the most technically valid in comparison with other offers. A compromise was finally reached: the Marconi Company would build the stations which would then become the property of the State, with Marconi and his shareholders receiving royalties. In 1912, a preliminary contract was negotiated to this end for the first six stations. The contract was never concluded, however. While the House of Commons was in the process of ratifying the agreement, the Marconi scandal brought the inventor's grand plans to a grinding halt.

## A Journalist on the Offensive

The whole story started with an article by an obscure journalist named Wilfred Ramage Lawson, published in the scandal-mongering newspaper *Outlook*, on 20 July 1912. In the article, Lawson stressed the fact that the Company had enjoyed its first real boom shortly after Godfrey Isaacs, a friend of the Marconi family, assumed the reins of the firm's administration. Isaacs, Lawson was quick to add, was none other than the brother of the Attorney General. Since he had taken control of the firm, the society shares, which in 1908 were worth only 6 shillings and three pence each, were now selling at £9 each.

Because of the reputation of *Outlook* and the author's lack of credentials, the article did not have any significant effect. The following month, Lawson renewed his campaign against the company with a series of weekly attacks, but these too attracted little notice. Things changed, however, when Lawson began contributing to the *National Review*, continuing his campaign from that more prestigious platform. The most important papers, from *The Times* to the *Daily Mail*, continued to ignore the story. But Lawson was determined to get his message to the public; he wrote a long open letter to the *Daily Mail*, accusing the Marconi Company of corruption. At this point, the weekly *Eye Witness* and a number of other publications took up the story, and the whole affair blew up. The parliament refused to ratify the contract, serious charges were leveled against members of the government, and an investigating committee was appointed to conduct an inquiry. Called as a witness at the inquiry, Marconi easily proved that none of the shares he owned had been bought or sold. He was fully acquitted and received formal apologies. Soon after—perhaps in compensation for the indignity of the inquiry—he was awarded the Grand Cross of the Victorian Order of Knights, a decoration which was very rarely conferred on a foreigner. From that moment, Marconi's name was accompanied by the title "Sir."

The Marconi scandal faded away. The inquiry also proved that his company's executives had had no part in the speculations on the Stock Exchange, which had created its own run on the Company's stock, but Guglielmo would remain shattered and embittered by the experience for a number of years

## The Sinking of the Titanic

In January 1912, Godfrey Isaacs had obtained permission from the Company's board of directors to realize an ambitious project: building a new and bigger radiotelegraph equipment factory near a smaller one existing at Chelmsford. Work was to proceed as fast as possible, because in June of the same year, a world congress on radiotelegraphy was to take place in London. Isaacs wanted the factory to be ready by that date with the hope that it might attract many of the delegates. It would be an excellent public relations and marketing operation.

But things turned out very differently from the way Isaac had planned. The new factory was ready when the congress started, together with elegant new offices in the city. By this time, however, the attention of everyone at the congress was focused squarely on the sinking of the Titanic and the technological preparations that might prevent such disasters in the future.

Built for the White Star Line, the Titanic was launched as the first "unsinkable ship." The vessel incorporated the most advanced naval engineering and was equipped with watertight compartments. In case of collision and damage to the hull, the ship would reportedly keep afloat by shutting off the damaged areas with water-tight bulkheads.

The maiden voyage began on 10 April 1912, and Marconi and his wife were to be among the passengers. The managers of the White Star Line's, whose ships were equipped with Marconi stations, had invited Guglielmo and many other celebrities to be their guests of honor—an invitation that the inventor fortuitously declined. Before a forthcoming trip to America, Marconi needed first to tend to a pile of unanswered correspondence, tidy up a lot of documents, and work on some technical problems concerning his overseas stations. Marconi's secretary at the time, a man name Magrini, suffered from seasickness, and would have been utterly useless on such a lengthy sea voyage. Consequently, the inventor opted for a speedier transatlantic liner, the Lusitania.

The invitation to sail on the Titanic was accepted by Beatrice, however, who would reach her husband in New York to spend a short holiday with him. In fact, she had already packed, when preparations were interrupted by the sudden illness of young Giulio. Refusing to leave her son to the governess's care, Beatrice gave up the trip across the Atlantic and her holiday with her husband.

Four days after its departure the great ship sank after colliding with an iceberg in the middle of the night: the breach in the hull was so large that the watertight bulkheads were useless. One thousand and five hundred people died; seven hundred were saved thanks to a call for help launched by Marconi's radiotelegraph. Many more people would have escaped death if the California, which was sailing nearby at the time, had been equipped with an additional radiotelegraphist. Exhausted by a sixteen-hour shift, the ship's only operator had turned the device off and gone to rest, and the California never received the Titanic's call for help. After reaching New York, the survivors put on an unprecedented display of gratitude to Marconi, bringing his name and work once more to the attention of the world.

## A Dramatic Car Crash

As soon as Marconi settled his business in New York, he returned to Europe, where even more important deals were awaiting him. Near

Aranjuez, Spain, a powerful radiotelegraph station had recently been built. Marconi had been invited to visit the new fracility and deliver a speech at Madrid University. Following the speech, King Alfonso XIII decorated the inventor with the Grand Cross of the Royal Order.

In May, Marconi traveled to Portugal, returning to England in June for the International Radiotelegraph Congress, where he helped compile the rules for a uniform procedure at sea. Learning from the sad experience of the Titanic, Marconi made the following proposal: each passenger ship should carry an emergency automatic radiotelegraph system. Another decade would pass, however, before such a device could be presented to the public.

At the end of the summer, Marconi had returned to Italy for an on-the-spot inspection of the huge radiotelegraph station at Coltano, which had been installed to link Italy with Italian Eritrea, four thousand miles away. Guglielmo and Beatrice decided to make the trip by automobile.

A motoring enthusiast, Marconi enjoyed driving at high speeds, often taking the wheel from his chauffeur. Everything went smoothly on the trip from England to Italy. Once in Italy, Marconi was received by the King on the royal estate at San Rossore, and Beatrice was appointed lady-in-waiting by Queen Helen. The Coltano station fully met Marconi's expectations, and all the experiments were successful.

With his usual foresight, Guglielmo had ordered his men at Cape Breton in Canada to send a deferential message to the king of Italy as soon as they had received the first signals from Coltano. Everything went according to schedule, and Vctor Emanuel III was quite pleased when he received the message, "The directors of Marconi Company of Canada send by Marconi telegraph humblest homages. Glace Bay." That evening great celebrations were organized at San

Rossore. Along with Guglielmo and Beatrice, many high-ranking navy officers were invited. Among the guests was Luigi Solari, who had become an official agent of the Marconi Company around the world.

After dinner, Marconi, Solari, and Beatrice drove back to Pisa. From Pisa, Solari took a train for Genoa, where a center for communications with passenger and cargo ships had recently been set up. Marconi was scheduled to arrive the following day.

Unfortunately, that plan was thwarted. The inventor, his wife, and their chauffeur left Pisa at about ten. As usual, Marconi took the wheel, with Beatrice beside him in the front seat. Guglielmo drove so fast that Beatrice complained that the wind was ruining her hair style.

Around 12:30 a.m., at a bend in the sharply winding road, their car suddenly crashed into another vehicle speeding from the opposite direction. The collision was so violent that the two vehicles were reduced to a heap of wreckage. At first, Beatrice and the chauffeur seemed more seriously hurt, while Guglielmo had only a trickle of blood running down his cheek from his right eye. The passengers in the other car seemed to be completely uninjured.

When Beatrice recovered from the shock, she asked her husband how he was feeling. Guglielmo answered, "I think I have lost an eye." Someone rang up the military hospital in La Spezia and the Duke of the Abruzzi immediately sent a military ambulance to help the injured.

Here is how a newspaper reported the news sent by its La Spezia correspondent:

Last night at 1:20 Cavalier Antenore Beltrame was brought to this hospital. 54 years old, born at Arzignano, he has been resident in Milan since his return after 30 years in the States. In the crash between the two cars he suffered some contusions, but his condition is relatively good and he will be fully recovered in about twelve days.

His child Arrigo, traveling with him, Mrs. Beltrame and another ten year-old son suffered only light bruises. Further details have now reached us. Marconi's car, with a fifty horse-power engine, number 6-61, was proceeding at moderate speed, near a place called Cavanella; at about two hundred meters beyond the village of Borghetto di Vara, on a sharp bend, it found itself facing Beltrame's car, number 69-320. Both were on the correct side of the road, but it seems that a moment of uncertainty either from Marconi who was driving or from the chauffeur of the other car, brought the two cars head-on making the collision inevitable.

All the passengers were thrown out, while frightened screams for help came from the children, Mrs. Beltrame and the few villagers who had seen the tragic scene from the fields nearby. The two cars were locked together. Cavalier Beltrame who, at first, did not realize he had been hurt, addressed harsh words to Marconi, whom he did not know, accusing him of causing the accident, though unintentionally. Marconi gave him his name and address. Hearing it, the other was dumbfounded. And he said to Marconi: 'I have long tried in vain during my stay in America to meet the famous inventor, whose reputation has crossed the ocean, and only today on the occasion of such a serious accident have I the opportunity to get to know him. Let's not talk of this any longer.' And he warmly shook hands with Marconi.


**One Eye Is Lost**

Reporting Marconi's condition soon after his hospitalization, the same newspaper pointed out that the hospital director, Professor Montano, had issued the following medical report:

Serious contusions to the right eyeball and because of the serious
swelling, examination is difficult and prognosis uncertain. Light
contusions to several parts of the body. Good general condition.
Fully conscious.

The article continued:

No sooner had Guglielmo Marconi reached the hospital, than he
was visited by the acting Commander-in-Chief of the Department,
Vice Admiral Bertolini, Chief of the General Staff naval officer
Mengoni-Ferretti, Subprefect Cavalier Masino and Cavalier Prati, a
member of the town council, representing the mayor of La Spezia.

After mentioning the telegrams and the messages from all over
Italy and the world, and announcing that further visits had been
prohibited by the doctors, the reporter added that:

Mrs. Marconi herself, for whom a special room has been prepared
close to her husband's, only goes to see him at rare intervals, so that
he does not get tired talking or moving. Movements of the head,
even if very slight, could damage the condition of the eyeball which
at present doctors diagnose as serious contusion to the eyeball with
yet to be specified injuries.

In fact, the chief consultant and his assistants indicated that the
optical nerve had been so seriously injured that it was necessary to
remove it in order to save the sight of the other eye. Solari dashed
back from Genoa, immediately contacting the most distinguished
eye specialist in Italy, Professor Baiardi of Turin.
Biardi fully confirmed the diagnosis and the need for an operation, even securing the corrobarating opinion of another famous eye
specialist, Professor Fuchs of Vienna. Marconi took the news calmly

and with relief, perhaps because he assured that, after the surgery, he would no longer experience the agonizing pain which had afflicted him since the accident. He walked to the operating theater unaided, accompanied by his wife and Solari, who were there only because they insisted on being with him.

Ten days later, when the bandages were removed, Guglielmo feared that he had lost his sight completely. The doctors reassured him his sight would return. Expecting the worst, however, he planned to retire to the Villa Griffone and let his work proceed under the direction of his leading assistants.

The accident had been a hard blow for Marconi's health and work, but it certainly helped solidify—at least for a time—his union with Beatrice, who remained at her husband's bedside night and day. Guglielmo had her read as many newspapers and magazines as possible, not only to follow the news but also because he enjoyed the sound of her voice. Little by little, Marconi was able to distinguish dark from light, until the sight of one eye was fully recovered.

### Love and Money

When his health was satisfactory, Guglielmo returned to Eaglehurst with Beatrice. The artificial eye was so realistic that it was impossible to tell it from the real one.

He did not return to a peaceful home life, however. The "Marconi scandal" was not yet over. The inventor was easily irritable, mistrustful of everything and everybody. He often took his frustrations out on his wife, provoking endless quarrels with her. Every time Marconi caught one of his friends—including such previously trusted associates as Filippo Camperio, Prince Gino Potenziani and

Godfrey Isaacs—paying a compliment to his wife, angry disputes ensued.

To complicate things further, one of Beatrice's sisters, Moira Harvey-Bathurst, who worked as a stage designer, offered the Marconis a pied-à-terre in Sloane Square in London. Because of her job, Moira had connections with members of the fashionable theater world of the time, and Guglielmo became very friendly with many beautiful actresses and entertainers. More and more frequently, he stopped in London for the weekend after finishing his work commitments, instead of running back home to Eaglehurst. With her connections to London society, Beatrice was naturally informed of her husband's actions, and now it was she who was jealous of her husband. Because of the two children, however, Lilah was able to persuade her sister to endure her husband's short-lived escapades.

At the beginning of 1913, another tragic event occurred to upset his already shaky family life. Beatrice's mother, Lady Inchiquin, suddenly died. Lady Inchiquin was a woman the inventor highly esteemed and had frequently turned to for advice. Through her work as journalist, Beatrice's mother had managed to support her unmarried daughters in the manner to which they were accustomed. With her death, things became more complicated. To his dismay, Marconi now inherited the responsibility for the financial security of his sisters-in-law. Beatrice's only brother, Lord Inchiquin, refused to share the expenses and Marconi was forced to provide a permanent annuity for the unmarried girls. Marconi hated this type of obligation on principle. Being an industrialist, he was compelled to assume financial responsibility for a rapidly developing industry, and he therefore could not rely on a fixed income. It was one thing to hand over large sums from time to time—as Marconi had previously done on more than one occasion; it was a totally different thing to supply more modest sums on a long-term basis.

The consequences for the Marconi's relationship were so serious that Beatrice decided to leave England for Rome with the children, where she would assume her role as lady-in-waiting in Queen Helen's court. Marconi fully supported his wife's decision; he had his own problems to deal with in Italy at the moment.

## A Volunteer for the War

Beatrice was given a hearty welcome in Rome, where she had taken rooms with her children at the Regina Hotel in via Veneto. She was received with every honor at court and in the most exclusive families of the capital. Lilah had also come to Rome to take painting lessons from Onorato Carlandi. Absorbed as he was in his business affairs, Guglielmo rarely paid visits to his wife and children. Things went on this way until the spring of 1914, when Guglielmo and Bea decided that life in a hotel, for all its attractions, was not the best atmosphere for their children. Returning to England, they reopened the home at Eaglehurst, and, for a time, domestic relations were quite calm. The scandal had passed and business was thriving again.

Events were occurring in other parts of Europe, however, that would soon disrupt the family's peaceful life together. On 28 July, Francis Ferdinand of Austria was assassinated at Sarajevo. The following month, Austria declared war against Serbia. Within weeks, Austria and Germany declared war on Russia, Belgium, and France. On 4 August, Great Britain entered the war against Germany and Austria. A member (with Germany and Austria) of the Triple Alliance, Italy decided to remain neutral, an attitude which aroused suspicion in France and England. Despite their popularity, Marconi and his family were subject to the same treatment as any other foreigner.

In spite of the war, Marconi's work continued to flourish. After completing the first radiotelephony tests on the warship Regina Elena, establishing contact with other ships over a distance of seventy-one kilometers, Marconi was again experimenting with thermionic valves—particularly useful both for safety reasons and for their small size.

Marconi soon found a new reason to return to his native country. On 30 December 1914, Marconi was nominated Senator of the Kingdom of Italy. At only forty, the minimum age for eligibility, the inventor was happy and flattered to be selected. He was also thrilled to spend time in the city where he had acquired so many interesting friends.

Although Italy had at first declared its neutrality in the war, the country soon joined cause with the Allies with the signing of the Treaty of London on 26 April 1915. By signing the treaty, Italy committed itself to declare war by the end of May.

Marconi was in America at the time, following one of the many lawsuits in defense of his patent rights. When he heard that Italy was at war, he immediately announced his intention to volunteer. Back in Italy, he placed himself at the government's disposal, and on 19 June, was appointed reserve lieutenant in the airship engineers with the predictable task of directing telecommunications.

### Short-Wave Experiments

Meanwhile, Beatrice was in England with the children. Guglielmo returned to Eaglehurst to say goodbye and to decide with his wife whether the family should move to Italy together or remain apart. The couple chose the second alternative, and the inventor returned to Italy on his own. Like most fervent interventionists, Guglielmo shared the view that war would last only a few months. On 27 July, he was appointed captain for special merits, charged with inspecting the radiotelegraph apparatus on the Italian front.

Guglielmo devoted himself passionately and conscientiously to the task. He also engineered radiotelegraph mechanisms to meet the new requirements created by the war and built the first apparatus for aviation. Since the radiotelegraph systems for circular transmission of long waves had shown considerable shortcomings, Marconi also resumed his earlier attempt to build the first short-wave instruments.

His daughter Degna notes that these tests were carried out in one of the long corridors of Genoa's half-empty Miramare Hotel, where Marconi was confined to bed with tonsillitis. With him at the time was Luigi Solari, who was in charge of building the reflectors at the Marconi factory and setting up the laboratory in the hotel.

The war lasted more than the expected few months. A year had already passed since Italy had entered it and the conflict was far from reaching a conclusion. It was a long, demoralizing war of attrition. The Germans were preparing for the offensive, resulting in the terrible battle of Verdun on the French front, from February to June 1916, in which more than half a million soldiers died.

Far from his family, Guglielmo was particularly worried about Beatrice, who was expecting the couple's child. Finally, on 10 April he received the news that a baby girl, Gioia, had been born and that everything had gone well. Once again, Marconi was away from home during the birth of one of his children.

Beatrice, who had moved to London to receive since medical assistance, returned to Eaglehurst. But she did not remain there for long. Marconi insisted that his family now join him in Italy. The trip was rushed and poorly planned, causing great hardship for the inventor's family. According to Degna's report, Marconi summed up the difficulties of the makeshift journey with a humorous observation at the Italian border at Domodossola. "All you need is a parrot," he shouted to his wife and children, who were loaded up like pack horses.

## A Fashionable Salon

In Italy, Guglielmo did not simply rent a house for his family, but almost the entire fifth floor of the Hotel Excelsior. The inventor spent many of his days and nights in a special room that had been equipped as a laboratory. In order to proceed with his studies and experiments, he asked to be assigned to the General Staff, and was promptly admitted as reserve naval officer, registering on 31 August at the military department of La Spezia.

This time, however, the separation from Beatrice and the children was neither long nor painful. Despite the wartime situation, Marconi could easily travel the distance between Rome and La Spezia; he was already accustomed to constant travel and enjoyed many of the privileges he was granted, such as special cars and reserved seats on trains.

He often stayed in the capital for several days at a time, spending evenings with friends and important personalities. Marconi had become a particularly close friend of Lilia Patamia, a leading figure in the elite Roman society of the time. Patamia had also become one of Beatrice's closest friends, introducing her to a number of celebrities. In her salon, she entertained leading figures of the government and the arts, such as Gabriele D'Annunzio, Saverio, Nitti, Enrico de Nicola, and Trilussa.

In the summer of the same year, the Marconis spent their holidays at Viareggio for the first time, returning to Rome at the end of the season. Beatrice and her children returned to the Excelsior, while Guglielmo busied himself with numerous jobs for the Army. When the United States entered the war in the spring of 1917, the Italian government sent a "good will" mission across the Atlantic to ask for solid financial help. The Italian delegation was led by the Prince of Udine, nephew of the king, and Marconi was invited to take part. He was very popular in the United States and had many solid personal and professional connections in the country. He was also one of the few Italians on the mission who could speak English. Marconi's success during the trip was so extraordinary that he sometimes overshadowed his colleagues. Whenever the head of the delegation or any other participant rose to speak, the audience would shout, "We want Marconi!"

The American mission lasted until the end of the summer. When Guglielmo returned to Italy at the beginning of autumn, he decided to move the family to the Villa Griffone. The offensive against the Allies was at its peak and Italy had been forced to retreat from Caporetto. Life had become more difficult, particularly in the larger cities. The population was asked to make greater and greater sacrifices, and there was apprehension and fear everywhere. Food was scarce and many lines of communication were interrupted.


## A House on the Janiculum Hill

With the situation deteriorating so rapidly, it was no longer wise to live in the capital, especially in a hotel in the center of town. Life would be easier at the Villa Griffone until the war was over. The move was delayed, however, when the family decided to stay with the Count and Countess Gregorini at the couple's splendid seventeenth-century villa at Casalecchio, near Pontecchio. There they remained until the summer of the following year. Marconi visited his family whenever he could, warmly welcomed by everybody, especially his eldest children. For Degna and Giulio—who were quite grown up by then—the inventor's arrival was always a cause for great excitement, not only due to the presents he brought them but because he took them to visit the places where he had spent most of his childhood.

In the autumn of 1918, Marconi decided to bring his family back to Rome. This time he purchased a house: the Villa Sforza Cesarini on the Janiculum Hill. Marconi had the top floor equipped as a laboratory, while Beatrice took care of furnishing the rest of the house. On 22 September, the inventor's ongoing experiments paid off once again, when he transmitted the first radiotelegraph messages between England and Australia, making use of the "continuous wave system" he had first conceived in 1912.

Following the battle of Vittorio Veneto, which ended on 29 October 1918, the war was over for Italy. In less than a month, the bloody tragedy which had cost more than 10 million lives would officially come to an end. The old Europe had been destroyed by the war, however, and it was now necessary to think about what was to take its place.

Despite euphoria over the victory and the optimistic outlook for his work, Marconi was going through one of the most difficult periods in his life. The anxieties of the war years—along with the family's frequent changes of residence—had prevented him from devoting himself fully to his research. He was increasingly dissatisfied and easily irritable. He wanted to work but felt a need for diversions. He enjoyed himself, especially in the company of beautiful women, but then he felt empty, regretting the time he had wasted. Naturally all this affected relations with his family, particularly the inventor's already-fragile relationship with his wife.

## A Disappointing Experience

After the war, Nitti organized a diplomatic mission to London to secure a loan for the reconstruction of Italy. As a result of Marconi's success on his trip to the United States, Nitti now invited the inventor to join the diplomatic mission. Guglielmo was pleased to accept and took Beatrice with him. Once again, he thought a journey might heal his family crisis. Bea was happy to follow her husband and did everything she could to help him. Things did not go well, however. Using his many friends and acquaintances in the upper reaches of British society and government, Marconi did a great deal to help the mission. Then Nitti suddenly decided to suspend everything and leave for Rome. Guglielmo returned to Italy even more frustrated and embittered than when he had departed—a state of mind that would only worsen during the following year.

Meanwhile, the Peace Conference opened in Paris, with only the representatives of the winning powers in attendance (Wilson for America; Lloyd George for Great Britain; Clemenceau for France; Orlando for Italy). The conference's aim was to lay out a new order for Europe. Orlando felt on an unequal footing with the other statesmen, both because they represented more poweful and important countries and because he did not speak any English and little French.

Once again, Nitti turned to Marconi. Wishing as always to be useful to Italy, the inventor forgot the disappointing experience in London and decided to accept. He put himself under Orlando's orders, had himself received by President Wilson, and tried to convince the Italian representative to adopt a more resolute line in defense of Italian interests. All his efforts were in vain. Orlando doggedly reiterated the Italian nationalists' requests, namely the demand of territories that had been promised to Italy by the Treaty of London—among them Dalmatia. But the Treaty had been signed when it was impossible to foresee both the formation of a Slav Nation and the ninth of Wilson's "fourteen points," specifically addressing the "Rectification of the Italian frontiers according to nationalities." And there was also the principle of self-determination, advocated by the American President himself, as a decisive element in the new European order.

Dalmatia was mostly inhabited by Slavs and it was therefore denied to Italy; which raised the problem of Fiume—a town lying between Istria and Dalmatia, whose inhabitants were largely Italians. If it was right to give Dalmatia to Yugoslavia, Fiume should have been given to Italy. But no agreement could be reached. Orlando was not up to his task; he lost his temper and, with a theatrical gesture, abandoned the Peace Conference just when the Allies were working on the partition of the former German colonies. Not a foot of territory was assigned to Italy. Marconi left Paris nauseated, determined in the future to keep away from politicians, for whom he had lost all respect.

Soon Marconi would get the chance to withdraw into his scientific world. In February 1919 a large yacht which had been built in Scotland for the Archduchess Maria Theresa of Austria had been put up for sale. It was a fine ship, called the Rovenska, seventy-five meters long and weighing seven hundred and thirty tons. During the war it had been requisitioned by the British Admiralty and transformed into a mine-sweeper.

Marconi decided not to let the opportunity pass. The yacht would enable him to fully enjoy his ongoing passion for the sea and provide him with a perfect place to carry on his studies and research in any part of the globe, without depending on anybody's favors. The yacht would become his home, his laboratory, his world.

## Freedom on the "Elettra"

Marconi spent quite some time deciding on a name for his newly-purchased. At first he thought of "Scintilla" (spark); but after much talk and argument with Beatrice, he was convinced that very few Englishmen—no matter how hard they tried—would pronounce the name correctly. H finally decided on "Elettra".

Meanwhile, the new Prime Minister Nitti—succeeding Orlando, who had disappointed everybody with his weak policies—reached the following agreement with the Allies: Dalmatia would become part of Yugoslavia. The Italian troops would move out of Fiume, and an international army would take their place until a diplomatic solution was found. The nationalists and the war veterans—all those who had favored Italy's participation in the war because they saw it as the last of the wars of Independence that had started in the nineteenth century—felt betrayed and rejected the agreement. Among the fiercest supporters of Italy's sovereignty over Fiume was Gabriele D'Annunzio. In a typically defiant act, the famous poet assembled a group of "legionaries." With the tacit support of a small cluster of military leaders—among them the Duke of Aosta—they set sail for Fiume in September 1919 and occupied the town.

Marconi regarded the Fiume adventure sympathetically. Marconi held D'Annunzio in esteem; the two men were friends and the inventor took pleasure in the high-sounding praises with which the poet addressed him. But Marconi did not extend D'Annunzio any public declaration of support. Guglielmo was devoting all his attention to the ship; he looked forward to the moment when it would be ready to sail the globe, far from everybody except some pleasant company of his own choice.

Meanwhile Marconi had also been offered the presidency of the Banca di Sconto. The post was offered to Marconi by Nitti himself; the Italian Prime Minister intended to compensate the inventor for his contribution to the two missions abroad and also to "make amends" for his foreign policy, which Marconi had harshly criticized in the past. To ensure that Marconi would accept the position, Nitti appealed to both his vanity and his patriotism, convincing the inventor that his name would lend prestige to a bank whose activity was fundamental to the reconstruction of the country.

## The Last Defense

His private life too was enjoying a moment of real tranquillity. For the first time in his life, Marconi bought a house—a lovely place in via Pietro Raimondi, near the Villa Borghese—and entrusted Bea with the task of making it a safe and stable shelter for their family. Located in the heart of the Italian capital, the house had a large garden and an English lawn. It represented the realization of all Beatrice's dreams for Guglielmo, the children and herself. She took care of the furnishings with joyful enthusiasm and, in a short time, was able to open her house to their friends and important acquaintances. But as on previous occasions, the peace did not last, as Marconi added yet another beautiful conquest to his growing list of affairs.

When Beatrice sensed that the current affair was more serious than her husband's previous adventures, she refused to keep silent. There were angry scenes. Her strong personality and aristocratic Irish pride found the offense all the more unbearable when she thought of her husband's jealousy in the past.

As time passed and the affair became a matter of public knowledge, her grief over the new adultery became more intolerable. The inventor was widely admired and his life was followed by the press; his movements and his social habits did not pass unnoticed. News of his most recent affair soon made its way out of the Roman salons and onto the front pages.

During these stormy episodes, Beatrice had one refuge: the house and the children. Sooner or later, she reasoned, the new infatuation would pass and Guglielmo would return to her, just as he had done on previous occasions. Things might have taken that very course—if the other woman had not anticipated the same possibility and persuaded Marconi to get rid of the villa in via Raimondi. The inventor needed little convincing. Spending more and more of his time on the Elettra, he had already begun to question the heavy financial burden of his residence in Rome. By selling the house, he could retrieve a handsome sum of money and save the cost of its maintenance.

## The Gravest Loss

Realizing that the last line of defense was slipping from her hands, Beatrice resisted with all her strength. Guglielmo insisted that the family could now live together on the Elettra, where he felt totally at ease and where they would have a home, a laboratory and the joy of the sea.

Seeing that her opposition was useless, Beatrice tried to persuade her husband to delay the sale of the house—suggesting they first try a cruise together. Marconi accepted the idea. The children were left with a governess in a villa they had rented at Posillipo in Naples. The Elettra would dock in Naples and there Beatrice would embark.

But before the voyage began, Marconi suddenly suffered a great and agonizing loss. On 3 June 1920, Annie Jameson Marconi died in London, in the little house where she had withdrawn with her memories. Her first-born, Alfonso, who had settled in Great Britain as an executive of the Marconi Company, was with her. Annie suffered from the same disease that would take the life of her son: angina pectoris.

Marconi was informed of the tragic event by radiotelegram, but he did not leave for London. Urgent business, the preparations for the ship, and the ongoing problems with his marriage—all conspired to keep him from attending his mother's funeral. The inventor's failure to pay his last respects to his mother is disconcerting. Perhaps Marconi simply could not bear the idea of returning to his past and acknowledging his loss under the curious eyes of the British media and public.

Twelve days after Annie's death, on 15 June 1920, Guglielmo succeeded in sending the first radiophonic transmission from his Chelmsford station. This time the "message" was a tribute to his mother—a concert by the famous Australian singer, Dame Nellie Melba. Finally, the bel canto that had so enamored Annie could span space—received and transmitted in every corner of the earth—thanks to her son's work.

Soon the Elettra was fully prepared, and the cruise began. On board the beautiful ship, however, all white and crowded with guests, Beatrice was horrified to discover that her rival was already there among them.

# 11

# A LABYRINTH OF EMOTION

## An Awkward Cruise

It is difficult, if not impossible, to understand why a man like Guglielmo Marconi should decide to have on board both wife and mistress. Perhaps it was an attempt to compare the two women and decide to whom he should devote the rest of his life. Perhaps he wanted to test Beatrice's patience, or was genuinely attempting to see whether the "trio" could live together in the future.

It was to be a very distressing cruise for Beatrice—all the more so because the other woman frequently enjoyed acting the "vamp" and being the center of attention. These, after all, were the occasions where Beatrice had once stood out, thanks to her upbringing, Lady Inchiquin's teachings, and the antiquity of her family. Her only comfort against the series of humiliations during the cruise was Pippù Camperio's friendship.

Every time the situation became particularly unbearable, Marconi sought refuge in his laboratory. While the ship sailed past the Bay of

Biscay, he broadcast records of Portuguese songs to Monsanto. This was a pleasant surprise for Luigi Solari and the other technicians on land who had been asked to record the transmissions from the Elettra and who, wearing their earphones, were expecting the usual Morse code signals.

If Guglielmo Marconi had hoped to solve his emotional and personal problems, he had deluded himself. His only success during the cruise was with the radiotelegraph tests. He had obviously misread his wife's personality and psychology. By the end of the cruise, Beatrice had lost any desire to struggle. She had realized that, as great and generous as he was, the man to whom she had devoted most of her life could no longer be a husband to her, even if he remained the irreplaceable father of her children.

Beatrice no longer recognized in Guglielmo the passionate lover who had sailed over to Brownsea to meet her; nor did she recognize the jealous husband who had extracted from her the exact list of the shops she was planning to visit so that he could find her. She no longer admired the tender affectionate father who, though plagued by countless worries and commitments, would play with the children in the park of their house at Eaglehurst. Beatrice's mind was now filled only with a series of very sad recollections: the loneliness at Glace Bay; her husband's long absences; his more or less unconcealed amours; the affront suffered as she hurried to meet him in mid-ocean with the news that she was expecting a second child.

Weary of Guglielmo's adulteries, Beatrice had perhaps already decided to give a new direction to her life; but she did not rush into anything. When the cruise came to an end, she made no further objection to the sale of the house; perhaps because she saw that it would be useless. It was to be the end of the Marconi household. Guglielmo went to live at the Grand Hotel in Rome; Beatrice and the children moved to the Hotel de Russie.

## The Magic Hero

The inventor immersed himself even more in his work and business. He accepted a pressing invitation from Nitti to go to Fiume with the Elettra to persuade Gabriele D'Annunzio to leave the town in order to avoid further international complications and the possibility of a local civil war. The poet had occupied the hotly contested town with his "legionaries" the year before, creating an unbearable situation for the Italian government. Marconi accepted Nitti's assignment on the condition that he could act "according to his conscience." This argument suited Nitti perfectly, protecting him from the responsibility of failure in case Marconi did not succeed in convincing D'Annunzio to end his campaign.

When Marconi's white ship reached Fiume, Marconi and his collaborators were welcomed with scenes of indescribable enthusiasm. If Nitti had really believed in Guglielmo's desire and ability to get the Italian "poet-soldier" to change his mind, he was to receive a rude awakening. Marconi's visit to Fiume was merely another chance for D'Annunzio to reiterate his determination to resist the policies of the Italian government.

Here are the most important passages of a speech he made during the occasion:

Citizens, Legionaries! Let us greet and honor in Guglielmo Marconi the Italian genius who has flashed across the universe with the speed of star light. I greet him from this platform from which many words of faith and confession have gone out, words which perhaps deserve to be launched into this crazy world from the sensitive top of his serial antennae.

One evening I told you: Since September twelfth there is another tower in Fiume, another lighthouse.

We have suffered, Guglielmo Marconi, magic hero, because we have not had on that tower, on that lighthouse, one of your metallic spires, the vibrating peaks of the propagated spirit.

But today in Fiume, now that he has landed on the last shore of heroic beauty, does he not seem to carry with him all the resonances of the most mysterious message, oh, citizens of the city of life?

He comes to build on our barren stones one of the most powerful of his iron spires.

He comes to lend wings to our defiance, our rejoinders, our protests, the affirmation of our rights, our courage, our pertinacity, all the appeals born of our grief and ardor.

Let us greet in him the genius of Italy, great, free, just, humane. And, as we are doubly Italian, today in honoring him, we feel ourselves Italians three times over."

D'Annunzio then described a visit he and Marconi had earlier made to Centocelle:

The magic hero was there among his iron towers, his gossamer wires, the thin walls throbbing continuously to the electric vibrations, shaken by the shocks of the terrible spark. His attendants in their white coats and naval insignia, pale, trembling, stood spellbound, their deep dark eyes burning with I know not what mysterious fever.

He examined the apparatus, with a familiar glance, touching it with an almost caressing hand as an enchanter might stroke the animals he bewitches. Immense cosmic energy, constrained within those exact instruments, measured and subdued, spoke to that man, so quiet and powerful, a language he understood like the babbling of his own child. Batteries of accumulators, Leyden jars, commutators, condensers, dischargers, switches, detectors, all that concentration of energy, that precision of function, that intensity of movement, that symphony of sounds unknown to Pan's pipes and to Wagner's vast orchestra, seemed to obey the secret will of that man alone, they seemed to beat to the blood in his veins.

We were side by side near the receiver: each of us holding up his saber so that it would not trail the floor.

We listened attentively. Signals were coming through, transmitted by the most remote stations, identifiable by the pitch; a message from France, a message from England, a message from Russia, a message from America.

Suddenly the man in charge whispered, recognizing the tone: 'It is an Austrian marconigram!'

And he took off his earphones to give them to me. I and my great friend gazed at each other sharing the same thought, the same feeling, the same throb in our veins and the very marrow of our bones, our souls leaping away, in a common impetus, towards the frontier, lands where our brothers were fighting, towards lands which had once been bathed in the purest Italian blood, transfigured by the deepest Italian passion. O naked Alps of Trento! O regal sea of martyred Trieste! O our imperial Aquileia, for too long desecrated by the Barbarians! O our Dalmatia, as narrow as the hem of a gown, but that gown a Roman toga! O our Fiume, our Fiume, Fiume desperately ours!

Yes comrades, yes brothers, this is the cry which rings through space.

Do not all the serials in the wide world vibrate to our acclamation?

Listen. Earlier, when the Magician was descending from his now-white ship, you were like those simple soldiers I saw one day crowded round him as he passed, forgetful of the rules, heedless of discipline, anxious to see him face to face, to recognize in his features some sign of his supernatural power, with a superstitious fervor which moved to tears the simplest among them.

Around him, calm and smiling, soldiers were talking of his secrets, they saw in him the miracles of victory, the triumphant messages.

Well, if his magician has his secrets, Fiume too had her own secret.

Listen. Tomorrow from his white ship which truly sails through a miracle and animates the ethereal silences of the world, my voice will go out to reveal that secret to the world. Citizens, legionaries, Italians, three times Italian. For Guglielmo Marconi, Italy's glory in the world, and glory of the world in Italy—eia, eia, eia, alalà.


## Radiotelephony

Marconi left Fiume full of enthusiasm for D'Annunzio's faith and work. As a memento of the visit, the poet had a machine gun fitted on board the Elettra. Away from Fiume, Marconi carried on his experiments and his tours of inspection at the various stations which his company had installed in the meantime. He visited England several times, where his engineers had set up a series of instruments for the transmission of short-wave signals over long distances. The results were encouraging; he succeeded in transmitting at a distance of over one hundred and twenty kilometers. The short (high-frequency) waves were more reliable than the long waves which he had used in the past. The inventor therefore decided to start replacing the old equipment in his stations, beginning in England, with the assistance of a young engineer named Charles Samuel Franklin. Research which had begun for wartime requirements and especially for aviation, was now intensified for commercial purposes.

Guglielmo returned to Italy on the Elettra with Beatrice's youngest sister, Dorrien, as a guest on the ship. The destination was Naples.

Beatrice, Lilah, and the Marconi children—having accepted Guglielmo's invitation to embark on a cruise—were waiting at Posillipo. The ship made a leisurely passage from the Tyrrhenian to the Adriatic Sea. This time the other woman was not on board and the days passed happily; but it was not to last for long.

When the Elettra reached Francavilla, Beatrice, Lilah, and the children decided to disembark and return by train, while Guglielmo, because of his various commitments, would sail on to Venice with the youngest of the O'Brien sisters. Dorrien, however, had an unpleasant surprise in Venice; her sister's husband took his mistress on board, with whom he had obviously arranged the rendezvous. Dorrien O'Brien shed no tears, but she was highly indignant. She left the yacht without so much as a goodbye, and rushed back to Naples. Dorrien was determined to tell her sister about what she had seen and to help her to find a way out of an unbearable situation. Beatrice told her that the only thing she could do was to pretend to know nothing, so that she could keep up at least the appearance of a link with her children's father. Dorrien did not understand this attitude; for days she argued with Beatrice and Lilah, protesting violently against these "continental habits" and finally left for England in a rage.

Dorrien's uninvited intervention did nothing to reconcile husband and wife. More serious efforts were made by one of Beatrice's friends, Princess Elsie Torlonia.


## Eagerness to Live

Elsie Torlonia spent the holidays with her family in a beautiful villa near Deauville in Normandy, and she graciously invited Beatrice and the children to join her at the villa. Guglielmo was in England at the time, and it was easy for him, with the Elettra, to visit his family whenever he wished. Marconi went to see them from time to time, but his visits were always short. At the end of the summer, he took the whole party on board, and they all sailed for Naples.

Beatrice, who was not yet forty, was still a beautiful woman, full of life and charm. Now that her husband was openly having an affair, even in front of her own sister, she began to see herself with new eyes. She no longer felt the slightest bit of sympathy or understanding for Guglielmo. Instead, she discovered an overriding need to assert herself, along with an understandable desire for revenge.

Years later, she recalled that her last violent argument with Guglielmo took place in a hotel in Naples. In her sharp Irish accent, Beatrice had shouted at Marconi: "I have put up with everything, but now my patience is over. You can go your way and I shall go mine, even if it's into the arms of the first man I meet." The inventor did not raise any objection; at the time he probably felt that Beatrice was making a decision he was too weak to make himself.

But Beatrice did not fall into the arms of the first-comer. Sometime before, the marchese Liborio Marignoli, a charming Italian who also lived in Posillipo and had associated with the Marconi's circle of friends, had been struck by Beatrice's beauty and vivacity. At first he only expressed a deep admiration for her. When Guglielmo's affair became common knowledge, however, he felt himself—in keeping with Italian customs—entitled to make his feelings known. At first Beatrice rejected him—just as she had done with Marconi. Like Marconi, Liborio persevered, even after Beatrice turned him down again.

December 1921 brought the scandal over the bankruptcy of the Banca di Sconto. Since he was president of the bank, Marconi found himself at the center of the controversy, even though he had no real responsibility in the running of the institution. These new anxieties came at a time when post-war Italy was going through its own troubling years of uncertainty and insecurity. The old ruling class was unable to control the deep social and political upheavals generated by the war.

A serious economic crisis brought the country to its knees, while bloody strife among opposing factions threw the nation into confusion. Uncertainty and ineptitude seemed the only constant features of the various factions competing for leadership in the political parties and in Parliament. Fascism started to spread rapidly, feeding on the disillusion of ex-servicemen. Fascist action squads in black shirts, weak on ideas but not short of brute strength, roamed the streets and the authorities had no power to stop them.

The social and political situation in Italy was tragic. Marconi, disappointed by politics on several occasions and disheartened by the people around him, did not take sides with any of the political groups. He found his only satisfaction and happiness on board the Elettra, where he could carry on with his research and experiments on Hertzian waves and at the same time enjoy the company of the people he liked.


## Separate Journeys

After observing the effects of deflection and reflection caused by metal obstacles on electromagnetic waves, Marconi decided to investigate the phenomena thoroughly and to examine their possible applications. The experiments proved to be both interesting and encouraging. He carefully gathered his most important experimental data in a report, which he decided to present at the important meeting of the American Institute for Electrical Engineers in May 1922.

The Atlantic crossing lasted longer than Guglielmo had anticipated, but when he finally arrived, he was welcomed with such enthusiasm that he felt compensated for the hardships of the journey.

Encouraged by the reception, Marconi gave a lecture in New York
on 20 June, that in many ways anticipated the invention of radar. He
told the audience:

> It seems to me that it should be possible to design apparatus by
> means of which a ship could radiate or project a divergent beam of
> these rays in any desired direction, which rays, in coming across a
> metallic object such as another steamer or ship, would be reflected
> back to a receiver screened from the local transmitter on the send-
> ing ship, and thereby reveal the presence and bearing of ships, even
> though these ships be unprovided with any kind of radio.

Beatrice was also in the United States at the time, visiting friends.
For a few days she joined her husband in New York to share his triumph, but the two were not formally reconciled. The two separated
again after the return trip to Italy, with Beatrice and the children
moving back and forth between Baveno, Viareggio and Florence, and
finally settling at the Pensione Gonnelli. Liborio Marignoli, who was
also in Florence at the time, stepped up his courtship of Marconi's
wife. Although Beatrice was flattered by his attention, she was also
concerned about what she should do, and decided to inform her
husband of her fears and misgivings. Here is a letter from Guglielmo
to Beatrice, dated 6 June 1923:

> I do not understand what is the serious trouble and danger you
> write me about so persistently, unless it is caused by the abnormal
> thoughts of someone under whose influence you are at the
> moment. [...]

Please remember that whatever is troubling you, I am always ready to support and help you in any way and to do whatever is best for us and the children.

It seems obvious from this that Marconi was still fond of his wife. In addition to his response to her concerns, he gave her a detailed account of his recent experiments on board the Elettra. The letter ended with these words: "If it were not for your troubles, I would have gone to Brazil."

Perhaps at that moment it might still have been possible to start again. Marconi had just ended his relationship with his current lover, with accounts differing about who left whom. But Beatrice no longer had faith in her husband. She decided to sue Guglielmo for divorce and live with Liborio Marignoli, .

Though the news came to Marconi like a bolt from the blue, he did nothing to make her change her mind. He was well aware that it was he who had destroyed both his marriage and his wife's love for him, and he did whatever he could to organize the divorce as quickly and discreetly as possible.

## Divorce in Fiume

Separately, both Guglielmo and Beatrice traveled to Fiume and established citizenship. According to the Treaty of Rapallo signed by Giolitti with Yugoslavia, Fiume had become a "free territory." D'Annunzio had been forced to surrender, but the town had preserved the more liberal constitution that the poet and his "legionari" had promulgated. Since Fiume admitted divorce, many Italians crossed the Adriatic to settle their marital problems. This activity had, in fact, become so intense that it formed a noticeable source of income for the town. It was Mussolini himself who first suggested the solution to Marconi.

By this time, Mussolini was confident that he could obtain from Yugoslavia a recognition of Italian sovereignty over Fiume, and he reassured Marconi that he would not risk his citizenship by changing his nationality.

The divorce proceedings were quickly completed, with Beatrice becoming the "marchesa" Marignoli and moving to Spoleto with her children. Degna Marconi was now sixteen years old, Giulio fourteen and Gioia eight. The new family arrangement was far from easy for the children. Their parents had agreed they would live with their mother, since Marconi was constantly sailing around the world and education on board a ship could not be the best for the children. But they would spend their summer holidays with their father. Marconi also took care to send regular monthly allowances and continued to correspond with both Beatrice and the children. Here are some passages from letters written during the period:

> I have also been thinking a lot about Degna, and cannot help thinking that a year or so in a good school in England, where she could get plenty of out-of-door exercise would do her worlds of good in every way and greatly improve her chances in Life. . . .
> Degna still suffers occasionally from seasickness, but is on the whole I think getting better. . . .
> I shall write you more, especially about Degna in a few days. I think she studies too much, and does not get quite enough of fun for a girl of her age. She so often looks sad, poor darling, and is so awfully shy of people. . . .
> In regard to the plate, I've got to find the receipt given to me for it by the Banca di Sconto, but I wish and hope you will be able to do without it, as I really would like to have it for the children. . . .

I would very much like to have the children in Rome, as soon as possible, as I may have to return here in two or three days. In regard to my plans Giulio and Degna might come to me in England after their exams, and as I expect to come to Italy later with the yacht, Gioia might come to stay on board for a week or two later. If absolutely necessary on account of Giulio and Degna's examinations, I might remain in Rome over Saturday and perhaps Sunday, but please write or telegraph me to the Hotel Eden on my arrival in regard to what you think is possible.

## The Human Voice

The couple had parted on friendly terms and for a time, their relationship remained cordial. Work and business were going well for the inventor. The English government had granted him permission to build several short-wave radio stations in various parts of the Empire. It was a triumph for Marconi's work on the short-wave beam system. On 30 May 1924, he achieved the first regular transmission of the human voice between Poldhu and Sydney, Australia. Technical advancements now allowed Guglielmo and his staff to broadcast over 4,130 kilometers from stations with only twelve kilowatts of power. The result was so important that the British government asked the Marconi Company to set up the Imperial radiotelegraph network as soon as possible.

Marconi achieved still more success in 1924. While on board the Elettra in the port of Beirut, he noticed that, contrary to his expectations, the radio signals transmitted from his Poldhu station covered a distance of 2,400 kilometers, both at night and in the daytime. At the time there was no explanation for the phenomenon. Realizing that the explanation involved some natural, but still-unexplained occurences, the inventor carried out several tests on varying wave lengths, each time changing the position of the Elettra. Experiments were made with the collaboration of the stations he had set up in Argentina, Australia, Brazil, Canada and the United States. Each time and from each new position, he achieved the same results, as long as he operated on a wavelength of thirty-two meters. At that time Marconi could not possibly explain—nor was he interested in explaining—the cause which science would eventually discover: the impact of the F2 layer of the ionosphere. As they had always been in the past, Marconi's intentions were strictly practical. Once he discovered that a particular type of wave behaved in a paticular way, he immediately drew practical conclusions from it. He would leave it to future scientists to understand why.

On 5 October of the same year, the Italian Minister of Communications authorized the Italian Radiophonic Union Company (S.U.R.I.) to start a regular service of circular radiotransmissions in Italy.

Despite all these activities, Marconi did not neglect his duties as father, and the children were often guests on the yacht during the summer. There they were able to join his spectacular cruises—meeting interesting celebrities, going to parties and generally living a life which was strikingly different from provincial Spoleto.

Some further extracts from Guglielmo's letters to Beatrice at the time show that the correspondence between the two continued to be constant and affectionate:

Degna arrived from Paris this evening looking very well and happy. I have taken her to Clare who is putting her up for a few days, as it was impossible for me to have Degna here, because I've got to go away for experiments in a day or two, and of course I would not leave her in a hotel alone. . . .

I arrived here yesterday evening after a very good journey. I left Degna at the Ozanne's in Paris: we had such as nice time together in the train as far as Paris, and in the evening she dined with me, Myriam Potenziani, and her nanny at the Ritz. Degna was so sweet and looking quite lovely. In the morning before starting for London I bought her a little leather hand bag which she loved. . . .

I'm sure, however, that Degna and Giulio have already written giving you all our news. I was fortunately able to just manage two and a half days at Cowes with the yacht. I attended the King's dinner at the R.Y.S. and was able to take Degna and Myriam to two dances, one, a small but very nice private dance at Lady Baring's, and the other, a very large one in Cowes. Lady Baring was most kind, and Degna got lots of partners and I feel sure enjoyed herself hugely! The party on the Elettra consisted of myself, Myriam, Degna, Giulio, Gino, and Noel Corry (who asked himself!). I could not fix up with anybody else as I was, up to the last minute, so uncertain as to whether I could go to Cowes at all. We had luncheons and dinners on board and heaps of people came including Brenda Dufferin, Lucia Monckton-Arundell, Nada Milford Haven, Edwina Mountbatten and her husband, the Birkenheads, the Duke of Sutherland, Lady Eva Baring and Poppy, Imogen Grenfell, besides lots of men of many of which I can't remember the names. I'm sure Degna and Myriam enjoyed it all very much. Degna wants to come on to Italy in the yacht with the Potenziani. I do so hope the sea won't make her too ill, but I must say that she seems to stand it very much better this year. What do you think of her doing this?"

## Another Love

These letters reveal how much Marconi wanted to keep Beatrice informed of how he spent the time with the children and of the interest he took in their lives. As usual there were several women around him, but these were superficial episodes, often caused by the ambitious women who, as Beatrice later said in an interview for BBC, "were ready to crawl at his feet in order to be close to Marconi."

In the summer of 1925, Marconi finally fell in love and decided to marry again.

Betty Paynter was only seventeen years old. Guglielmo probably saw in the younger English woman a kind of sincere admiration and submission that gratified him. He soon wrote to Beatrice about his decision to marry again:

> Don't be surprised or upset if you hear I have become engaged to Betty Paynter. I care for the girl an awful lot, more than I ever thought I could. I have been fighting against myself over this for a long time but I am afraid it's of no use. After all even you know how lonely I am.

Beatrice's response was so disapproving that it deeply distressed Marconi, and he sent her a telegram asking to meet him in Florence to discuss the subject at greater length. During the meeting Beatrice reaffirmed her point of view. How was it possible, she asked, that he decided to set up a new family when the destruction of the first had resulted from his great need for freedom and independence? Didn't he remember his constant complaints about family responsibilities that prevented him from devoting himself fully to his work? Did he seriously think that a new marriage would escape the problems that had made him so unhappy and intolerant? And why, she concluded, had he found it necessary to consult with her about the decision?

"Because you are the only person in the world who will tell me the truth," he answered simply.

Marconi followed Beatrice's advice and ended the relationship.

## Love at First Sight on the Elettra

Marconi was soon attracted to another woman. This time she was Italian, very pretty and clearly a product of Roman nobility. Her name was Maria Cristina Bezzi-Scali.

Daughter of Count Franceso Bezzi-Scali, a high-ranking dignitary in the Vatican, and of the Marchesa Annetta Sacchetti, Maria Cristina was no longer a young girl when she met Marconi, though she was still half his age.

The two met at a party given on the Elettra off the town of Viareggio during the summer of 1925. Whenever he reached that port in Tuscany, Marconi was in the habit of organizing splendid receptions and elegant dances for the society people who spent their holidays at the famous resort. After a number of years, a kind of ceremonial had gradually evolved. The military and civil authorities of the town would go to meet and pay homage to Marconi, after which invitation cards would be distributed to the leading people of the town and to the most prominent guests at the resort. Invitations to Marconi's parties were enviable possessions—not only for the dances, which were the main topic of conversation under the umbrellas on the beach, but also because they provided the opportunity to see and meet the inventor himself.

Maria Cristina was on vacation with her aunt, who—according to the recollection of one of Marconi's engineers, Giovanni Gallarati—did her best to obtain an invitation for herself and her niece. The young woman boarded the Elettra in the afternoon. For both Guglielmo and Cristina, it was a case of love at first sight. The reception was a great success; champagne flowed abundantly. But even in the midst of the celebration, no one could miss Marconi's attentions toward the lively and attractive young woman from Rome. Sensing this, he soon took her to visit his radio cabin and the rest of the ship, away from prying eyes.

By the time that the evening was over and the guests returned to town, something more than a simple friendship had already developed between Guglielmo and Cristina. From that moment on, she was always the first to be invited on board the yacht. Soon afterwards, Marconi organized a round-trip cruise from Civitavecchia to Montecarlo; once again, Cristina was on board, chaperoned by the Prince and Princess Del Drago.

Meanwhile, the inventor was still on friendly terms with his former wife. In February 1926, Marconi sent Beatrice his affectionate congratulations when she gave birth to a girl named Flaminia.

In June 1926 in Bologna, the thirtieth anniversary of wireless telegraphy was marked by great public celebrations. Marconi was awarded a gold medal. He made an unusually brilliant and inspired speech, summarizing all his past work and dividing his life into three long periods. The first (from 1896 to 1906) was characterized by ups and downs, successes and failures, but had finally been crowned by the victory of the Marconi radiotelegraph system. The second (from 1906 to 1910) was characterized by further developments made possible by Fleming's thermionic valve; during this time, particularly after the sinking of the Titanic, radiotelegraphy had become tremendously important because, as he reminded his listeners, "everybody had realized the great value of the radio in saving human lives at sea." The third period marked yet another turn, in which the long-wave system was replaced by short-wave transmission.

"It took us a lot of courage to do this," Marconi explained to his fellow citizens, "considering that we had previously invested a lot of money in long-wave stations. But the Bolognese will not find this strange, because they too, after building one of the highest towers in

Italy [the Asinelli] did not hesitate to build right next to it a lower tower. I had to do the same."

The following summer—though he was very busy preparing for the October opening of the first link of the Imperial British radiotelegraph network—Marconi arranged to meet Beatrice and Degna in London for his daughter's coming out. He also followed all the proceedings necessary for Giulio's admission into the Naval Academy, and even sent a pony to Gioia, a gift which cost him considerable time and expense. We find references to these events in his letters to Beatrice:

Forgive me not answering your long letter of the 16th before now, but I have always been awfully busy travelling all over the country to look after the tests which are being carried out with my new system. In regard to money, I am now glad to tell you that I hope to pay over to you, within December or January at latest, the third million Lire which you are to receive in accordance with what was stipulated when certain proceedings were decided upon.

This payment will therefore be made a full year, or more, before the expiration of the time within which I promised to make it, giving you thereby the benefit of the interest of one million for one extra year amounting to 40 or 50 thousand Lire.

I have received a letter from Giulio in which he tells me that he has passed all his exams, which I'm delighted to know, but at the same time he tells me he would prefer not to go to the Accademia Navale as he says, 'non mi sento affatto attratto dalla vita di mare.' This is quite a surprise, and a great disappointment to me, as I had always thought he loved the sea.

He also says that the pay he could get in the Navy would be insufficient, and less than what he would get if he obtained the laurea d'ingegnere. I agree with this, but you perhaps know too, that if he passes the Accademia examinations, he gets the rank and position of Officer, which brings with it the certainty of employment by the Government, whilst if he becomes an ingegnere he may fail to get a satisfactory position for years. I think you will agree with me that the general education is much better at the Accademia than at the universities, where many of the graduates they turn out are very poor specimens indeed. In any case I should like to have your views on the matter."

## An Ugly Episode

Marconi decided to marry Maria Cristina. She was happy and untroubled by the difference in age, and her family would have been open to the marriage—except for one, nearly insurmountable difficulty. Guglielmo was divorced, the father of three children, and for Count Francesco Bezzi-Scali and his wife—both of whom were members of the conservative Roman nobility, with strong links to the Vatican—a civil marriage was unthinkable.

There was another obstacle, perhaps not so insurmountable but even more delicate: though he had been baptized in a Catholic Church, Guglielmo had been brought up by Annie Jameson according to the Waldensian faith and, when he was twenty years old (in Leghorn in 1894), had been "confirmed" by a Protestant clergyman. This last hindrance was easily overcome; thanks both to his work and to the many acquaintances he had made in the upper levels of Roman society, Marconi could count on the friendship of many influential representatives of the Vatican hierarchy—from Cardinal Gasparri (who in 1929 signed the Lateran pacts between the Vatican and the Italian State) and Cardinal Pacelli (later Pope Pius XII) to the Pope himself. And besides, Marconi was ready to convert to the

Catholic faith. The more serious problem was the issue of his first marriage and the divorce obtained in Fiume.

The only solution was to obtain an annulment of the marriage by the Sacred Rota. The most eminent experts on the subject were consulted, a distinguished team of lawyers was set in motion, and bishops, archbishops, and Vatican dignitaries were approached in the search of a solution. The task was to undo (as if it had never existed) a bond which had lasted for twenty years and been cemented by the birth of four children. The best solution was to demonstrate that, while they were engaged, Beatrice and Guglielmo had considered the possibility of an eventual divorce. According to the Catholic Church, any marriage celebrated with this mental reservation is not valid. If this could be proven, Guglielmo and Beatrice's union could be declared null; the inventor would then be a bachelor and could therefore marry Signorina Bezzi-Scali in a religious ceremony.

Marconi was obviously ready to sign any declaration on the subject; but his declarations were not legally valid without a similar statement from Bea and her relatives. Guglielmo tried every possible means to convince his wife to support his efforts; he talked to her at length. He wrote her a long series of letters urging her to cooperate. He even asked for Liborio Marignoli's help. Acting on the suggestions of his ecclesiastical advisers, he even provided Beatrice with word-by-word responses for her interrogators. He searched for witnesses who might help him, writing down conversations and episodes from the time of his engagement which might favor his case.

Beatrice was distressed and disconcerted by her ex-husband's request. On the one hand, her inborn honesty led her always to tell the truth. On the other, she felt obligated to help her former husband. After all, she now had a new family of her own and could not prevent Guglielmo from marrying whomever he chose. The inventor also reminded her that it was he who continued to support the family; the children's present and future financial stability depended on the declarations she made to the Sacred Rota.

Money had become a sore spot in the relations between Beatrice and her first husband after the divorce. The following letters sent by Guglielmo to his wife in the period between June 1924 and August 1926 illustrate the problem:

14 June 1926

Am much perturbed over what you say in regard to money matters. You certainly read and understood the agreement which was entered into between us.

As I told you in a previous letter, I had to make a very big sacrifice to pay you the two million lire as agreed, and to do this I was compelled to sell shares at a very unfavorable time and price. Things are so bad at present that the Company is not doing as well as was expected, and if I paid the further million at once I would be left without a penny and no prospect of leaving anything to the children, even if I had to sell the yacht!

You know that you absolutely declined to guarantee anything for the children out of the moneys I was to pay, and that the real responsibility for what they may have in the future rests entirely with me. Of course, I will pay you when I get to Rome the 10,000 Lire which you say I owe you for the rent of furniture.

Don't forget you got this furniture too, and that it represents quite a substantial amount.

6 December 1926

In regard to presents for the children, I think it's better, as you suggest, that you should get them, and of course I'll join you, but I must just now limit my contribution to two thousand lire. I can't afford more, after the pony and other things. Someone gave Degna a fur fox for her neck, which I brought over with me to Rome last time, but in the rush of things, forgot to give her. I however sent it on to her at Spoleto before I left and hope she's got it all right."

According to a document Liborio Marignoli left at his death, Marconi eventually progressed from blandishments to actual threats, perhaps under strong pressure for a quick solution from Bezzi-Scali, who certainly did not like the idea of being the object of Roman society gossip.

Finally the annulment was declared and Marconi led Cristina to the altar in her white dress on 15 June 1927, at a ceremony attended by the most important people at the time. A few days before, on 12 June, a civil ceremony had taken place in the Campidoglio.

"It was the wedding of the century," Marconi's second wife boasted more than half a century later.

# 12

# AN IDOL OF THE REGIME

## Political naiveté

In the years before the rise of Fascism, Marconi was one of the many Italians who had grown disillusioned by the country's political and economic situation. A friend and admirer of D'Annunzio, he was a true patriot and ardent nationalist. Accustomed to life in Victorian England, he also found himself uneasy with the social upheaval that marked Italy in the years immediately following the war. Marconi had never belonged to any political party; after his experience as a member of the plenipotentiary commission for the peace treaty of Versailles, Marconi harbored an extremely low opinion of politicians, viewing them as little more than corrupt manipulators who were incapable of subordinating party interests to the good of the country as a whole. He certainly saw Mussolini—a man quite unlike himself in both character and temperament— in the same light.

Nevertheless, the two men would soon develop a cordial relationship. The truth was that Marconi was useful to Mussolini, just as the Duce, in his turn, often served as a powerful ally for Marconi.

Along with many of his fellow countrymen during the years between 1918 and 1921, the inventor was honestly afraid of the so-called "red peril," and when Mussolini introduced himself as the restorer of law and order and the defender of the "strong state," Guglielmo enthusiastically embraced the fascist movement.

The psychological motives behind Marconi's commitment to Fascism can be seen less in his declaration of faithfulness to the regime—required of him by his position—than in the following words from before 1922:

> I don't understand how one can fail to see that the people are much happier in America than in Russia. Why prefer ruin to prosperity? Why apply the principle of equality in the sense of leveling down rather than leveling up? As long as there exists in the world one man more intelligent than another, or one woman more beautiful than another, absolute equality will never be possible. So it's a question of where to draw the line, and given the choice between a party which tends to raise the standard of living and one which tends to lower it, I think an intelligent people must prefer the first, and it is for this reason that the Italian people, who are intelligent, will always be more faithful to the party of order and work than to that of destruction and disorder which degrades the human race.

At the time, Marconi's political ideas were vague and simplistic, corresponding neither to the real intentions of Fascism (as he would later discover) or to the "ideals" of communism. Marconi almost certainly had never read or understood Marx for himself—just as he had never studied nor analyzed what was presented as "fascist philosophy". He was far more preoccupied with the technical problems in his own work, and his criticism of Marxism, like his adherence to Fascism, was extremely superficial.

At the time he also wrote:

Fascism is a strong regime, necessary and salutary for Italy. I, therefore, am a fascist by conviction and not simply out of convenience. Though as for convenience, I can say that the interests for which I have some responsibility in Italy have never been so much sacrificed as at the moment when Fascism assumed the government of our country. But I am not here concerned with the measures taken by the fascist government, measures which I have accepted as a discipline. I bring them up to show that my commitment to Fascism was sincere, since I believe above all in the good which its leader will bring to Italy.

## Sincere Commitment

Marconi was never involved in any of the violent enterprises in which the fascists specialized, and he often went out of his way to avoid Mussolini's requests for assistance. On more than one occasion, he made sure he was far at sea on the Elettra in order to avoid an invitation he did not wish to honor, rather than give the Duce a direct refusal. At such times, Marconi's actions were not the result of an aversion to Mussolini and Fascism, but because there was something else about the proposed event which did not appeal to him.

Marconi originally joined the cause in 1923—for which the Duce remained grateful to him—but it was only in 1928 that he received his first official appointment from Mussolini's government: president of the National Council for Research. Two years later he was chosen as the president of the Royal Academy of Italy. Neither of these nominations was awarded to Marconi, "for services to Fascism." The inventor was being honored at the time stricly for his extraordinary achievements. It took years for Marconi to begin making public speeches and private statements in which, quite sincerely, he went out of his way to praise Fascism and its leader.

The period between the end of the First World War and 1931 saw a great number of developments in the field of radiotelegraphy and radiotelephony in which Marconi was again prominent. From 1922 to 1923, he established the possibility of short-wave communication at a distance of four thousand kilometers in a series of experiments carried out between the Cape Verde islands and the Elettra—brilliantly overcoming what had seemed the insuperable limitation of solar interference during daylight hours. A year later he constructed a network of short-wave stations for the English government, presiding over the first transmission of human voice between England and Australia. Radio links between London and Buenos Aires would soon follow, and many countries, including Italy, set up circular radio transmission systems, making use of Marconi's innovations. In a spectacular display from aboard the Elettra, which was harbored at Genoa, Guglielmo switched on the lights of the Sydney town hall in Australia with a radiotelegraphic impulse. During this period, Marconi also installed a high-powered radio station at the Vatican, from which Pius XI could share the first pontifical radio message with the world.

On 17 June 1929, the king of Italy invested Marconi with the hereditary title of Marquis. Guglielmo was flattered, but his happiness was clouded by the discovery that his friend Gabriele D'Annunzio had been made Prince of Montenevoso, an even higher rank of nobility.

In spite of his resentment, Marconi asked D'Annunzio to compose a motto for his new coat of arms. The fiery poet, however, was either too busy or too uninspired to meet the inventor's request at the time, and the father of radio remained temporarily without a motto. After Marconi's death, D'Annunzio finally provided the words that Marconi had requested during his lifetime: "Audere silenter" (to dare in silence).

## A Changed Man

Mussolini had the highest regard for Marconi, appointing the inventor as the first president of the Academia d'Italia (replacing the Accademia dei Lincei) on 19 September 1930. The inventor had been a senator since 1914, however, and existing law barred members of the senate from serving in the academy. Mussolini ignored the law and upheld his appointment, with Marconi automatically becoming a member of the Fascist Grand Council by virtue of his new position.

For a time, Marconi's attitudes and behavior were dramatically changed by his new position in the government. In the archives of the Royal Academy of Italy, there are countless letters and memoranda which demonstrate that Marconi was preoccupied with trivial matters such as dress and protocol—things that had nothing to do with his intellectual gifts and scientific achievement. For example, the inventor was extremely concerned that his rank always be recognized at official ceremonies and in correspondence. He often spent whole days at the tailor's so that uniforms appropriate to different occasions might fit him to perfection, and he was routinely tormented by the problem of choosing the correct dress and decoration for different public appearances.

In a memorandum which the chancellor of the Royal Academy, Arturo Marpicati, circulated to the various organs of the regime, one reads: "In letters directed to His Excellency Marconi the following mode of address should be adopted: 'To his Excellency the Senator

Marchese Guglielmo Marconi, president of the Royal Academy of Italy, Member of the Fascist Grand Council.'"

In another note to General Mario Zucchi, Commander of the Military Division of Rome, dated November 12th, 1932, Marpicati wrote:

> In a friendly and confidential spirit I am passing on some observations made by His Excellency Marconi on the review which took place yesterday in Via dell'Impero on the anniversary of the birthday of H.M. the King. His Excellency had the pleasure of being present on the platform designated for the authorities, but found it awkward and displeasing that the Marchesa his wife was excluded and that her ticket allowed access only to platform D, while it was noticeable that similar rigid exclusion was not applied impartially to all wives. Guglielmo Marconi is a person who has the right to be placed together with his lady, above protocol; if the officials of the Divisional Command have not made an exception on this occasion, presumably it will be possible to do so in the future without anyone finding such deference to Marconi inappropriate.

To a lesser degree, Guglielmo had always attached great importance to matters of form. One humorous anecdote involves an encounter between Marconi and Queen Victoria, while he was installing a link between Buckingham Palace and the yacht Osborne. While the young inventor was hard at work connecting the aerials in the garden, the Queen passed by. The inventor bowed deferentially but received no response. Taking offense, he immediately abandoned his work. When the Queen learned of his actions, she simply shrugged and snapped, "Get another electrician." It was then explained to her that the impressionable and easily offended young man was not just any wire-puller; in fact, his efforts were quite irreplaceable. Victoria diplomatically invited Marconi to dine with her, and peace was restored.

## His Wife's Influence

Some have linked Marconi's second marriage with the change in the inventor's character and the slowing down, not to say the abandonment, of his technical work. Certainly Cristina Bezzi-Scali had her part in bringing about this change of course in the inventor's life. She was not a wife willing to accept long periods of solitude, as Beatrice had been, while her husband was carried by his work to Cornwall and Canada, Cape Cod, or round the Atlantic on some ship or other. From the first days of the couple's honeymoon, one could see that Marconi's second marriage was very different from his first one.

After the wedding in London, the couple had spent only eight days on the impressive, yet solitary estate at Dromoland. Then the pressure of work, the continuous series of inventions, the affairs of the Company, the defense of his patents, and so on, had carried Marconi back into a whirlwind of feverish activity. After the wedding in Rome, however, the honeymoon lasted several months: after a month of peace at the Villa San Mauro in Rieti, then England, then America, the final destination. Marconi and his second wife traveled from Italy to London on the Elettra, which, moored in the Thames, was the scene of numerous social engagements. Certainly the change in Marconi's lifestyle was brought about by the presence of this woman, so different from his first wife in character, education, outlook and age.

Two other factors had contributed to the change in Marconi's temperament and behavior; his age and maturity, and the new turn—almost a change of nationality—taken by his economic and industrial interests. Although the greater part of Marconi's industrial and commercial activity remained in Britain with the original Marconi Company, both his public life and a good part of his business interests bound him increasingly to Italy.

Since 1925, the Marconi Company had been the cause of endless worries for its founder and president. That year, Godfrey Isaacs had retired from his position as managing director, after brilliantly handling the "Marconi scandal," and carrying the Company to still greater industrial and economical levels. Forced to retire for health reasons, Isaacs had soon afterwards died, leaving the management with grave difficulties—not financial ones but political ones.

After its numerous, much publicized commissions from the government and the installation of a network of short-wave telecommunications throughout the British Empire, the Marconi Company now had the opportunity to pursue a whole series of projects and cooperative ventures with other companies. Along with Isaacs, Marconi realized that the moment had now arrived to make peace with cable companies and enter into agreement with them, perhaps even forming an amalgamation. Demoralized by the success of the short-wave beam system, Marconi's competitors were not in a position to ask for anything better.

### English Misunderstandings

Marconi's advice went unheeded by the administrators of the Company, however—perhaps because he had lost his former persuasiveness; the Company's advisors, while appreciating his merits as an inventor, may have judged themselves more perspicuous in the fields of economic strategy and commercial policy.

Kellway, the former Postmaster General, had been nominated to succeed Godfrey Isaacs and the whole board of directors had been replaced with illustrious figures from the world of finance and diplomacy. These men had little in common with the pioneers of the old Marconi Company. The former board had hung on Marconi's every word; the new men, while admiring his genius, viewed him as a troublesome president, and one, moreover, who was increasingly absent from board meetings. In short, relations between Marconi and those who ran the Company became extremely cool. Yet the Marconi Company continued to grow.

The merger with the cable companies, when it did occur, was brought about by a government decision—and not by the perceived self-interest of the parties involved. It did not prove to be a profitable change for the Marconi Company. While increasing its capital, the Marconi Company found itself with only forty-four percent of the shares in the new Company. Had the merger taken place when the inventor suggested it, at the moment when his company was in a strong position, the operation would have been concluded much more favorably. Even so, the British government, wishing to reserve exclusive state rights in telecommunications, had recently suppressed by law all private activity in the field. The Marconi Company could no longer transmit messages; it was left only with the tasks of research, experimentation and the manufacture of apparatus.

Finally, once Marconi's dream of short-wave beam communication had been realized, the inventor felt drawn toward other fields of research, including the concept of radar and the possibility of guiding ships solely by radio waves. On a scientific level, Marconi began to lose his interest in telecommunications and radio, and found less and less time for study and experimentation. Hence Lord Mountbatten, an expert in radio communications, after a reception on board the Elettra, was able to write:

I was present in my own yacht at Cowes and the invitation from Marconi was a purely social one. I do not think he had any idea that I was a specialist in radio, and after lunch when he was showing guests round his ship, he took us into his main wireless office which of course absolutely fascinated me, being full of the latest developments. He gave a very general description of what was going on in the office, and when I started going round and asking specific questions about various sets, he expressed great surprise at my interest and knowledge and then sent for his Senior Radio Officer to answer my questions.

The impression I had was that at this stage, which I think was about 1926, he had lost close contact with all the developments, although they were being carried out under his aegis."

Lord Mountbatten failed, in his report, to take account of the fact that, even in his earlier years, Marconi had often left the task of developing techniques and equipment to his assistants, engineers and other researchers. Once the inventor had exhausted an idea, it no longer engaged his curiosity and he would move on to something new.


## It Was Not Influenza

When Marconi married Cristina, he was certainly in need of a long vacation. Unhappily, the honeymoon, when it finally occured, came to a dramatic and unpleasant end.

Guglielmo and Cristina sailed for the United States, where the inventor was once again given a triumphant welcome. Marconi and his young bride were delighted by the great enthusiasm and affection that greeted the inventor's lectures and public appearances.

When the two left once again for Europe, it was already late autumn. The crossing was made in intense cold and storms. Guglielmo, not troubled by seasickness, was quite at home on a ship in mid-ocean, and spent many hours walking the deck enjoying the sight of the open sea, unwary of the icy wind. Perhaps because of the cold, or perhaps because of some lingering disease contracted in his earlier travels, he was suddenly afflicted by stabbing pains in the chest and violent attacks of fever.

At first, Marconi thought it was influenza, but the pain recurred several days after he had disembarked in London. A celebrated physician was called and immediately diagnosed a severe case of angina pectoris. This was the first appearance of the disease that would later take the inventor's life.

Marconi was taken from the Savoy to a nursing home where he spent a fortnight, apparently recovered at the time of his departure. Back at the hotel some days later, he collapsed under the effect of another series of attacks, so violent and incapacitating that one rash newspaper even announced his death.

Once again, Marconi recovered from his illness, but the convalescence was lengthy. Degna Marconi later described her father's condition during this period:

> As soon as he was able to travel, his wife took him by easy stages to Rome where two excellent Italian physicians, Professors Bastianelli and Frugoni, gave him devoted care. At the end of several months he was pronounced well enough to resume the regular routine of his life, though he never again was able to work with the unrestrained buoyancy he gave to his early achievements. Nor was he able to pick up the thread of his active experimentation again until 1930. In the meantime he had to content himself with consolidating what he had done before instead of pioneering new trails.

Through this time Father was no easier a patient than when he had lost his eye. It must have been trying for Cristina. During the next couple of years, Giulio and I got to know her and indeed saw a great deal of her the summer of 1928, when we were on the yacht for many weeks together. Towards the end of that summer, at Viareggio, her parents joined us on the Elettra and her mother was particularly friendly to me. At twenty I was still so shy that I did everything I could to disappear when I saw the launch bringing gay and fashionable friends out to the yacht.

In view of the agreement about sharing us that had been made at the time of Father's and Mother's divorce, we took it for granted that we would spend our summers with Father until we were off on our own. Since our parents' relations were conducted with meticulous politeness on both sides, Mother invariably waited for a specific invitation to arrive from Father before she made plans for our summers. For two years we were asked and went to England to cruise with Father and Cristina for whatever periods of time suited everybody's convenience. Then, with no explanation, the invitations ceased."

Her account continued:

Cristina was young and she gave convincing evidence of being overpoweringly excited by the prominence of her husband, in which she shared and took frank and unabashed pleasure. Under her influence the aloof man, the man who had been too "terribly busy" for personal publicity, no longer avoided it. Instead he embraced the honors and distinctions that once embarrassed him. Beside him, radiant and proud in the limelight, stood his young wife. Outward manifestations of fame, so sedulously and so long discouraged, were Father's daily bread in this last phase of his life. He opened fairs and cut ribbons; he "appeared" in public and lit distant beacons in Sydney and Rio by pressing wireless keys. Wherever the

Marconis went he submitted without cavil to endless picture-taking by film as well as still photographers.

At Cowes for the Royal Regatta, he posed with Cristina smiling at his side. Beneath his black-visored, white-topped yachting cap, his expression is slightly strained and the wrinkles under his eyes and from his nose to his mouth are deeper etched. He walks with a cane now but briskly, one can see, a cigarette in his hand. His wife, as tall in high heels as he, looks pretty, assured, satisfied.

"I think his chief delight was in pleasing her. His great working years were over and Cristina gave him an illusion of the youth that had slipped away. His first marriage ended in failure. This one would prove that it was not altogether his fault.

## The Lights in Australia

Marconi seems to have found, at least in the early days of his second marriage, an emotional tranquillity which he had rarely known. Years later, Cristina Bezzi-Scali was genuinely shocked by questions concerning her husband's fidelity, insisting that he had always been faithful to her. She also maintained that Guglielmo was an ideal husband and that there had never been any friction in the marriage. Her assessment was almost certainly true, at least in the early days of the marriage. Though there were the inevitable arguments and differences of opinion, these never extended beyond the family circle.

Most significantly, the second marriage was no longer marred by the amorous, and often very public affairs, that were so common in the inventor's earlier relationship. Along with Marconi's deep love for Cristina, there were at least three reasons for this change in behavior. First, he had finally learned to respect his position as an important public figure. His new social and political position had

made him scrupulously attentive to his public appearance and reputation. Second, his behavior was also restrained by Cristina's chaper-
oning of him in public. Either she accompanied him herself or—on
those rare occasions when she could not be with him—she left him
under the watchful eyes of the Bezzi-Scali family at their ancestral
home in via Condotti. The third reason was the deteriorating state
of Marconi's health; the angina pectoris was now dormant, but
always present as a threat.

The years between 1930 to 1932 passed quietly for Guglielmo
Marconi, but not without a number of extraordinary achievements
and awards. On 26 March, he switched on lights in Australia from
on board the Elettra. On 19 September, he became President of the
Royal Academy of Italy. At the beginning of 1931, again on board the
Elettra, he began experiments on microwaves. On 12 February, he
opened a new station at the Vatican. Pius XI gave the first papal
radio message and appointed Marconi to the pontifical academy. On
13 October, a radio beam from Rome controlled the lighting of a
huge statue of the Redeemer on the summit of Corcovado in Rio de
Janeiro; in the same autumn the inventor carried out his first demon-
strations of microwaves between Santa Maria Ligure and Sestri
Levante and then increased the range as far as Levanto. On 15
January 1932, the king of Italy bestowed on Marconi the order of
Knight of the Grand Cross of St. Mauritius and St. Lazarus. On 10
March, the city of Philadelphia conferred on him the John Scott
Prize through the American ambassador in Rome. On 3 May, in
London, he received the Kelvin gold medal presented to him by
Lord Rutherford, the most famous scientist of the day. In June, he
was elected as an overseas member of the American National
Academy of Sciences. The same month, the National Italian
Lifeboat Society paid solemn homage to Marconi with a great gold
medal bearing an inscription of apotheosis: "To the prophet of

radio, savior of ships and men . . . is offered the golden pledge of maritime recognition."

But certainly the most joyous occasion was the birth of his last daughter, Elettra. The happy event took place in the Villa Odescalchi at Civitavecchia, where Marconi and Cristina spent their holidays from time to time.

The infant was given the names Maria Elettra Elena Anna, each for a precise reason. Maria was the mother's first name; Elettra was to record the site of the prophetic first meeting between Guglielmo and his second wife; Elena was out of indebtedness to the queen of Italy who had agreed to act as godmother; and Anna honored both Guglielmo's and Cristina's mothers.

The baptism was as solemn a ceremony as the marriage had been; the secretary of the pontifical state, Cardinal Eugenio Pacelli, the future Pius XII, officiated. He had become a personal friend of Marconi, and in the reorganization of the state secretariat, he entrusted the inventor with the task of constructing a powerful short-wave station. As a result the church was assured its independence from the Italian state in telecommunications. Pius XI was already composing the encyclical *Quadrigesimo anno*, with which in 1931 he warned Catholics against the systematic action of the new regimes—the reference to Fascism was clear—which fostered in the young an exclusive devotion to the state.

The birth of Elettra put even more distance between Marconi and the members of his previous family. Beatrice and Guglielmo did not meet again after 1928. The children continued to see him from time to time, but finally even this contact came to an end. As Degna later recalled:

My mother watched them from afar, and whatever she may have felt, she kept her thoughts to herself. But she was seriously discomfited by the complete breach which, as time passed, succeeded the early and friendly mutual consultations about us. Marconi, the man who hated making hard-and-fast financial agreements, had declined to make any for her children. She brought the matter up in letters, since this was the only way she had left to communicate with him, and he brushed off her queries, assuring her that he would take care of us. Mother reluctantly concluded that it was safe to believe him, if only because failure to provide for us would make an ugly impression in the eyes of the world. In the meantime, we had our allowances as proof that we were not wholly forgotten.

The year that the invitations to visit Father ended, our pocket-money was also reduced, causing Mother fresh alarm about our futures. The time had come, she felt, to press Father to confer with her on money matters and she wrote him urgently to that effect. Father at first replied courteously that he would be glad to talk to her and made appointments. These he failed to keep and left later letters urging a settlement unanswered. Frantic, Mother summoned her lawyer. This was the signal for open war, and in Father's eyes we all had to choose sides. He had every reason to assume that, since we still saw Mother, we had lined up with her, conveniently expunging from his memory that it was he who had severed his ties with us.

In fact we two older Marconi children, Giulio and I, were physically removed from the scene by the time the struggle reached its height. I was living by myself in London and Giulio had gone into the Navy. Even Gioia—Puffett, as Father called her—had left home and was in school at Florence. We did, however, spend some of our holidays with Mother and were cast in the unhappy and unwilling role of ambassadors from one to the other of our parents. The chief mission with which Mother charged us was to at least get the full amount of our allowances reinstated. This Father categorically refused to do.

When none of our embassies availed and the lawyer was equally ineffectual, Mother appealed to Cardinal Gasparri to use his good

offices with Father about our welfare. This, too, miscarried woeful-
ly. Father was incensed rather than moved, and chose to see Giulio
and me as conniving in the maneuvers.

However, he did send me [the following] card dated, July 20,
1930:

> My Dearest Degna,
> Just a line to tell you today at 5:05 p.m. a little girl arrived. She
> is quite pretty and both she and Cristina are getting on very well.
> With best of love in haste.

Scratched in the lower left-hand corner are two Xs, for kisses.
They recur through his letters to me, a shy indication of the affection that somehow survived between us. He was a man who found it
impossible to put his feelings into words and I sense, rereading his
letters, strangely formal though they were, that he was trapped by
his British background in a language of understatement. When
indeed, he did manage to set down some part of what was in his
heart, he slipped, unconsciously, into the easier, warmer vernacular
of Italian, in which he finds it possible to say, "So much love and so
many kisses from your affectionate, Babbo"—"Tanto amore e baci
dal tuo affettuoso, Babbo," or "A million kisses,—Un milione di
baci." In English it was more likely to be, "Ever your Aff., Daddy."

"She was born, this baby, at the Villa Odelscalchi, near Civitavecchia, a country house beside the sea that Father had rented. A
few days later she was christened Maria Elettra Elena Anna by
Cardinal Pacelli, who was to become Pope Pius XII. I would have
loved to see my baby half-sister. I did not and we have never yet."

Beatrice was also deeply unhappy about the situation, and from
Marignoli's home at Spoleto and probably on his advice, she began
to takeserious measures. Once again, it was Degna who recalled the
details:

Mother, desperate at Father's failure to honor his pledge that he would provide for us financially, was tempted to use any means she could to force a showdown. The means were hers. Father's letters to her at the time of the annulment were so susceptible to being misconstrued that they might cause the Roman Catholic authorities to question the validity of his second marriage. I have serious doubts that she would ever have used them to hurt him publicly but she had every intention, I think, of invoking them privately to get her way. Without the knowledge of any of us children, she consulted a lawyer in Rome, who advised that she bring action against Father.

"When, at the eleventh hour, we were told what was impending, we were horrified. As Mother had no real wish to be vindictive, she readily acceded when we begged her to withdraw from her position.

Father, alas, did not know what role we had played and allowed himself to be persuaded that it was not Mother but we who were the real culprits in what he may well have thought of as blackmail.

All love for us was erased, or so it seemed, when in 1935 my father wrote a will bequeathing everything he had to his wife Cristina and his daughter Elettra.

Giulio and I were beyond the pale and, by association, Gioia, branded in Father's mind as callous and indifferent to him."

Elettra's birth did not prevent Cristina Bezzi-Scali from remaining at her husband's side on his various travels. When Guglielmo needed to go abroad, the daughter was entrusted to her grandparents, who were always happy to take care of her. The most spectacular of the thousands of voyages the inventor made during his life was the world tour he undertook with his second wife in 1933.

## A Triumphal Progress

The tour lasted from the summer of 1933 to the beginning of 1934. The object of this long journey was "Marconi Day" at the great Exposition of science and technology in Chicago, dedicated to the "Century of Progress." The lights of this international gathering were switched on by Marconi with a rather more complicated system than the one he used for the illuminations at Sydney and Corcovado. From the Arcetri observatory in Florence, Galileo's telescope was pointed at the star Capella; the star's rays, through the lens constructed by the founder of modern science, struck a photoelectric cell which controlled a radio beam, and rebounded to the radio station at Rome and from there to Chicago, where the entire Exposition was illuminated. Guglielmo, however, felt the need to add spectacle to spectacle. Using an improved radio telegraph apparatus, he sent into space the three signals of the letter "S." From Chicago they rebounded to a station in New York and from there to London, then to Rome, Bombay, Manila, Honolulu, and San Francisco, and finally back to their point of departure, completing the circuit of the earth in three minutes and twenty-five seconds. The return of the signals set off the automatic detonator of a huge fireworks display.

From Chicago, the Marconis traveled to San Francisco and then set sail for Japan. From there, they sailed to China, Manchuria and India, and finally back to Italy.

Marconi was encouraged in this venture—which had little to do with real science—by Mussolini himself, who was proud to show off to an attentive public so prestigious a representative of Italy, and one who was also a fervent supporter of Fascism. For his part, Marconi was pleased with his triumphs and happy to serve his country.

To this period belong those of Marconi's speeches and writings which were most adulatory of Fascism. Some examples appear below, beginning with a message he broadcast to the world in French, English and German on 15 October 1932:

> On the tenth anniversary of the Fascist regime, the Royal Academy, which includes among its members distinguished representatives of the arts and sciences united in their faith in Mussolini, extends the sincerest invitation to the exponents of every art and the practitioners of every science that they look for inspiration to the Eternal City, restored by Fascism to the majesty and splendor of the Augustan Age, thanks to the indomitable will of its leader. Intellectuals all over the world, who recognize how in the spirit of ancient Rome lies the foundation of modern civilization, will be moved at the sight of the ancient monuments uncovered by the fascist government in recent years (Curia, Temple of Vesta, Scipio's Tomb, the Capitoline Hill). A magnificent road links the heart of Rome with the beauty of the surrounding hills. And on all sides, you will find a modern Rome with museums, streets, new districts, the Foro Mussolini and the motorway. And throughout our beautiful peninsula, you will notice how, not only in Rome but everywhere on Italian soil, remnants of our ancient history have been brought to light (Paestum, Pompei, Herculaeum). And you will be astonished by all the achievements of civilization and progress built by Fascism (roads, railways, bridges, factories, schools, hospitals, gymnasiums, reclaimed marshes). In a word, everywhere are the signs of a peaceful economy and flourishing educational system. All this bears witness to the great effort and to the blood spilt by the fascist youth for the renewal of their country. The Royal Academy of Italy feels confident that the invitation will be accepted by intellectuals all over the world: they will be honored guests of the Italian people and they will be able to feel the spirit called into

being by the force of an idea and by the actions of a man of Genius.

And here is what he wrote in *Il Popolo d'Italia* on 28 October of the same year, on the tenth anniversary of the March on Rome:

I have never been able to understand how in some foreign circles there has grown up a myth of Fascism's scant sympathy for science and culture in general.

There is nothing more unjust than this false myth. Neither as doctrine nor in government has Fascism ever opposed science, let alone culture. On the contrary I undertake to show how the organization and encouragement which the fascist government has given to science, and the scientific research on which all science rests, is both thoughtfully considered and productive.

All governments take pains to give the means and renewed energy to the silent army of their men of science who faithfully and tenaciously undergo the long trials of meditation, observation and experiment. The fascist government has done this, is doing this, and will continue to do this.

With clear-sightedness it has recognized that the seedbeds of culture are incalculable elements of strength for a people. Only yesterday the Duce gave assurances that these seedbeds, created over the centuries in our universities, often painfully overcoming grave difficulties, living proof of the high civilization of our people, will not be touched. The fascist regime intends to build, not to destroy.

Although the times are hard for us all, we see in the universities a ferment of life and renewal. Our old universities with very great sacrifices made by the state, as much by the generous intervention of the local institutions as through the untiring efforts, full of self-denial, of our scholars, have been, one can say, completely renewed, with a far-sighted vision of the high significance they have in the life of a Nation, proud of their wonderful traditions.

MARCONI

And the whole undertaking depends on the passionate concern of the government, which has one of its best and most capable departments directing higher education.

I remember the document in which the head of the government introduced to Parliament the bill for the rebuilding of the University of Rome, settling a vexed question which had dragged on for years, and cutting short delays and difficulties which previously would have been insurmountable.

But the fascist government does not restrict its activities to the development and improvement of the universities.

It has founded two great institutes with different but interrelated objectives of the highest importance for the scientific life of the country. The Royal Academy of Italy in the mind of the Head of the Government who promoted it, represents, and I quote his words, a living center of national culture, to nurture and stimulate intellectual activity in the light of the genius and the traditions of our people, but making itself felt beyond the confines of our country and contributing above all to that intellectual community which makes it possible for Italians to affirm that primacy in the arts and sciences which has been theirs before, reconstituting that universality characteristic of the Italian mind which shines out in Dante, Thomas Aquinas, Galileo and Leonardo da Vinci. This conception is translated into practical terms in the law which institutes the Royal Academy of Italy and lays down its aims. . . . Linked with these is the clearly defined role of the Council for Research.

The fascist government has taken a notable step forward in the training and encouragement of promising inventors. The new legislation on intellectual ownership constitutes considerable progress in this direction, but above all it is with the standardization of examinations for patents, now realized through the initiative of the National Council for Research, that the problem has been reduced to practical terms.

This is the Government's work.

## The Inventor as Hero

That Marconi acted in good faith writing and speaking in the name of Fascism can be demonstrated by other documents which have little or nothing to do with politics. From these it seems that the father of radio pursued an ideal in which he was able to reconcile both his love for Italy and his emotional links with the Anglo-Saxon world.

In the early 1930s, when the political relationship between Italy and United Kingdom was still good and the English government continued to admire Mussolini, Marconi looked forward to a union between what he defined as the Latin and the Anglo-Saxon spirit in the name of the advancement of mankind. An early example of these sentiments can be found in a eulogy Marconi wrote for Thomas Edison, which was published in the periodical *Gerarchi* at the time of the great American inventor's death:

> With the fate of Thomas Edison, the ideal and constant inspiration of my own activity is lost.
> His luminous figure represents a new kind of human genius, giving characteristic expression to the best features of the American spirit. A type which, balancing and harmonizing theory and practice, loftiness of thought and ardent love of mankind, remains throughout the world the precursor of new and universal forms of civilization.
> Science is no longer pure thought alone, the privilege of a few superior minds, but action in the service of mankind, the very symbol of progress.
> Edison's light bulb illuminates not only the streets of the cities but the remotest mountain villages, the most humble dwellings. It spreads safety and light, where before there was darkness. So many

MARCONI

of his countless inventions have yielded incalculable moral and
material benefits.

The steadiness, the perseverance, the tirelessness of Edison are
the peculiar virtues of a nation young in years but already mature
in deeds. The projects of his fervid imagination have all the mag-
nificence of a nation with a whole continent for its home. Through
his work science becomes the daily conquest of the world we live in
and the space which surrounds it.

I end this heartfelt tribute to the great American who has
renewed the glories of Benjamin Franklin, with the hope that the
Latin spirit and the Anglo-Saxon spirit will draw ever closer
together in the common ideals of scientific progress and human
solidarity.

The dream of a reconciliation between the Latin and Anglo-Saxon
spirit was expressed most fully on the occasion of an exceptional
European cultural initiative: the reconstruction of a map to the scale
of one millionth of the Roman Empire in the period of its greatest
expansion. The initiative had various supporters beside Marconi,
among them a famous Cambridge scholar, G.S. Crawford, who had
been promoting the idea at his own university since 1928. The fascist
authorities were determined not to let the opportunity pass, and on
the tenth anniversary of the March on Rome, they set up the
International Commission for the map of the Roman Empire. The
commission was presided over by General Wintherbotham, Director
of the British Geographical Institute, and included distinguished
scholars and educators from throughout Europe.. The project was
officially inaugurated at an opening ceremony in the Campidoglio,
on 21 November 1932.

As president of the National Council for Research, Marconi gave
the opening address:

Your Excellencies, Gentlemen, at the International Convention of the Volta Foundation which has just taken place in Rome, eminent orators from all nations have recognized and declared that the foundations of European civilization lie in the civilization of the Roman Empire: not only for those things that are strictly Roman handed down to the world, in the law and institutions, in architecture and language, in the coordination of strength of thought and action as in the dignity of life, but also because, what the civilization of today owes to the Hellenic and Oriental world, it owes in great part to Roman thought and reinterpretation.

It is now our duty not to abandon the study and research of what Roman civilization represents, what it has achieved, the forms and the limits of its action, the methods and the forces which operated within it.

A celebrated English scholar, who I am pleased to see here with us today, Mr. G. S. Crawford, has understood perfectly that one cannot really know the history of a civilization without a thorough knowledge of the territory where it operated.

The successful outcome of an undertaking of so much interest as that which concerns us today depends above all on two factors: a sharp-sighted vigilance on the part of those who direct the work and a harmonious cooperation on the part of those who carry it out. The first, entrusted to a special office at the Ordinance Survey at Southampton under General Wintherbotham and his collaborator Mr. Crawford, is absolutely assured. The second, in our opinion, can only be obtained with frequent coordination between the organizations and persons responsible.

This is the reason for the present gathering, and I hope that this international cooperation will continue beyond the strictly topographical work of the map, through research and investigation in the fields of economics, language, military science and social life so that it will be possible to arrive at general conclusions about Roman civilization.

Meanwhile I am happy to be able to report that Italy, for its part, has already made a start through the assiduous and expert work on the map of Professor Lugli and through the interest of both the Institute of Antiquities and Fine Arts and the Institute of Military Geography and, above all, of its director, the Hon. General Vacchelli, one of the moving spirits behind the undertaking and whose absence today we deeply and sincerely mourn.

To the map of the Roman Empire as the to the great archeological map of Italy [. . .] and to many other initiatives at once cartographic and cultural, Vacchelli had dedicated the best efforts of his intellect; consequently his loss represents a real sorrow for science and for us all.

"I end by thanking most sincerely His Excellency the Governor of Rome for having given us his hospitality on this sacred Capitoline Hill where all the roads of Rome and the world come together, and from which, since the days of Ovid, Jove has looked out over the whole world to see the sign of Rome."

Much of this speech is clearly not the work of Marconi's own hand. A letter preserved in the Royal Academy of Italy, sent by Chancellor Marpicati to Umberto Di Marco, the inventor's secretary, reveals the circumstances of the speech's composition. Dated 14 April 1931, the letter refers to the proceedings of the Academy scheduled for the 18th, 19th, and 21st of the same month. Di Marco had written to Marpicati for the remittance of 120,000 Lira in repayment of expenses, informing him that the inventor was in London at the time, but would be arriving in Rome on the 17th or 18th after a brief stop at the Hotel Miramare in Genoa. Di Marco asked Marpicati to send a note directly to Genoa describing what was expected of Marconi.

The Chancellor of the Academy replied promptly, announcing that the Academic Council would be in session on 18 April; on the

19th, the general session of the Accademia would officially open, and on the 21st, the formal anniversary of the founding of Rome, the General Session of the Academicians would be held in the presence of the king of Italy.

Then Marpicati went on to brief the inventor:

> Your Excellency, it seems appropriate that you should open the formal session with a few words; you will thank the king for his august presence and say, "No one can be better entitled to the prize given by the 'Corriere della Sera' than Mussolini, since Benito Mussolini embodies for the new Italy the spirit of the nation and the most certain hope of the reconquest of that spiritual primacy which belonged to our ancestors and towards which the most lively and vigorous powers are moving, animated and sustained by the Regime."

Marpicati's letter continued with other verbatim instructions for Marconi's speech. Marconi faithfully made the speech without changing so much as a comma.

The following urgent message, circulated to the editor in chief of the *Popolo d'Italia*, Sandro Giuliani by the Chancellery of the Royal Academy of Italy, evidently at Marconi's request, provides additional proof of the diligence with which Marconi executed the tasks entrusted to him by the regime and of the care he took that his speeches should be published in full, rather than in synopses which might misrepresent his ideas:

> In case the Stefani agency should circulate the communication in less than its entirety, here are His Excellency Marconi's words at the opening of the general assembly of the Academy on January 17th, 1932:

"Distinguished colleagues, at the opening of the work of the present session I believe I am expressing the feelings of the whole assembly in renewing our profound condolences to the head of the government on the sudden and untimely death of his beloved brother Arnaldo. It has been a sorrow for the whole nation, particularly felt by the Reale Accademia d'Italia, created by the Duce and lovingly sustained by him. Arnaldo Mussolini has left a void in Italian journalism which will not easily be filled. For ten years at "Il Popolo d'Italia" he was a penetrating commentator on all the major political events at home and abroad. The regime and the party owe much to him. Arnaldo Mussolini was an honorable man, an ardent and pure spirit. He filled his difficult and delicate position with direction and moderation, seeking neither honor nor office, content simply to collaborate in the immense and weighty tasks of his elder brother."

Marconi's theatrical effectiveness as a spokesman was cleverly used by the representatives of Fascism. Given the inventor's acute intelligence, it is unlikely that he was unaware of this. He probably lent himself, as far as possible, to the various requests that came to him from the fascist federations all over Italy or directly from the Grand Council for conflicting reasons—partly because he clearly enjoyed being surrounded by admirers and covered with honors, partly because he saw all this as in keeping with the duty of his high offices. Three telegrams illustrate this. The first two concern a "cultural" manifestation by the young fascists at the Augusteo in Rome; the third, a visit to Fiume which Marconi was asked to undertake in 1934:

Rome—February 28th, 1934—Fascist Federation—Rome. To His Excellency Marconi, President of the Royal Academy of Italy. Many thanks for your agreement to preside over the two cultural reunions which took place at the Augusteo. The words and presence of

Marconi lent important significance to the occasion. Federal secretary Vezio Orazi.

Marconi's reply followed three days later:

I thank you for your expressions of kindness and wish to record my lively appreciation for the opportunity of finding myself among the fascist masses of Rome.

On 9 May 1934, Guglielmo sent the following telegram to the faithful Marpicati: "Alright for the visit to Fiume—please telegraph details of the appropriate dress."
The chancellor's reply was to Marconi's secretary, Di Marco:

Given the political nature of the occasion, it seems appropriate that Marconi wear fascist uniform with full braid and other Italian decorations. As for the dates, the 22nd is a Saturday; it would be advisable to fix on Sunday, the 23rd, because the holiday would allow greater public participation. For Saturday, the 22nd, the council of the party has been convened and [Marpicati] will not be able to be present at the ceremony."

In addition to these services to Fascism at home, others had an even greater impact abroad. In September 1935, Marconi was invited by the Brazilian government to inaugurate the new Tupy radio station. In a letter of 18 July, Mussolini urged the inventor to take the opportunity to inagurate the new "Case del Fascio" (Party Headquarters), one at Rio de Janeiro and the other at São Paulo. This would provide Marconi with an opportunity to expound "Italy's good reasons" for the recent invasion of Abyssinia. The Duce strengthened his case by assigning Marconi an "expense account" of 250,000 Lira.

Feeling himself fully fit, the inventor ignored the advice of his doctor and left for Latin America. In Brazil, he received enthusiastic responses from both the Brazilians and, even more, the large Italian community. Here are some extracts from Marconi's speech at Rio on 27 September 1935:

> I feel the need and the duty, although I am not an orator, to say a few words to you, above all at this time when we have left Italy and the Duce in the middle of a harsh diplomatic and political struggle, just—and indeed sacred—for our natural and necessary expansion, for the security of our colonies, for the prestige of the name of Italy in Africa.
>
> The whole Italian people is taking an active part in this struggle, from the veterans of the Great War won gloriously on the banks of the Piave and on the sacred heights of the Grappa, to the younger generations who have grown up in the brilliant and stimulating climate created by the Duce and the Black Shirts.
>
> No one can understand better than you, settlers in this generous land, the good reasons and the right to life of a young country, full of healthy ferment for action, like Italy. Because you have left, have felt a duty to leave the joys of the beloved country, to seek work and bread beyond the vast ocean!
>
> Why for this people, old and young, rich in military honors from the recent world conflict, so ungenerously neglected at the Peace of Versailles why should the way forward be barred?
>
> Yet in thirteen years of Fascist government, this people has achieved, in spite of scant resources, an immense transformation, not only of the face of Italy, but of the spirit. The Duce has created a national sentiment in the mass of Italians within and beyond our borders which has meant greater political evolution in this last decade than in the previous fifty years.
>
> You all know and recognize this; many of you have seen it with your own eyes. You can be proud, Italians, to have given your talent

and your strength, your ardor and your faith to contribute to the greatness of this vast country which shelters and helps you.

To my warmest greetings I add the brotherly advice to you, always to be worthy of your past, of your achievements and of mother Italy who follows and loves you, and who needs to feel the generous and vigorous beating of the hearts of all her sons for her future victories and place in the world.

Long live Italy! Long live the King! Long live the Duce! Long live Brazil!

At the inauguration of the "Casa del Fascio" in São Paulo on 1 October 1935, Marconi greeted the crowd:

Fascist comrades, fellow nationals all! The inauguration of a casa del fascio in a city like São Paolo is the culmination of many important ideals. In this center of Italian life, the casa del fascio must mean and embody unity, must be an example of national and human solidarity, must shine out with brotherhood and fascist faith!

The times are hard, but splendid, because they carry to the world the battle, so long suspended, of our historical and natural rights to win for ourselves a place in the world!

In the name of the Duce, I declare the casa del fascio of São Paulo open."

During Marconi's trip to Latin America, Italian troops invaded Ethiopia. Even before leaving Brazil, whilie Mussolini was still amassing his troops for the campaign in East Africa, Marconi had asked to be enlisted in the Black Shirts. It was a calculated gesture, of course, given the inventor's poor health, but it did not fail to impress the Duce.

## Disappointment in London

On 18 November, the League of Nations declared sanctions against
Italy as punishment for the attack on Ethiopia. Mussolini entreated
the inventor to use his international prestige and high standing in
the Anglo-Saxon world to explain Italy's actions.

Firmly convinced of the justice of Mussolini's undertaking,
Guglielmo left immediately for London, where he was scheduled to
read a message in English on the BBC. His was shocked to discover
that, in spite of his requests, he was forbidden to speak to the
English people The denial of Marconi's freedom of speech by the
English authorities was strongly criticized, even in *The Times*.

Barred from addressing his English neighbors, Marconi used the
microphones of Rome Radio to address the American people:

Italy is being accused of violating obligations she has entered into.
For 40 years Italy has tried to open up friendly relations with
Abyssinia (the proof is the conclusion of the treaty of friendship of
1928). Abyssinia, however, has not carried out a single clause of
that treaty. Italy's friendly intentions have been met with 40 years
of refusals and hostile actions. The truth is that there are those
who want to blame Italy for seeking her place in the sun. This
place cannot be denied. Her recent advance is an advance for
progress and peace. The proof is that the population and the chiefs
of the Tigrai have presented themselves of their own accord to our
representatives in the sacred city of Axu, while one prince of that
region has offered his sword to Italy to free the victims of
Ethiopian chaos. Civilization advances with our soldiers, bridges,
roads, power stations and electric cables, provisions. We have carried the abolition of slavery into the occupied territories.

Between primitive Abyssinia and Italy, with its civilization and centuries of glorious history, a hurriedly assembled tribunal (the
League of Nations) wishes to assign the blame to Italy with the
verdict: sanctions! They have never been applied in similar cases;
they amount to a declaration of economic warfare and are themselves the greatest injustice this century; the U.S. cannot look on
with indifference. Italy calls on the American people for impartial
justice and humane understanding of her vital needs."

But as with many of his other public declarations on behalf of
Fascism, this speech was not Marconi's own composition. In the
archives of the Royal Academy of Italy, "His Excellency Marconi's
Radio Message to the American People" is credited to Marpicati.

Perhaps the most exhaustive and sensitive account of Marconi's
relation to Mussolini—and to Fascism—was given in *The Times*
obituary to the inventor:

The Duce loses in Marconi a devoted admirer and a trusted friend,
and the Fascist Party one of its staunchest supporters. The
Marchese, who, before the advent of Fascism to power, had never
taken an active part in internal politics, joined the Fascist Party in
1923, at a time when other prominent Italians were either opposed
to or lukewarm towards the government of Mussolini. The Duce
greatly appreciated Marconi's gesture, and, besides bestowing
numerous honors and distinctions upon him, treasured a friendship
which grew deeper and deeper with their increased contacts. The
Marchese was a frequent visitor to the Palazzo Venezia, and he
kept the Duce regularly informed of the progress of his scientific
researches, receiving from him constant encouragement. As a testimony of the trust placed in him, the Duce appointed him a member of the Fascist Grand Council. A further signal honor was
accorded when, in 1930, Mussolini nominated him a member of

the Italian Royal Academy, despite the fact that Senators could not belong to that body, and appointed him President of the institution. Marconi's devotion to the Duce and to Fascism was best seen during the Ethiopian crisis, when not only did he volunteer for service in East Africa, but became an active propagandist of the Italian cause.

13

AT THE FRONTIERS OF ELECTRONICS

## The Conquest of the Microwave

When Marconi returned to Italy after his triumphant tour of the world in 1934, he started a new series of experiments on the transmission of centimetric waves. These tests—which later would lead to the development of modern radio systems—had begun many years before, in 1922, when Guglielmo first demonstrated that short waves could reach the longest distances in daytime. From this stage Marconi had rapidly progressed to further experiments on the characteristics and possibilities of shorter and shorter waves. By the end of the 1920s, Marconi already recognized that the most important results and progress would come from this part of the spectrum of electromagnetic waves.

In 1932, using waves ranging from fifty-five to fifty-eight centimeters, Marconi received messages from a transmitter placed on the terrace of the Meteorological Observatory at Rocca di Papa (four hundred and fifty meters above sea level). The experiment was conducted on board the Elettra in the Tyrrhenian sea between Civitavecchia and the Gulf of Aranci. The signals covered a distance of two hundred and seventy kilometers and the results were so important that Marconi presented them to the Royal Institution on 2 December 1932:

> In regard to the limited range of propagation of these microwaves, the last word has not yet been said. It has already been shown that they can travel round a portion of the earth's curvature, to distances greater than had been expected, and I cannot help reminding you that at the very time when I first succeeded in proving that electric waves could be sent and received across the Atlantic Ocean in 1901, distinguished mathematicians were of the opinion that the distance of communications, by means of electric waves, would be limited to a distance of only about 165 miles.

## The Transmitting Dipole

In 1932, Marconi supervised the construction of the ultra-short-wave station connecting the Vatican City, Rome and the summer residence of the Pope at Castelgandolfo. Though the distance involved was small, Marconi had to overcome a number of other difficulties, such as the presence of several high buildings between the two stations. The solution to these problems involved an even deeper understanding of electromagnetic waves. The following year, on 14 August 1933 during an exceptional session of the Class of Physical Sciences at the Royal Academy, Marconi made a special announcement to Italian scholars:

> Electromagnetic waves less than a meter long are commonly known as micro-waves; and are classed as quasi-optical waves because it has generally been thought that radiotelegraph communications

were possible with them only when the transmitting and receiving apparatus were within sight of each other; their practical utilization would consequently be very limited.

"In the course of these experiments, carried out in July and August last year, I was able to discover that the useful range of these waves was by no means restricted to the optical geometric distance, which depends above all on the height of the instruments, but that they could be received and detected beyond the horizon at twice the optical distance and also between two positions screened from one another by hills rising in between.

Between the 2nd and 6th of this month, I have been able to carry out further radiotelegraph transmission tests by means of microwaves approximately 60 cm long, between a transmitter sited at Santa Margherita Ligure and a receiver set up on the Elettra sailing off the Tyrrhenian coast. The transmitting dipole, broadcasting a power of approximately 25 watts, was placed on the Hotel Miramare at Santa Margherita, 8 meters above sea level and near the focus of a parabolic reflector having an aperture of 2 meters. The receiving dipole was in a similar reflector located on the Elettra and was placed 5 meters above sea level.

Although the optical distance was only 30 km., the radiotelegraph and radiotelephone signals of the transmitting station were received on the yacht clearly, strongly and regularly at a distance of 150 km., five times the optical distance. Yet, during last year's experiments, although the instruments were installed at a higher level above the sea (50 meters), the longest distance reached by the Morse signals was only 52 km.

It was not possible to carry out constant tests beyond the mentioned distance of 150 km. during these experiments because of the contour of the land, which prevented the Elettra from sailing with its reflector towards the transmitting station. The Morse signals were, however, detected very feebly, and sometimes rather indistinctly, but it was often possible to read them as far as the anchorage at Porto Santo Stefano, 258 km. from Santa Margherita, nine times the optical distance, although in this case on the direct route between the two small stations there was land interference for 17 km.—the high hills of the Piombino promontory for 11,842 km. and the small headland of Troja for 5,556 km.

The longer range reached with these tests seems to have been possible thanks to the improved efficiency of the transmitting and receiving apparatus and the reflectors adopted. Carrying out these experiments, both last year and this, I have been very considerably helped by engineer Gaston-Antoine Mathieu who has personally been responsible for the construction and the initial tests of the new mechanism, and by the technical staff of the Marconi Company.

In my opinion, the theoretical explanation for the results we have obtained, considering the wavelength adopted, presents serious difficulties, even applying the computation of diffraction and refraction indicated by Pession in his paper "Considerations on the propagation of the ultra-short and microwaves."

The speculations deriving from it affect the whole theory of radio-transmission over distances exceeding the optical range.

After further, more detailed and extensive tests, I intend to publish a specific account of the methods adopted and of the results obtained. I also hope that, apart from the theoretical conclusions which could be of scientific interest, today's results may lead to new and substantial progress in the field of communications."

## The Experiment at Santa Margherita

In this same period Marconi also perfected Langevin Fleurisan's echo sounder, a complex system which uses ultrasonic waves to measure the depth of the water where a ship is sailing and to determine whether there are obstacles around or beneath the ship. The principle on which this system is based is exactly the same as that of the echo; a train of waves, after bumping into an obstacle, is reverberated back and then measured.

Most spectacularly during this period, Marconi demonstrated the possibility of "radio navigation", or "blind air navigation" by means of radiophares. Within a few years, this discovery would open the way to a new method for improving the safety of sea voyages and air travel. The man with whom Marconi worked most closely for this purpose was the Belgian engineer Gaston-Antoine Mathieu, who had created the first truly successful radio-phare— a transmitter capable of broadcasting electric signals of a specific wavelength at a constant sequence, exactly like the light beams of an optical beam.

The experiment took place on 30 June 1934, off Santa Margherita Ligure. The radiophare had been set up at a strategic position on a hill; on board the Elettra Marconi's collaborators had placed a special receiver connected to the small hand of a dial. Two buoys, fifty meters apart, had been moored in a suitable position on the sea surface as points of reference.

The Elettra was to pass between the two buoys without any other guidance except the radiophare. All the portholes of the upper deck were covered with thick black curtains after the instruments were activated. The ship passed between the two buoys three times, after making a series of circles and changes of directions to show that it was possible to "pick up" radiophare signals from any position and return to the prescribed route. The famous American physicist Arthur Compton was among the many personalities from the scientific, military and political world who were on hand to greet the success of the experiment.

## The Death Ray

In the second half of the 1930s, news spread through Europe of a phantom death ray—an emission (it was unspecified whether it was electromagnetic or of some other kind) capable of stopping cars, planes and ships and of killing men and animals. In Italy the fantastic ray was naturally attributed to Marconi and there were persistent rumors that the inventor had successfully tested it in Mussolini's presence. It was also whispered that Marconi had secretly discussed his new achievement with the Pope and committed himself, on the Pope's advice, not to reveal the nature of the ray and the method of producing it. Among all these improbabilities, a still greater one was imagined—that Mussolini had magnanimously accepted the Pope's counsel and Marconi's qualms of conscience.

The truth was quite another. Marconi had been fairly successful in experiments that used radiophares to locate vehicles on ground. Mussolini, concerned as always to demonstrate "the genius of the Italian mind," deliberately allowed rumors about the death ray to circulate, with the assistance of the Fascist secret police. While news of the "death ray" was officially denied, great efforts were made—through false information given to the international espionage community—to ensure that the public really believed Marconi's had created the fantastic ray.

But the possibility of such a phantom weapon was cherished not only in Italy. Also in England, the idea had assiduous supporters. Within a few months, the number of so-called inventors and pseudo-scientists claiming success grew so rapidly that the British Ministry of Aviation decided to stop the endless claims about the mysterious "black boxes" once and for all by offering a prize of several thousand pounds to anyone who could kill a sheep at one hundred meters with one of the deadly weapons. No one claimed the prize.

False information concerning the death ray also had a positive effect, however, when the British Committee for Air Defense decided to present an accurate report on the real scientific possibilities of building such a ray. Among the scientists involved in the report was one of the day's most distinguished experts in radio communications: Richard Watson-Watt. After demonstrating the impossibility of concentrating sufficient energy to stop or destroy an animal or machine at a great distance, Richard Watson-Watt went on to point out that by means of electromagnetic waves it was possible to signal the presence of airplanes at a great distance and to measure their speed and direction.

This would involve sending out a signal from the ground into space, while determining the time necessary for the return of the reflected signal to the transmitting station. This would, of course, be a very short interval, since radio waves travel at the speed of light. The detector employed was an oscillograph, an instrument that had already been used by E.V. Appleton to measure the ionized layers in the higher atmosphere.

A first experiment was tried in 1935 at Daventry and was a great success; an airplane clearly revealed its presence, though flying at a great distance and hidden night and day by the clouds. The first steps in the development of radar (radio detection and ranging) were under way. The British kept their results secret, and Marconi and his staff were kept in the dark. In a matter of a few years, the onset of World War II accelerated the final development and practical application of the invention. The British were joined in their work by the Americans. The Germans and the Italians soon got wind of the enemy's scientific progress, but they had been left too far behind.

Radar was one of the most powerful weapons in the hands of the Allies. It allowed their anti-aircraft defense to detect the German bombers soon after take off. The Navy could also pursue Hitler's ships even in thick fog, as in the case of the battleship Bismarck, which was followed for thirty hours, and at the battle at Cape Matapan, where Mussolini's fleet was the target of the radar-guided British fleet. In the Atlantic, the German fleet of "pocket submarines" had no better luck than the Bismarck, since the radar installed on the American and British ships were already so accurately devised that they could spot the submarines below the water's surface.

## The Birth of Short-Wave Therapy

Marconi deserves the credit for inventing another non-military application of the micro-wave. The inventor was the first to discover that the large amount of energy condensable in a powerful microwave emission could be used for therapeutic purposes. He also predicted that waves could penetrate the human body and, if sufficiently powerful, even generate heat. Grasping these possibilities, Marconi accepted an invitation to the International Congress of Radiobiology which opened in Vienna, on 10 September 1934. There, he presented his ideas, summarized above, initiating the form of physical therapy which still bears his name: in Italian, short-wave therapy is still know as "Marconi-therapy."

14

## The Final Days

### Warning Signs

The Congress of September 1934 in Venice exhausted Marconi, but he still insisted on delivering his speech to the expectant crowd. As soon as he finished talking, he felt an acute pain in his chest and realized that he had suffered another attack of angina pectoris. The leading Italian cardiologist, Professor Cesare Frugoni, was called in from Rome. The doctor helped Marconi to recover sufficiently to return home. Frugoni's orders were clear: a quiet life with no heavy commitments, no tiring journeys, no excitement and no smoking. In his current state, Guglielmo agreed to follow the doctor's orders, but after two months, he felt better and decided to resume his traditional hectic routine.

In November 1934, Marconi traveled to England for the wedding of Princess Marina of Greece and the Duke of Kent. After that, he went to Scotland for a ceremony installing him as Chancellor of the University of St. Andrew. A few days later, on a damp and foggy afternoon in early December, the inventor attended an international soccer match at Highbury. With the combination of cold weather and fatigue, Marconi suffered another attack of angina pectoris and he was taken to a London clinic. In Italy, the news of his illness was kept secret; the leaders of Fascism did not want the public to know that its idols were mortal.

Marconi soon recovered and was able to return to Italy, where he devoted himself to his numerous duties with the National Research Council and the Royal Academy of Italy. When the inventor's cardiologist learned that his patient was defying his orders, he instructed a nurse to follow Marconi like his shadow.

1935 was another year crammed with public commitments. The most important were the visits to Brazil, London, and Paris to defend Italy's position in Ethiopia, as we have already seen.

On 16 December, Marconi left Paris by train, on the Rome Express, together with Cristina and his personal secretary Di Marco, who later gave the inventor's daughter an account of what happened:

> On the journey between Paris and the Italian frontier, your father had very little sleep. Yet he turned up for breakfast, very pale but meticulously dressed, calm and kind as usual.
>
> There was a journalist on the Paris-Rome express who was determined not to pass up such a fine chance for an interview and made me promise to ask Mr. Marconi for it. When I broached the subject, I remember the resigned mood in which he responded and I was surprised when he said he would talk to so-and-so.
>
> After he finished breakfast, he talked to the newspaperman and retired to his compartment, not to emerge again until lunch time. At the table in the dining-car, he sat opposite his wife. I was some distance away in the non-smoking section of the car and lunch was being served when the waiter came to me and said "His Excellency" was not well.

When I rushed to the Marconis' table I found your father sitting up looking quite normal except that his eyes were closed and his head was lolling slightly to one side. Marchesa Marconi was coming round the end of the table to him. For a moment I believed that he had fainted as a result of his sleepless night and I was trying to feel his pulse when a gentleman who had been sitting at the next table go up, saying that he was Dr. Pace of Genoa, and offered his assistance.

The three of us carried your father's unconscious form to his berth, striving as best we could to soften the jerks of the speeding train. As soon as we got back to the compartment, Marchesa Marconi unlocked a bag in which she always carried heart stimulants for her husband. Suddenly your father opened his eyes, looked at us all and said, 'What's the matter?'

He was persuaded by his wife not to get up and Dr. Pace gave him an injection. For the rest of the journey he kept to his berth. Dr. Pace, whose destination had been Genoa, decided to proceed with us to Rome.

On arrival Mr. Marconi showed no signs that anything untoward had happened. He walked quite steadily from the train to the exit gate, greeted several people who had come to meet him and nothing more was heard or said about the incident. The doctor, however, ordered him to stay in bed for several weeks.

"Ironically," Degna Marconi later added to Di Marco's account, "the day after the return to Rome, the newspapers published the news that he was present at a meeting of the Fascist Grand Council. In fact he was safely in bed."

## A Guest in His Wife's House

This time, recovery was much slower and Marconi had to give up long journeys. On 25 April 1936, the inventor's brother died suddenly in London. Alfonso, who had continued to work uninterruptedly for the Marconi Company, suffered an attack of angina pectoris, exactly as his mother Annie had done. Marconi was particularly shaken by the fact that Alfonso and his mother had both died of the same illness that was plaguing him.

The last part of Guglielmo's life was probably the worst. Though he was still one of the richest men in Europe, his financial affairs were not going as well as before. Psychologically, he was distressed for other reasons. With the passing of the years, his estrangement from the children of his first marriage became more unbearable, and he grew depressed when he remembered other episodes in his life. His present marriage was not very happy, and he was forced, according to Degna's recollections, to spend long periods of time in the Bezzi-Scali's Roman palazzo, a place where he always felt uneasy. There was also the absolute ban on cigarettes and the strict diet—all things which inevitably irritated him. Marconi had grown increasingly bitter over the bad relations between Italy and Great Britain after the war in Ethiopia, and a decreasing faith in Fascism and in its founder made him even gloomier and more disenchanted.

Years later, Degna recalled her encounters with her father in this period:

[From the boarding school,] I returned to Rome whenever I could. There I saw Father frequently and, shyly, we two grew close again. His gentleness towards me was the more remarkable since he was, in general, fretful at the ill health. I began to realize that he had a sense of guilt at my having become an outcast and was trying to ameliorate the unhappiness he had allowed to come into my life.

I went back to Rome in the winter of 1937. It was troubling to see how much Father had aged, though I still had no definite idea of how ill he was. He never talked about it and Cristina confided nothing to us. By now the old affection had returned to replace our bruised relationship and the kindness I had so desperately missed was mine again. Misunderstandings vanished and by mutual consent we forgot them. Like all people who have been separated for a long time, Father and I reminisced.

We talked the afternoons away with complete freedom and candor. Father always received me alone. In all my visits to him I never laid eyes on Cristina nor heard the voice of my half-sister, Elettra.

One change in Father raised my spirits and gave me hope for the future. His mind turned again and again to London, and incredulous though I was at first, I began to be sure that he intended to leave Rome and move there, so that he could once more enjoy the old independence to work. His plans, as he unfolded them, were clear and concise and centered on taking a house where Giulio and I were to live with him. To my joy, he wanted us once more, not fleetingly, but entirely, regretting much that had occurred and determined to wipe out all memories of past divisions between us.

That spring, three minor heart attacks frustrated them. In May they were followed by one so severe that Mr. Di Marco told me in some detail about it. I went to his house in the morning and found him lying in bed, though quite cheerful and ready to go through the usual work of sorting correspondence and instructing me how to reply. Suddenly he showed me some bloodstains on his pajama sleeve and said with a smile: 'See what this bloodthirsty doctor of mine has done to me. If things go on like this, I shall really give up the ghost soon.'

It was, however, impossible for any doctor to make an invalid out of Father. In June, walking slowly, his face ashen, he went with Solari at his side to inspect the new wireless station at Santa Colombia near Rome. An unfortunate dispute had arisen between him and the Marconi Company Managing Director, H.A. White. At issue was whether the Company or Marconi should pay Di Marco's salary and traveling expenses! Since the formation of the Company it had always borne the costs of Father's private secretary. Now, it seemed, it was no longer prepared to do so. What, then, would the next move be? A cut in Marconi's salary, the disposal of the yacht (for which he was allowed a minimum of £5,000 a year)?

Father felt, however, that the disagreement would be settled sensibly if he himself went to London and thrashed it out. Its resolution might, he well understood, affect his entire position with the Company. At the same time he could make arrangements for returning to London to settle there permanently at the end of the summer.

The doctors in Rome vetoed the journey, to my lasting sorrow. They wanted him to remain in Rome, or within easy reach of Rome. A compromise was finally effected. Father would go to Viareggio where he could stop at the comforting Hotel Astor, with the Elettra moored in full view of the front windows. Game to the last, he firmly informed his doctors that this would only be a postponement. He intended to go to London as soon as his stay at the seashore was finished.

It was typically hot in Rome that July, and Elettra had already left and was with her grandmother, Countess Bezzi-Scali, at Viareggio.

## The Last Audience with the Pope

Guglielmo remained in Rome for two important reasons: on 17 July, he was to have an audience with the Pope at Castelgandolfo and, two days later, a meeting with Mussolini was arranged for. Cristina remained in the capital until the morning of the 17th. Marconi saw her off at the station where she left for Viareggio together with a maid. The two were loaded with presents for Elettra, who was going to celebrate her seventh birthday the following day. Guglielmo was expected in Viareggio two days later, on Wednesday the 21st.

Degna had this to say about this last meeting between Marconi and the Pope:

> What they talked about no one will ever know. It was said that Father wanted to give the Pontiff news of recent developments in wireless. That could have waited. I am convinced that Father was impelled by more personal and pressing motives. He was on the threshold of a new life. As he had made clear to me, he had decided to live alone and to transfer himself and his work to England, despite his abiding love of his own country. At such a juncture he would have turned to a man of elevated spiritual insight who had repeatedly shown him understanding and friendship."

Signora Bezzi-Scali later denied that there had been the slightest misunderstanding between her and Guglielmo, even during the last period of their life together. She also denied his intention of moving to London for good. The bulk of the evidence, however, supports the position presented by Degna Marconi.

For example, on 29 July, Marconi, having no other commitments, could have gone to Viareggio with his wife to celebrate his child's birthday. Yet, it was decided they should leave Rome separately, with Marconi reaching Viareggio the day after Elettra's birthday.

On the morning of 19 July, the inventor went to his office at the Royal Academy after taking his wife to the station. He dictated some letters and then spoke with Professor Carlo Romichi, who, as vice-president of the Academy, was to replace him in his absence, until one o'clock. Then he went with Di Marco to the Company's offices. Here Di Marco left him and Guglielmo went to see Solari. Pale and very tired, he slumped on a sofa until he felt better, when he and Solari discussed at length the problems involved in the experiments on micro-waves. Tthen he said: "There is still a lot to do in this field. I would like to have the energy I once had . . . the energy that I no longer have."


## The Crisis

This was the last time Marconi and Solari met together. Guglielmo got up, left the office, came slowly down the stairs and went home. At four o'clock in the afternoon, he received his lawyer, Carlo d'Amerio. An hour later, Di Marco brought him a few letters to sign. At six o'clock an appointment was scheduled with Mussolini at Palazzo Venezia, but Marconi suffered another violent attack. A nurse and his father-in-law were with him, and they immediately called the doctor. Frugoni was away from Rome for the day, and his first assistant, Dr. Arnaldo Pozzi, came in his place He examined the inventor, giving him the necessary medicines, and the crisis seemed to have passed. When Frugoni arrived later that evening, Guglielmo's condition had deteriorated.

Here is Dr. Pozzi's clinical report of Marconi's final illness:

In January 1937, one evening I had an urgent call. While he was getting ready to set off for Palazzo Venezia to meet Mussolini, Marconi had had an attack of angina pectoris. Without showing his sufferings, concealing the pain with iron will-power, he managed to walk across the wide hall of the Mappamondo, go down in the lift, get into his car and reach his residence.

I found him exhausted in the armchair, in his shirt sleeves and bathed in cold perspiration, in severe pain. I had him immediately taken to his bed and I gave him an injection of morphine. But the excessive physical effort he had made certainly affected the strength of the attack, so that I had to give him other injections of morphine before the pain finally disappeared. The attack lasted more than one hour, so that when the crisis was over he was worn out. He had certainly been very close to death.

The following morning when I went to see him with Professor Frugoni, Marconi was in an excellent mood. Evidently he had either not fully realized his serious state or he wanted to forget, otherwise he would not have resisted so strongly Professor Frugoni's kind but firm advice that he should rest for a few days. Finally he was persuaded and promised that he would not leave his bed or his chair for a week.

From that moment and for some time after, Marconi seemed to get a new lease on life. The only thing which troubled him was the strict prohibition on smoking. This was to him such an evident strain and made him so nervous that Professor Frugoni gave him a special formula for the preparation of cigarettes without nicotine (based on dried vine leaves, sage and eucalyptus). Marconi found them so much to his taste that as soon as he saw Frugoni he was full of praise and compliments for his excellent formula and, jokingly, he advised him to put the cigarettes on the market adding: "We shall call them Salus cigarettes, from the Marconi and Frugoni Company, and we shall make a fortune!"

One night in March he had just gone to bed when he was suddenly woken up by a feeling of oppression in his chest and a lack of air which made it almost impossible to breathe. I was called urgently and discovered he had suffered a severe attack of lung oedema, which unfortunately was the first of a series.

On July 19th, he was to go and talk to the Head of the Government at the Palazzo Venezia, when, suddenly—it was 5:30—he succumbed to another extremely violent attack of angina. Soon the pain was unbearable so he went to bed. I was sent for and in a few minutes I was at Marconi's side. I found him very pale, holding his hand against his heart. As soon as he saw me, he pleaded: 'I can't stand this any longer. Help me.' He had already taken two grains of tinitrine, but the pain was still bad and his forehead was beaded with two huge drops of sweat. An injection of spalmalgina given immediately had no effect, so that soon afterwards, I gave him one of morphine. The pain persisted violently, spasmodically: it was certainly a serious heart attack. Immediately afterwards the lung oedema started.

Marconi's condition was more than serious; my therapeutical resources were drying up. I knew that Professor Frugoni was absent from Rome for a consultation and would come back only late at night; I could therefore not count on his immediate intervention, so that the responsibility for such a precious life lay on my shoulders alone. I arranged things so that on his arrival Frugoni would be informed, without delay, of Marconi's critical condition; he reached Via Condotti about nine o'clock, a few minutes after returning to Rome. Marconi thanked him for his trouble and told him he was feeling better.

After examining him and hearing what I had already done, he advised a continuance of vasodilatories, sedatives and some heart analactics; he reassured Marconi, telling him his state was not serious, but that he would stay for any eventuality which might occur during the night. Some contractions at the corners of his mouth revealed that the pain had not ceased. But he suffered in silence, as was his habit. Suddenly a sharper pang wrung a cry of pain from him while the anguish and difficulty in breathing compelled him to sit up. Frugoni was quickly at his bedside and, thanks to oxygen and other suitable treatment, the crisis was once more averted.

Marconi was lying motionless. Suddenly he whispered slowly: "Frugoni, tell me, how is it that my heart has stopped beating, and yet I am still alive." (By a strange anomaly, Marconi's left radial artery was clearly visible on the surface so that he could usually follow the pulsation quite easily without feeling the vein with this fingers.)

"It is because of your position," answered Frugoni to calm the dying man.

"My dear Frugoni, you know better than I do that this might happen with veins but not with arteries."

With such an argument, so clear and precise, Marconi demonstrated once more the serenity with which he was facing death. One o'clock, two o'clock, three o'clock came and went.

Thus passed the first hours of July the 20th.

Sitting at his beside, I felt his hand occasionally seek mine and heard him ask the time.

He remained conscious, always in control of himself. From time to time a quiet groan indicated that his sufferings still continued.

From the street one could hear the noise of the town beginning to wake up. Very important people had telephoned, sending their kind wishes for his recovery. From Castelgandolfo the Pope had sent his benediction.

## It was three o'clock

Count Francesco Bezzi-Scali had informed his daughter of her husband's illness. Cristina set off on the first possible train; unfortunately, she did not arrive in time to see her husband alive

The bells of the nearby church of Trinità dei Monti rang three o'clock that night and they were the last that Marconi heard. The air was heavy although the temperature had gone down during the evening. In his bed Guglielmo was suffering excruciating pains, all the more cruel since he was fully conscious.

Marconi's room consisted of a small bed with a carved headboard, a few square meters of floor space, a high ceiling typical of old buildings, a wide window with panes screened by white curtains, and rather bare furnishings, although the actual pieces and the faded tapestry were valuable antiques.

At 3:45, his forehead wrinkled and his body shaken with tremors, Marconi said, "I am feeling very bad."

The corners of his mouth contracted even more tightly and he added, "Anyway, I don't care any more."

By this time, his voice was only a feeble whisper, an imperceptible death-rattle, but Frugoni and Pozzi could still hear the few last words, "I don't care at all. . . ."

A moment later, his body contracted once again and he drew his last breath. Thus the great genius, a man whose affections had been so full of contradictions towards those who loved him, died in a house which was not his own—surrounded by devoted and thoughtful strangers, yet deprived of the comfort of those to whom he was linked by the ties of blood. The priest, who was perhaps not called earlier in order to avoid upsetting the dying man, administered

Extreme Unction post mortem. A breathless Cristina reached her husband's side just three hours after he had died.


## The Funeral Ceremonies and the Apotheosis

The news of Guglielmo's death was known throughout the world in minutes, thanks to the radio waves he had so brilliantly developed. Tributes were solemnly paid to him all over the globe. Degna was told of her father's death while she was in England, staying with friends. Giulio heard it on the radio in the States; he immediately sailed for Italy, but neither he nor Degna arrived in time for the funeral, which took place on the afternoon of 21 July.

In Italy the fascist regime used Marconi's death and the funeral ceremonies to stage a demonstration in support of the regime. Guglielmo's body, dressed in the imposing uniform of President of the Royal Academy of Italy and the insignia of the Fascist Grand Council, lay in the hall of honor at the Farnesina. An endless line of people filed past to pay their last respects.

Hidden among the crowd, Beatrice O'Brien also came to bid a last farewell to her first husband. Strictly disciplined guards controlled the flow of the mourning crowd. The soldiers allowed everybody only a few minutes in front of the catafalque. When Beatrice finally reached Guglielmo's coffin, she kneeled beside the body of her former husband. A carabiniere instructed her to move on, but when she gave her name she was not troubled any further.

Here is how she described her last encounter with Marconi in a letter to Degna written the following day:

My darling Precious Child,

The first moment of peace to write you what's happened. My thoughts have been all the time with you and poor Giulio, away at this moment and I wish you could have been here to see and feel the touching love and tributes to him—lying there at the Farnesina, looking so peaceful and serene.

The ambiente was simple and austerely pious, no flowers, no candles just one continuous flow of people of all classes, nationalities, to render their last grateful tribute.

I went along and mingled with the crowd and it helped me and gave me a sense of peace and that all the pettinesses and misunderstandings of this material life had slipped away and that he understood so many things better now. I wished with all my heart and soul you and Giulio could have been there.

I asked to be allowed to go up close and for a moment was overwhelmed, but I knelt until I could get hold of myself and then I left. Although there was a crowd all the time, a moving stream, I was unobserved and no one could have recognized me.

Those who saw the procession say they have never on any occasion in Rome seen anything to equal it. The dense crowds stood for hours and hours in the heat—the heart and soul of Rome and the whole nation seemed to go with him. It was the humble, loving thought that was so impressive.

Gioia, who was in Santa Maria degli Angeli next to Cristina, says it was awe-inspiring.

Thirty years later, on occasion of the centenary of her husband's birth, Beatrice had this to say on the BBC:

Marconi was something extraordinary, a wonderful man. And he had a fine character. We were separated, it is true, but I have never forgotten his eyes, his expression which struck me the first time we met, when I was a young girl. He had a way of looking quite his own, both on the world around and into his own soul.

On the same occasion, Cristina Bezzi-Scali said:

Though he was a man of science, he was full of humanity and he always thought that in doing his job he was all the time doing something for the good of mankind. When he was working he was totally absorbed, but when he was with his little daughter Elettra and with me he was always charming and cheerful.

For several days newspapers all over the world devoted extensive articles to chronicle his death and past activities. The *Corriere della Sera* wrote the following tribute on 21 July:

The sad news of Marconi's sudden death was immediately taken to the children of the deceased, 29 year-old Degna, who is in London, Giulio, age 27, in New York, and 17 year-old Gioia, at present at Acqui. At the same time Marconi's father-in-law, Count Bezzi-Scali, Professor Marpicati, the Academician Vallauri and the Prefect of Rome went to the Termini station to receive the Marchesa Marconi who was to arrive at seven o'clock and to prepare her for the bad news. In a state of deep depression the lady was taken to Via Condotti and led to the room where her husband's body was lying.

At 8:30 the Duce, with the Undersecretary to the Presidency of the Council of Ministers, Medici del Vascello, and the Chancellor of the Accademia d'Italia, arrived by car to pay his respects to the dead. After stopping in the entrance to sign the visitors' book, Mussolini went up to the private apartments and stopped in front of Marconi's coffin expressing his sorrow to the widow and the relatives.

"Soon after midday the coffin was taken privately to the Accademia d'Italia in a Government hearse. The crowd who had gathered along the pavement gave the fascist salute to the dead hero in reverent and moving silence. The hearse was followed by a few cars carrying Count Bezzi-Scali, Marconi's personal secretary, the Marchese Solari and the parish priest of Sant'Andrea delle Fratte.

Marconi's stature as Citizen was no less than his stature as man and Scientist. His love for his country was very strong; he was always ready to serve it in time of peace and in time of war, gloriously, humbly; in Italy and abroad; with the ever increasing authority of his name and with a pure Italian heart. A good Italian, he was also a convinced and valuable supporter of the Regime since its beginnings; this revolutionary in the field of science understood, loved and enthusiastically forwarded Mussolini's revolution.

Therefore the pennants of Fascist Italy together with the Italian Tricolor are dipped over his tomb; and the flags, flying at half-mast, of all the peoples he has benefited all over the world are united in a feeling of sorrow which is the deepest and sincerest sign of admiration."

Among the thousands of telegrams received there were those from the King, the Queen, Cardinal Pacelli on behalf of Pius XI, and one from Gabriele D'Annunzio. The poet addressed his message to Professor Formichi, vice-president of the Royal Academy. It read:

My dearest Carlo, I am with you today as in one of our conversations on immensity. I bring all my laurels to the ark and I watch over him all night. Remember comrade. Gabriele D'Annunzio.

The Council of the Royal Academy published this note:

Guglielmo Marconi died suddenly tonight in Rome. Italy, mother at all ages of geniuses and heroes, has lost one of her greatest and dearest sons and mankind one of its most generous benefactors. Victorious over space as no mortal before him, Marconi encircled the earth from one continent to the other, with marvelous links which no power will ever destroy. He who has saved countless lives from certain death among the treacherous waves of the ocean and amid the storms of the air lies motionless within the walls of the Accademia d'Italia who honored in its glorious President a great Italian and faithful fascist. But Marconi's glory will not die. The Italian race will honor him in the course of the centuries as one of its immortal geniuses and the civilized world will celebrate his name forever with gratitude and admiration. Glory to Guglielmo Marconi.

## Conclusion

Was Guglielmo Marconi really the matchless genius, the important scientist, the great benefactor of mankind, who was glorified by newspapers all over the world, by statesmen and men of culture, by learned scholars and common working people?

If by scientist we mean one who looks for the laws governing the world of nature, unconcerned with his discoveries' practical applications, then Marconi was not a scientist. As the documents presented in this work clearly indicate, he was only interested in uncovering the secrets of natural phenomena in order to draw general conclusions. He always relied strictly on experience; his experiments were a source of information to be turned to his own practical ends. He always left theoretical interpretations to others.

If by science we also mean applied research for practical purposes, however, then Marconi was certainly a great man of science.

For at least two-thirds of his life Marconi was able to conceive and manufacture with his own hands, often with rudimentary tools and instruments, and with no scientific theory outlined in advance. Marconi was also a remarkable captain of industry, a formidable organizer of research and production. He was a gifted "talent-scout," capable of gathering around himself the best minds and the most gifted young men; and when his research reached a point beyond his own technical and scientific capacity, he left to his collaborators— above all to the younger among them—the task of improving old equipment and developing new discoveries. At the same time, he always made certain that his Company retained the financial and technical advantages of the various patents.

As for the scientific value of Marconi's work we might quote Enrico Fermi, another Italian awarded with the Nobel Prize for physics:

It is well-known that Marconi's discoveries were at first received with a certain skepticism in the scientific world. Skepticism based on the belief that it was not possible to transmit radio waves between stations obscured from each other by the horizon. The reasoning behind this was more or less the following: electromagnetic waves used in radio transmissions are substantially analogous to light waves, differing from these only in their greater length; and the earth, being a good electrical conductor, behaves with them like an opaque body. The radiation emitted from a station and propagating in a direct line, cannot reach all the stations located beneath the horizon of the transmitting station; except for some slight deviation due to phenomena of diffraction. Luckily for mankind these arguments, which a priori sound reasonable and well-founded, did not deter Marconi from his experiments on long-distance transmission. The history of his first radio-transmission successes proves that in the study of natural phenomena, theory and experiment must go hand in hand. Experience can rarely—unless guided by a theoretical concept—arrive at results of any great significance; and it is certainly one of the most important successes for theory that the very existence and the essential properties of electromagnetic waves had been mathematically foreseen by Maxwell before their existence was proved experimentally and before they were turned to practical application thanks to Marconi's infinitive genius; on the other hand an excessive trust in theoretical conviction would have prevented Marconi from persisting in experiments which were destined to bring about a revolution in the technique of radiocommunications.

A survey of Marconi's own writings, his speeches and the recollections of his closest associates shows that in all his undertakings—though he was constantly aware of the need for commercial success in his industrial activities—Marconi was always preoccupied with the advantages that telecommunications would bring to humanity. His first concern was what his experiments would mean for others, whether it was for saving lives at sea or advancing mutual understanding among the people of the world. It is almost impossible to conceive of life today without Marconi's extraordinary contributions.

# INDEX

Alphonse XIII, king of Spain, 264
Appleby, E., 108
Appleton, E.V., 345

Baiardi, dr., 268
Ballentyne, family, 104
Bannatyne, J.F., 107, 108
Baring, lady E., 297
Barzini, L., 194
Bastianelli, R., 316
Battelli, 184
Battenberg, Louis of, 219
Battenberg, Victoria Eugenia (Ena), queen
  of Spain, 219
Belcredi, 200, 201, 202
Bell, A.G., 36, 164
Beltrame, Arrigo, 266, 267
Beltrame, Antenore, 266
Bennett, C.F., 107
Bennett, J.G., 120
Bertolini, admiral, 267
Bezzi-Scali, family, 304, 318, 352
Bezzi-Scali, Francesco, 298, 302, 357, 360,
  361
Bezzi-Scali, Maria Cristina, 298, 303, 312,
  318, 323, 353, 360
Bianco, captain, 92
Birkenhead, family, 297
Bizzarrini, G., 32
Blaserna, P., 171
Bollini, G., 25, 26
Borden, F, 219
Borden, R, 219
Boyle, C. (sir), 163
Bradfield, 126, 130, 132, 137
Branly, E., 39, 45, 46, 48, 124, 125
Braun, K.F., 254
Brian Boru, king of Ireland, 236

Brin, B., 89, 90, 94
Brusati, U., 213
Buller, R.H., 141
Bullock, Marconi's assistant, 139, 141

Calzecchi-Onesti, T., 38, 39, 48, 58, 125
Campbell, S., 69
Camperio, F, 32, 283
Camperio, G, 32
Camperio, S., 257, 269
Carignani, ambassador, 179
Caruso, E., 254
Castelli, P., 178
Ciano, A., 90
Clemenceau, G., 277
Collier, D.M.B., 93
Colonna, P., 228
Compton, A., 343
Corry, N., 297
Crawford, G.S., 329, 330

D'Annunzio, G., 274, 279, 285, 286, 288,
  293, 306, 309, 361
Davis, A.G., 107
Davis, family, 104, 105
Davis, H.J., 65, 66, 69, 102, 107, 108
De Nicola, E., 274
Del Drago, family, 299
Densham, W, 130
Dessau, B., 169
Dewey, G., 133
Di Marco, U., 331, 333, 348, 351, 353, 354
Dolbear, A.E., 135
Domville, C. (sir), 128
Douglas, admiral, 219
Dufferin, B, 297
Dundonald, lord, 219
Dunlap, O.E., 60